THE
POLISH ECONOMY

THE
POLISH ECONOMY

Legacies from the Past, Prospects for the Future

Raphael Shen

PRAEGER

New York
Westport, Connecticut
London

Library of Congress Cataloging-in-Publication Data

Shen, Raphael.
   The Polish economy : legacies from the past, prospects for the
future / Raphael Shen.
       p.   cm.
   Includes bibliographical references and index.
   ISBN 0-275-93886-7 (alk. paper)
   1. Poland—Economic conditions—1945-1980. 2. Poland—Economic
conditions—1980- 3. Poland—Economic policy—1981-   I. Title.
HC340.3.S54   1992
330.9438—dc20   91-16683

British Library Cataloguing in Publication Data is available.

Library of Congress Catalog Card Number: 91-16683
ISBN: 0-275-93886-7

First published in 1992

Praeger Publishers, One Madison Avenue, New York, NY 10010
An imprint of Greenwood Publishing Group, Inc.

Printed in the United States of America

 ∞™

The paper used in this book complies with the
Permanent Paper Standard issued by the National
Information Standards Organization (Z39.48-1984).

10 9 8 7 6 5 4 3 2 1

CONTENTS

TABLES AND FIGURE

TABLES

FIGURE

INTERVIEWEES

Askanas, Wiktor — Professor of Management, University of New Brunswick

Baka, Wladyslaw — President, National Bank of Poland

Beksiak, Janusz — Professor, University of Planning and Statistics; advisor to the Finance Minister

Bratkowski, Stefan — Chairman of Polish Association of Journalists; leading figure in the development of social and economic scenarios for development in Poland

Brzezinski, Stanislaw — Advisor to the Minister of Work and Social Policy

Bylinski, Janusz — Member of the Parliament; Chairman of the Parliamentary Committee for Agriculture (later Minister of Agriculture)

Dietl, Jerzy — Senator; Professor, University of Lodz

Goscinski, Janusz — Professor of Economics and Management, University of Warsaw

Johann, Wieslaw — Minister of Liquidation of Central Office for Publications and Performance Control

---

* The positions listed above were those held during the time of interviews, June-July 1990.

Jozefiak, Cezary	Senator; head of the Economic Commission of the Senate; Professor, University of Lodz
Lis, Krzysztof	Minister for Privatization
Machalski, Andrzej	Senator; President of the Confederation of Polish Employers
Obloj, Krzysztof	Docent, University of Warsaw
Pacuski, Jerzy	Director of the Department of Employment, Ministry of Work and Social Policy
Piotrowski, Zbigniew	President of Foreign Investment Agency, Ministry of Finance
Ploszajski, Piotr	Professor and Member of the Polish Academy of Social Sciences
Rosati, Dariusz	Professor and Director of Foreign Trade Research Institute
Staniszkis, Jadwiga	Author and journalist; advisor to Lech Walesa
Sterniczuk, Henryk	Associate Professor, University of New Brunswick and advisor to Minister Krzysztof Lis
Szemplinska, Ewa	Journalist (*Gazeta Bankowa*) and Specialist in Solidarity
Zoltowski, Przemyslaw	Vice Director of the Department of Social Insurance, Ministry of Work and Social Policy

ACKNOWLEDGMENTS

I wish to express my profound gratitude to Professors Janusz Goscinski (University of Warsaw), Wiktor Askanas (University of New Brunswick), and Ewa Kurylowicz (Warsaw Polytechnical University) for their generous assistance to me, from inception to completion of this book. Through them, the courage to write this book took form. With their assistance, doors to top Polish officials and academicians were opened. And with their wise counsel, the book finally came to be.

I am also deeply indebted to Attorney and Mrs. Wieslaw Johann, who on more than one occasion kindly obtained the needed documents for me from the Polish Parliament. Gratitude is also due to Kathlene Barrett, who edited the manuscript, to Ann Reilly and Carol Dockery, who typed the draft and revisions over and over again, to Jeanne Waeiss, who helped with typing the tables, and to my graduate assistant, Miroslaw Reczko, who spent countless hours assisting me with every aspect of this book.

Finally, I wish to acknowledge the goodness, kindness, and hospitality of the people of Poland. They deserve the best.

INTRODUCTION

Among Eastern European economies, the people of Poland led the way in pressuring for and obtaining political reforms within the Soviet bloc. Other than the Soviet Union, Poland is the largest nation among COMECON members, and the best educated and has the most volatile economy. In moving the country from a centrally planned economy to a free-market system, Poland's economic reform measures have been the most radical and most ambitious. The objectives are laudable, but, with good reason, concerns over the *modus implemendi* may be justified. The ramifications and implications that result could impinge on and, positively or otherwise, influence the thinking of many in the recently liberalized Eastern European economies.

This study assumes a two-pronged approach,[1] combining document research and field interviews into a synthesized study of the Polish economy, with particular concerns for the Poland of years to come.

A note of caution, however, is in order. Since the topics in this study are fairly extensive, in-depth research studies into each of the sectors and macroeconomic variables are needed in the future. Such individualized research projects can then provide more detailed analyses of Poland's economic transformation as it impacts diverse fronts of the economy, now and in the years to come.

For now, it is the studied opinion of this writer that measures and approaches of transforming the Polish economy from the *old* to the *new* should be paced over time rather than instituted overnight, and should be moderate rather than radical. Throwing the centrally planned system out and replacing it immediately with the free-market system would mean that the economy would have no system based in the concrete. The necessary economic infrastructure and basic institutions would have had no time to develop and to render the market system functional. The current experience in Poland has already led to extensive disillusionment and doubts among consumers. The Polish experience will be a useful and valuable lesson in economics for students and decision makers alike.

NOTE

1. This writer visited Poland during the summers of 1988 and 1990. During the more recent visit to Poland, he was able to interview twenty-one top academicians and officials. Among others, there were professors, three senators, two ministers, one member of Parliament, the president of the National Bank of Poland, the president of the Foreign Investment Agency, and the director of the Foreign Trade Research Institute. A list of the interviewees is provided at the beginning of this volume.

THE
POLISH ECONOMY

1

POLAND IN
HISTORICAL PERSPECTIVE

THE COUNTRY

The kingdom of Poland was founded in A.D. 966 by Prince Mieszko. Over time, the borders of Polish territory bulged and contracted with the advancing and retreating military maneuvers of the plains-dwelling Polish people. Before 1795, Poland was a military power of Europe, but it became prey to its expanding neighbors, Russia, Prussia, and Austria. By 1795, the nation-state was incorporated into the maps of these powers. Poland was to remain a pawn of foreign powers for a century and a quarter, until 1919 when sovereign nationhood was restored to the people of Polish heritage (Brumberg, 1983: 3-4). But this arduous task of reestablishing unity and developing the independent nation's economy lasted for only two decades. Stalin and Hitler signed an agreement on August 23, 1939, which caused the Polish nation to disappear from the political map of Europe once again. Stalin took territories east of the Curzon Line, and Hitler west of it.[1] During both periods of non-existence, only the fierce spirit of Polish heritage helped hold the people of today's Poland together.

The 313,000 square kilometers (121,000 square miles) of territory composing present-day Poland are a result of the Yalta and Potsdam agreements of 1945, called the bilateral Polish-Soviet Union Agreements thereafter (Barnett, 1958: 33). This definition of Polish territory after World War II was a blessing in disguise for the development potential of the future Polish economy. Vast territory east of the Curzon Line was ceded to the Soviet Union. At the same time, a sizable amount of land that used to belong to Germany--namely, the territories east of the Neisse and Oder rivers, was placed under Polish jurisdiction and administration.[2] Whereas Poland lost in terms of territorial size, since the eastern portion that went to the Soviets far exceeded in size what was acquired from Germany after World War II, it gained in potentially productive land.   Area east of the Curzon Line is predominantly nonfertile agricultural land; area acquired from Germany is both mineral rich and agriculturally fertile.   More important, the current map of Poland shows extensive access to the Baltic Sea, a bonus which Poland did not enjoy prior to World War II.   Before the war, Poland's shoreline was only one-fifth of what it is today.

Currently, Poland is bounded on the east by the Soviet Union, by the former East Germany on the west, and by Czechoslovakia on the south.   On the north, it is fronted by the Baltic Sea, which holds vast development potential.   Poland is the largest Eastern European nation outside of the Soviet Union.   It provides strategic importance to the latter, both militarily and economically: militarily it is a shield from Germany, which was in the habit of intruding into Russia;   economically, it is an important supplier of raw industrial materials and agricultural products, and also provides a ready market for Soviet finished products.   The Polish population, the largest among COMECON nations outside of the Soviet Union, is nearly 17 percent greater than the combined populations of former East Germany and Czechoslovakia.

The word *Polanie*, often expressed as "Polska," refers to the Slavic people who settled on the northern plains of Europe east of the Oder and west of the Vistula Rivers around the first century B.C.   From the Carpathian Mountains southeast, the plains slope northwest until they reach the coast of the Baltic Sea.   Though Poland possesses mountains of considerable height, nearly 90 percent of Polish land is no higer than 1,000 feet, with the more fertile agricultural land in the west and land of decreasing productive potential eastward toward the Vistula River (Barnett, 1958: 35-36).   The most richly endowed mineral deposits are found in the southwest regions of the highlands. The country is divided into forty-nine provinces, which are then subdivided into 813 towns.   The four largest cities, with half a million people or more each, are Warsaw, Lodz, Krakow, and Poznan.   These have also been hotbeds of political unrest in modern Polish history.   Of vital importance to the Polish economy are the coastal cities of Gdansk (Danzig), Gdynia, and Szczecin (Stettin).

The major population concentrations are in the capital city of Warsaw (1,664,000), the industrial city of Lodz (847,900), the cultural center of Krakow (744,000), and the once political hotbed of Poznan (578,100). Female population exceeds that of male by approximately 4 percent.   Urban population approaches two-thirds of the total.   Poland has a relatively high population growth rate of 1.4 percent, with a population density of approximately 120 persons per square kilometer.

POLISH SOCIETY AND ITS PEOPLE

Poland is a land rich in history. This sense of history is embedded in the souls of Poles, and being Polish is one of the few banners that can rally its generally independent-spirited people to action. It is understandable. For generations, the Polish people endured foreign domination. But even when its statehood was denied, Poland always existed and survived in the hearts and souls of the Polish people. "While we live, she exists"--the beginning of the Polish national anthem eloquently attests to the will of its people for an independent Poland.

Even in the twentieth century, citizens of Poland have felt deep suffering. The estimated population in 1921 after World War I was 27.2 million. In 1955, the population was estimated to be the same. In between, a large number of Poles moved: they fled, were conscripted into foreign armies, were shipped to neighboring nations as laborers, or were exiled, imprisoned, or summarily executed. Other than the Soviet Union, no Eastern European nation lost more lives during the second World War than Poland. Through suffering, the Polish people emerged, and today, conscious of their heritage and historical identity, they are more prepared than most to lay down their lives for the motherland.

Today's Polish population is one of the most ethnically homogeneous among nations. Prior to World War II, Ukrainians, Jews, Byelorussians, and Germans constituted a combined minority of nearly 30 percent of the Polish population. Today, less than 2 percent of Poland's population is of minority origin. The remainder are descendants of the same culture and the same language, espousing the same values. Among those more cherished values are individualism, personal respect, independence, freedom, religion, selflessness, and integrity.

Individualism

This is a trait cultivated in the formative years. Polish parents, who cherish respect by others, also respect their children as endowed with unique characteristics. Each child is encouraged to develop its individual potential. Rarely do Polish parents impose their personal tastes and preferences upon their children. Young people are guided to explore their own strengths and weaknesses, to make their own important choices and decisions in life, and to map their own destiny. Formed in such an atmosphere, Polish youth mature to be individuals rather than faceless people fitted into an obscure common denominator. Therefore, a value, a belief, or a practice imposed from above, unless palatable to personal conviction, often does not lead to its desired effect.

Personal Respect

The Polish people, though for a long time pawns of foreign domination, have pride and self-respect. They have risen from political oblivion to independent nationhood. It is described thus: "A Pole on horseback will charge a tank with pistol and saber for a cause" (Barnett, 1958: 3). Woe to the person who attempts to deprive the collective Polish people of their personal respect. A Pole is an individual, a master of self, not an entity in the hands of a powerful elite--especially if the latter is not held in deep respect. Therefore, personal respect is a cultural value that needs be accorded due consideration in devising any system of production.

Independence

The desire to be independent flows from the individualism mentioned earlier. It is also fortified through historical events. As youths mature they are encouraged to be their own masters. This constant affirmation of potential nudges young people forward to take explorative steps and test the unknown. Views of respected authority are sought, but decisions are personal. Adults likewise recognize the limits of their authority over their children. Forcing maturing youth to listen or to be dependent is relatively alien to Polish parents. Therefore, the Polish people rebel against a helpless, dependent position, whether imposed from without, such as by foreign domination, or from a domestic economic condition in which they have neither voice nor responsibility.

Freedom

Freedom from foreign occupation or domination is basic. Freedom from foreign supervision or intervention is desired. Freedom to be one's self is cherished. The Polish people have achieved political freedom. Now they seek economic freedom--freedom from wanting what should be there but is not. The relevant question is how to make the people recognize that freedom from financial and material need henceforth rests on their own shoulders.

Religion

In general, religious belief to the Polish people today means belonging to the Roman Catholic Church. This religious sentiment is embodied in Polish music, poetry, literature, architecture, and art. Through thick and thin, the

Catholic Church has been an advocate of what is good, right, and Polish. Intelligentsia may differ with Church teaching on given issues, but the Church symbolizes struggle, suffering, and unity for the Poles. To them, without Catholicism there is no Poland of today. In practice, Polish youth are the most religious among Eastern European nations. Being Catholic goes beyond the symbolism of opposing a system. It is a way of life; it is the source of hope; it is Polish. Although not all Poles practice their religion, their identity as Roman Catholic is indelible, singularly strong in more tradition-bound rural areas as well as among common laborers. For an issue to be popularly accepted, the seal of approval by the Catholic hierarchy is nearly indispensable--a factor to be reckoned with by aspiring politicians and policymakers.

Selflessness and Integrity

These are admired qualities everywhere, but particularly appealing to the Poles. A Polish individual may not be a person of selflessness and integrity, yet for an individual who wishes to command respect and whose voice will be heeded, these qualities are indispensable. For instance, the Roman Catholic hierarchy alienated the faithful, prior to World War II, because it was perceived as associated with the rich and powerful and as uninterested in defending the rights of the masses. Stefan Cardinal Wyszynski, with his humble and principled approach, won back the people's respect for the Church. His people, such as Father Popieluszko who defended the rights of Solidarity, brought Catholics closer to the Church. Conversely, public officials who indulge in privileges and abuse public trust can expect no following. The loss of public trust during communist administrations made policy implementation ineffective. To build up the Polish economy, therefore, civil leaders must show not only vision and intelligence but also place the well-being of the nation and its people above personal gain.

There are other cultural values dear to the Poles, but these are the more significant ones. In considering economic reform, policy formulation, and economic growth, it serves to bear in mind how these values can best be incorporated into the social energy needed for development and progress.

THE HERITAGE

Descendants of Slavic tribes, the Polish people took form in A.D. 966 as a political entity under the leadership of Prince Mieszko. To ward off German advances, the prince married a Bohemian princess, aligning himself and his subjects with the powerful Roman Empire. Thereafter, Catholicism became part and parcel of Polish history, and Western influence permeated its culture (Barnett, 1958: 9).

The people of Poland, not unlike the people of many smaller nations, have witnessed their share of short days of glory and longer days of subjugation and humiliation. A product of geographic location, social and political structuring, and the ebb and flow of foreign strength, Poland once expanded its territories east to include most of today's Byelorussia and the Ukraine during the Jagiellos dynasty, which began in the late fourteenth century. King Sigmundus III (1587-1632) went as far as setting his sights on the Moscovy throne and publicly laid claim to it (Barnett, 1958: 13). Universities were built, centers of culture and commerce established, and literary and scientific activities promoted. The Poles were among the promulgators of what was the new and progressive: it was the heart of Europe. As a whole, however, the people of Poland viewed themselves as victims of neighboring intruders and distant foreign powers. Historically, the Polish people have been intensely nationalistic and patriotic when faced with external threat, yet they have been unable to remain unified long enough to achieve a proclaimed national objective (Obloj interview, 1990). This may stem from the importance they place on individualism and independence.

Throughout history, the Polish people have been dominated by special-interest cliques. Peasants were strongly attuned to serving the landed gentry in the sixteenth century. The voice of one noble could negate the sentiment of the entire parliament *(liberum veto)*. Internal cohesion and continuity were sacrificed for personal gains. Even when neighboring powers preyed upon the Polish people, the interests of nobles were protected, and a pledge of allegiance to the invading monarch was not uncommon. This eventually led to repeated partitions of Poland by foreign forces, beginning in the latter part of the eighteenth century and ending after World War II. For more than two centuries, the people of Poland were denied self-determination: by Russia, Prussia, and Austria in 1772, 1793 and 1795, and by the Soviet Union and Germany in 1939. The reemergence of the state of Poland in 1918 was, in large measure, due to the proclamation of President Woodrow Wilson. The reemergence of Poland as a nation with its re-drawn boundaries came after World War II, the end product of efforts by the major international powers.

Poland is a nation that emerged from days of glory and eons of foreign domination, from serving the interests of local gentry or, worse, foreign lords; whose language was forbidden to be taught by Russia's Czar Nicholas I, whose people were drafted into foreign armies during Prussian occupancy, whose forefathers were deported to alien lands, and whose soldiers were slaughtered by nominal allies in the forest of Katyn. This is a nation whose writers and poets lamented the loss of its statehood and a people who, in one form or another, were seen as a dispensable lot by its towering neighbors.

After the war, Poland reappeared on the map of Europe but was, until

1989, in the shadow of a modern superpower that monitored its major political moves. As time passed, it increasingly became a nation of disillusionment-- about the theory and practice of decision makers, about promises, different from reality; about being able to fulfill one's productive potential, and about progress, seeing neighbors to the west growing exceptionally faster than itself. What the people of Poland have inherited are dreams long unrealized and aspirations long denied. Now, Poland has a chance to do what needs be done and to be what it can be.

THE CATHOLIC CHURCH

No important aspect of Poland's history, or Poland's future, can be meaningfully studied without taking into account the role of the institutionalized Roman Catholic Church. As the nation weathered political upheavals, the Polish Church had to withstand the onslaught of Reformation movements from the west and the north, as well as Eastern Orthodox oppression from the east. The Church was used to ward off contemplated invasion of its land by Prussia in the tenth century. It was repeatedly used by the politically powerful to form allies, to mediate, to appease, and to rally its people. The Church brought what is western to Poland, distinguishing itself from what is Eastern. It symbolizes what is good, moral, right, powerful, and beneficial.

In the quagmire of Poland's history, the Church has never been on the periphery. Critics never fail to point out the emotive aspects of the Church, which seem to appeal to less educated peasants and industrial workers, yet the overwhelming majority of white-collar workers and the intelligentsia profess allegiance to the Church. It represents the suffering Christ who will eventually rise victorious over its inimical opponents. And the Church is most influential in the face of national suffering and crises. For the Poles, the Church is the rallying point, the moral guardian over what is Polish. To persecute the Church is synonymous with attempts to alter the Polish identity. This was evident not only by the Nazis' rough handling of the institutionalized Church during the war but particularly during the 1949-1956 period of overt attempts by the then Polish government to suppress and control it. But measures aimed at weakening the Church only brought about stronger identification with it, defeating the original intent of any antagonist.

Aside from the moral force it exerts over its people, and its role in Polish history and culture, the Church is a wealth holder, an institution of privileges, and the only institution that is effectively expanding its visible domain. Until the fall of the Communist regime in September 1989, the fastest-growing industry in Poland was the remodeling of existing Churches and the construction of new ones. As it always has been, the Catholic Church is a powerful political force in Poland.

This recognition, however, came with a price. The memory of Church heroics is still relatively fresh, even in the minds of the younger generation. During World War II, Church leaders were actively involved in the Resistance Movement. Many were incarcerated and executed (Barnett, 1958: 72). The Church hierarchy valiantly resisted compromise or accommodation with the occupying force. With the installation of the communist regime in Poland, the Church deftly maintained its position while opposing an atheistic regime. Stefan Cardinal Wyszynski, a man held in highest esteem by the people, publicly denounced the government's moves and endured years of imprisonment. The elevation of Cardinal Wojtyla to the papacy further strengthened the people's tie to the Church. It was the Church that provided moral support to the Solidarity movement; it was the Church that assisted imprisoned leaders of Solidarity; it was the Church's martyrs, such as Father Popieluszko, who represented the Polish people's just cause; and it was to the Church that the general public went for counsel and moral support. As a result, even for negotiations between the communist regime and Solidarity, it was to the Catholic Church that both parties turned.

POST-WORLD WAR II GOVERNMENT AND POLITICS

The Polish Communist party, whose leaders had been exiled by Stalin in the late 1930s, reemerged during the war as the Polish Workers Party (PPR) under the leadership of Wladyslaw Gomulka. The party had no tangible following, no realistic chance of playing a leading role in Polish politics. Its only hope for gaining political ground was a Soviet invasion of eastern Poland. The dream was realized when the Soviets confronted the Allied Forces during the August 1944 Warsaw Uprising. The uprising, directed by the Polish government-in-exile in London, was crushed. The invading forces then entered Warsaw and recognized beforehand the so-called Lublin Committee--a resistance group that, under great pressure from the Soviet Union, included Gomulka's Polish Workers Party--as Poland's legitimate government. When a coalition government was formed, the PPR kept a low profile. Only after having secured key positions in the army and the police force did the PPR begin to move against its former partners in the government. Opposition was driven either into exile or into the ground. Anti-Soviet elements in opposition parties were liquidated 'a la Stalinesque' thoroughness; pro-Soviet elements in the party were privileged.

Stalin never permitted the Polish people to forget that it was Soviet troops who freed Poland from Nazi occupation, and that the Soviet Union was the benefactor and protector of this reemerged nation. The Soviet Union began its systematic control-purge and installed a communist government acceptable to itself. Gomulka, siding with Josef Tito of Yugoslavia in the latter's struggle against the Soviet Union, wanted to lead the Polish nation to a communist state in line with Polish culture and heritage. He was removed from office and placed under arrest in 1948. His successor, Boleslaw Bierut, consolidated the Polish Socialist Party (PPS) into the Polish Workers Party (PPR) to form the communist era's Polish United Workers Party (PZPR). The Catholic Church was still the only major moral political force capable of influencing the masses, so Bierut's administration began its campaign against the Church in order to break the people's passive resistance and active opposition to increasing centralism. It was in direct violation of the Church-state agreement reached during Gomulka's administration.

In 1956, three years after Stalin's death, Nikita Khrushchev publicly criticized Stalinism. The disenchanted Poles also began criticizing their own government. The only political figure capable of regaining the confidence of the general public was Wladyslaw Gomulka, and was recalled from oblivion on his own terms. His conditions were that reforms and policies pertaining to Poland be free from external interference. With the Hungarian Revolution in the making, and with general discontent in other Eastern European nations, Moscow had little maneuvering room. Gomulka returned to office, and he placed the blame for the Poznan riots of 1956 squarely on the previous administration and on complacent office holders: "The silent enslaved words began to shake off the poison of mendacity, falsehood, and hypocrisy. The stiff cliches previously predominant on party platforms and at public meetings, as well as in the press, began to give place to creative, living words. There is no escape from truth. If you cover it up, it will rise as an awful specter, frightening, alarming, and madly ringing" (Barnett, 1958: 31).

Perceived as a man of integrity, conviction, and honor, and above all, as a patriot, Gomulka reestablished himself as a rallying point for the people. His ascendancy brought about the temporary downfall of the National Group --political members who had resisted reform and had rested in the comfort of knowing that their position had the blessing of powerful figures in the Kremlin (Zielinski, 1973: 22-23). It was Gomulka's charisma, plus the Soviet crush of the Hungarian Revolution in 1956, that dissuaded the general public from voting against the Communist party in January 1957.

Gomulka's return to power was widely held as a beacon of hope: hope for greater independence from Soviet meddling and control of Polish politics, as well as hope for greater economic freedom. Economic reform, as promised, would not only have departed from the Soviet type of communist socialism but would have placed Poland on a solid foundation for economic freedom and development. It was not to be, however. Gomulka feared a possible invasion by the Soviet Union, as happened in Hungary, so he repeatedly reasserted that the PZPR was the guiding force of the nation. Some reform measures, such as decollectivizing farms and granting greater political freedom, were implemented, but no far-reaching economic reforms were carried out. Instead, fearing that a rationalized approach to economic development would lead to demand for greater political freedom and further economic reforms, Gomulka headed in the other direction with tighter control of more aspects of life in Poland. The economy stagnated. Discontent mounted. Students took to the streets in 1968, and workers went on strike in 1970. With brutal force, the dissenting voices were crushed.

But the support that Gomulka enjoyed upon his return to power in 1956 also eroded. Through interparty politics, Gomulka was replaced by Edward Gierek in December 1970. Recognizing the popular demand for "socialism with a human face," as heralded by the Prague Spring, Gierek's primary concern was to appease the masses by offering "consumer satisfaction." Wages were increased, but with that, inflation also followed. To meet an increased demand for consumer goods, Gierek borrowed heavily from the West to import foreign goods as well as foreign technology.

Because the system was inherently inefficient, waste became commonplace while foreign debt accumulated. With the energy crisis of 1973, energy costs soared and Polish commodities abroad lost competitive ground. Debt servicing increasingly became a threatening dilemma, and consumer dissatisfaction kept mounting (Nelson, 1984: 54-55). The Polish government verged on bankruptcy, making its economy and political actions more dependent upon the Soviet Union. In a desperate move, price adjustments on food items were announced in June 1976. Again, people took to the streets, and the intended price increases were immediately annulled.

Gierek lost effectiveness as a leader. Compounded by the merging forces of the Catholic Church, students, intellectuals, and workers, the regime caved in to popular demands and recognized the first workers' union--the Solidarity,--outside Communist party. Gierek was replaced as party secretary by Stanislaw Kania. Poland was then in the throes of internal upheavals and also suffering external threats. Demands by workers, farmers, students, and the intelligentsia kept the regime on edge while the country's big neighbor to the east was making menacing noises as well as gestures. Soviet Politburo members kept making friendly visits to Warsaw, while Polish leaders reciprocated with visits to Moscow. Polish internal affairs became the battleground for verbal exchanges between Moscow and the West.

Sensing the explosive turn of events, Kania solicited and obtained the assistance of Jozef Glemp, Catholic archbishop of Warsaw and primate of Poland. Worried that Poland could be dealt the same blow as Hungary in 1956 and Czechoslovakia in 1968, the government and the Catholic Church called moderation in demands. Solidarity's demand for a self-governing republic was seen as a direct challenge to Communist rule. During the party's Central Committee IV plenum, Wojciech Jaruzelski replaced Kania as party secretary, but efforts at reconciliation failed. Faced with a demand for a referendum on the government, and with strikes in all major cities planned for December 17, 1981, Jaruzelski imposed martial law on December 13 and outlawed Solidarity. The external threat was deflated. But Poland, nearly half a century after its reemergence from the war, was faced with a mounting economic crisis as well as a legacy of failures--failures that prohibited the people of Poland from feeling proud of what they could have accomplished.

NOTES

1. The Curzon Line was an attempt by the Council of Allied Powers of 1919 to delineate Poland's eastern borders with the Soviet Union. But the Poles insisted that the real border between the two countries was much farther east into current Soviet territory. Poland insisted that the border should have been as in 1772, when czarist Russia seized the eastern portion of the Polish kingdom (Barnett, 1958: 20).

2. In November 1990, German Chancellor Helmut Kohl agreed with the administration of Prime Minister Tadeusz Mazowiecki to ratify the post World War II demarcation of the two nations' existing boundaries.

2

THE STRUCTURE AND FUNCTIONING OF THE ECONOMY, 1945–1989

GOVERNMENT AND CENTRAL PLANNING

For historical reasons, the Polish people in general and the rural population in particular are not fond of governments, especially those perceived to constrain freedom and dictate activities. The memory of serfdom lingers, and the Communist government of Poland was perceived as such. It had been structured after the Soviet model (Johann interview, 1990). By constitution, supreme power was vested in the working people, whose interests and concerns were represented by a deputy whom they elected to the Sejm (Parliament). The process of nominating and electing deputies was a bone of contention between the Communist government and Solidarity. It was through roundtable negotiations in February 1989 that free elections were finally made possible.

Before these negotiations, Poland had the equivalent of the legislative, executive, and judiciary branches of government parallel to many Western governments. The functions of these three respective branches of government, unlike those in the West, were not distinct--all three branches were under the influence and direction of the Communist party. This was particularly true concerning issues of vital interest to the party. The justification was that the constitution had mandated the party as the guiding force of state affairs.

Comparable to government structure of the West, the legislative branch was the Sejm, with a chamber of 460 elected deputies. In name, deputies were counterparts to congressmen and senators in the United States or to members of the Parliament in England or Canada. Unlike the West, legislation was not initiated from an individual or a group of deputies. It was introduced by the Council of State, which served as a conduit for the concerns of the party.

The Council of State operated as a collective presidency, somewhat comparable to the executive branch of a Western government. Its chairman, four deputy chairmen, and council members were elected from among Sejm members. The council called the Sejm to session, nominally oversaw the operation of the Council of Ministers, and ratified international treaties (Nelson, 1984: 32-33). It could issue decrees in place of the Sejm when the latter was not in session. Depending upon circumstances, it could serve as a symbol (like the emperor of Japan) or wield real power (like the president of the United States). It had neither a purely ceremonial nor a purely substantive role.

After Wladyslaw Gomulka's second departure from office in 1971, political reform measures included the provision that a group of fifteen deputies or more could independently introduce legislation in the Sejm (Nelson, 1984: 231). An individual deputy was then also permitted to drill the administration on specific issues. However, the effectiveness of an individual deputy representing the interest of his or her constituents was functionally curtailed because the Sejm frequently was not in session. More time and energy were spent on committee sessions which were not open to the public for input or debate. Committee sessions conveniently catered to discussion of issues espoused by the Council of State. It would not be fair to assert that, directly or indirectly, the Sejm was a rubber stamp for the party apparatus, but it was a much less effective and assertive legislative body than its counterpart in the West.

Since the Sejm often was not in session, plus when sessions were called they lasted for only a day or two, there was a structural and functional vacuum, conveniently filled by the Council of State. One instance of such practices was the decree of martial law in December 1981. Although the Sejm was in session, the Council of State decided to hold a secret weekend meeting, declare martial law, and then impose the declared date, all without the Sejm's approval. That the Sejm possessed the ultimate power was theory more than reality.

The day-to-day operation of the state was in the hands of the administrative branch of government. The Council of Ministers was comparable to various administrative departments and bureaus in Western governments, in both structure and function. Ministers and their deputies were appointed by the Sejm. The council was a policy-making as well as an administrative entity, and each ministry was responsible for issues and policies pertaining to its respective sphere, but the council had prerogative over ministry decisions pertaining to laws and policies. Ministries were also responsible for administration on regional, provincial, and local levels. The hierarchial structure of government from state to region or province, and on to local or village levels was designed to ensure that the central policy of the council, and of the party, was implemented on a national as well as local level.

The state's Council of Ministers was composed of ministers, agencies, and state commissions, among which was the Planning Commission. Major concerns of the government revolved around foreign, defense, central planning, and finance. Of relatively minor significance to decision makers but of major concern to the general public were housing, consumer welfare, and the environment. High council offices were as a rule occupied by high party members; policy formulation and implementation by the council never wandered far from party philosophy and party dictates. The party de facto managed the affairs of state in accordance with its own visions. The party structure was established in such a manner that for each major government office, there was a corresponding party office. For instance, for the Ministry of Foreign Affairs, the party had a Central Committee Secretariat for Foreign Affairs. For the Ministry of Agriculture, there was a Party Secretariat of Agriculture as well. The rationale for such parallel secretariats was self-explanatory; who was administering state affairs was self-evident.

The third branch of the government was the Judiciary. It enjoyed greater latitude in decision making than the other two branches. In civil or criminal cases, judges were known to take a more lenient stand in favor of the defendants. Even in cases involving political dissenters, judges were not in the habit of conforming to party or government sentiments. It was only in major cases with potentially serious political implications that higher courts heeded government wishes.

In structure, the Polish government bore close resemblance to that of Western governments. The building blocks of the government, however, were different. In the West, members of the legislative body are elected. The administrative branch is appointed by the chief executive. In Communist Poland, members of the Sejm were nominated by the party-dominated National Unity Front. Administrative members were appointed by the Sejm, and nomination was invariably translated into election. It was a one- candidate-per-slot system, closely supervised by the Communist party. The National Unity Front's members were composed mostly of Communist party members. A few members of the two smaller parties--The United Peasant Party (ZSL) and the Democratic Party (SD)--plus a few government-recognized social organizations served as occasional token nominees. Such nominees were known to be sympathetic to and supportive of party doctrines, however. Once nominated, they were elected; once elected, they in turn helped to appoint administrative officers who, like them, would toe the party line. In office, perks and privileges accrued as a tacit reward. Desirous of continuing such privileges, they sought to assure their future nominations--they adhered to party policy. Consequently, dissenting voices were rare in either the Sejm or the Council of Ministers. Ironically, it became a transformed feudal system that had been given an egalitarian nomenclature. It was this system that produced unsatisfactory results, particularly with regard to the economy and political freedom. And it was this system that the people, through Solidarity, sought to reform.

CENTRAL PLANNING

Governments generally draw up plans for their respective economies. The market socialist economies of Norway, Denmark, and Sweden have economic plans. So do the socialist economies of the United Kingdom, Germany, and France. Planning for investment, manpower, trade, and other major economic variables is neither new nor unique to communist economies. However, the extensiveness of planning in the Eastern bloc varied vastly from planning in the West. In the latter, even though increasingly socialist, reliance is on marketplace forces. Market function, the market pricing mechanism, profit motivation, and competitiveness are instrumental in bringing about market equilibrium, efficiency, productivity, and growth. But in Poland, as in other former communist economies, the function of the market was replaced by centralized planning. The Planning Commission was an integral part of the Council of Ministers. It had more authority over more aspects of economic life than most of the other ministries. In fact, the Planning Commission had tangible authority over the activities of most of the ministries themselves.

With its economy destroyed during the war, the Polish government reasoned that only a concerted effort could rebuild the economy rapidly and orderly. A centralized plan, taking all key variables into account, could coordinate all economic activities for an envisioned objective. To accomplish its tasks, the commission drew up the plan, supervised its implementation and monitored its success. It is said that, at one time, the commission had more employees under its jurisdiction than any other government office. Warsaw even boasted of having a School of Central Planning and Statistics to educate the commission's future cadres. The commission delineated the sources of revenue and expenditure. It directed key investments areas. It apportioned production quotas to state enterprises and communes, allocated factors of production, and suggested which ministry was to have how much of the pie. Major changes in a given ministry's policy or function pertaining to economics and finance had to secure prior support and approval of the Planning Commission. Any call for a decentralized planning process and the liberalization of economic activity was invariably opposed by the commission.

The planning process was efficient; it was the implementation that was inefficient. The problem was that ideology was valued more than objectivity. On the one hand, the commission received a directive from the party and government regarding the direction and speed of economic development; on the other, it collected information from its subordinates on regional, district, and enterprise levels. It involved all sectors and subsectors of the economy. In a society where information flow was neither speedy nor accurate, miscalculation and misrepresentation unavoidably led to nonoptimal decisions.

Also, wage payments were a function of state budgetary solvency and not a result of worker productivity; recognition was given for fulfillment of production quotas rather than for quality performance. The funding of state enterprises was centrally allocated via sectoral production objectives, not market needs. Labor, supposedly the central force of a socialist economy, had become a cog in a mammoth state machine more concerned with privilege for the political elite than goods for the masses. To assure fulfillment of production quotas, enterprise directors resorted to production-factor requisitions over and above the efficient employment of scarce resources. To assure fulfillment of a value product quota, the product mix led to accumulation of unwanted inventories. This imbalance was further strengthened by the central purchasing policy of the Ministry of commerce which automatically purchased anything and everything produced by state enterprises. The economic linkages needed for the smooth functioning of the economy were forcibly reduced to an inflexible one: the state. Labor and management entertained neither the prospect of being materially rewarded nor the promise of being ideologically rewarding. Since profits from all state enterprises had to be diverted to the state, and all expenditures disbursed by the state, the concepts of efficiency, opportunity costs, or meaningful profit became irrelevant.

In every sense, the objective laws of value and of market were being violated. Prices did not and could not objectively reflect relative scarcity or abundance. There were neither objective measures of value nor the need for such measures to lead to efficient investment decisions. In brief, planning replaced the function of the market, effectively preventing the Polish economy from actualizing its productive and growth potential. At the same time, the culturally independent-minded Polish people could not be forced to be mechanized parts for the state-planned machinery's successful operation.

This "successful operation" began with the state's first plan, a three-year period (1947-1949) intended to implement economic recovery and reconstruction (Kolankiewicz, 1988: 101). By then, the Soviet Union had established itself as the guardian and mentor of Polish planning, rendering the Polish economy an economic satellite. Sectoral growth of Poland was planned to benefit the Soviet economy more than Polish society. Poland became a supplier of cheap raw materials, especially coal, while at the same time, a ready market for finished Soviet products. With the initial overemphasis on rapid industrialization and its concurrent overcommitment of resources to investment in heavy industry--which the Polish economy did not quite need at that stage of economic reconstruction and development --it became increasingly difficult to retrench. The subsequent Six-Year Development Plan (1950-1955) continued along this path of rapid expansion in heavy industries. The ground had been plowed; the seed of deformity had taken root. Corrections would become increasingly costly with successive plans. Consumer dissatisfaction, fueled by the Hungarian Revolution in 1956, led to riots against the government's development policies. *Reform* was the word on the lips of decision makers, but the word was not put into practice. The Office of Central Planning, a traditional foe to any attempt at paring down its functioning and authority, kept its pervasive influence on economic activities by churning out more detailed five-year plans, one after the other. Other widespread riots in 1970 brought some economic sense to Edward Gierek, who replaced Gomulka as the new Communist leader in Poland. However, old habits die hard and attempts to reform the economic system and to redefine the power base of the establishment proved unsuccessful (Obloj interview, 1990). Frustrated consumers, particularly workers and students, began taking to the streets. Protests, generally precipitated by announced price increases, became commonplace. That led to the formation of Solidarity, martial law, Solidarity suppression, and an economic crisis bordering on national bankruptcy. Throughout, Central Planning held onto its pivotal role in Poland's economic life. The Plan had to cover all major areas: industry, agriculture, investment, construction, health, education, transport, communication, trade, energy, fuel, employment, wages, prices, labor, and productivity. It specified how much each sector or subsector needed to produce for which year, and how much of the available factors of production was allocated to which economic or social activity. Conveniently, the human factor was taken as predictable.

Since a Plan must be in place at the beginning of a planning period, the commission was obliged to draft the plan long before its inception. There was a constant dissemination of directives, inquiries, clarifications, and guidelines flowing downward to thousands of planning bodies on lower levels, while an incessant series of reports, requests for clarification, petitions, calls for assistance, and permissions floated upward to the Central Commission. Even if every micro variable behaved exactly as planned, the coordination task alone would have proved superhuman. The economy, through the Plan, had been organized into a gigantic state enterprise. Any miscalculation in one of the key industries, or a breakdown in any of the vital links, could paralyze the system.

Material balance was one of the chief concerns of the planners, yet material imbalances were often the result. The commission planned to resolve economic stagnation and crises, yet stagnation and crises came. The Planning Commission revised growth rates downward for the late 1970s and early 1980s, yet negative growth rates were recorded instead. Accustomed to numbers crunching, planning officials lost touch with economic reality. Workable and more effective measures were bypassed owing to ideological fossilization. Planning with minimal regard for the well-being of producers and consumers led to growing social unrest. The formation of Solidarity was an expression of far deeper dissatisfaction, but dissatisfaction was not a Table quantified or quantifiable variable in the minds of economic planners. Their command style of planning dehumanized as well as detracted from the growth potential of the Polish economy.

Table 2.1 illustrates the ineffectiveness of command planning in Poland from 1966 through 1990. Planned growth for the 1976-1980 period in terms of real GNP was not officially given, but the contrast between planned and actual *net material product* for the same period is sufficiently telling. The Planning Commission's projection was for an annual growth rate of 7.0 percent; the actual performance was a dismal 1.2 percent. Even with drastically reduced expectations in the 1981-1985 plan, the actual annual growth for the period was a negative .8 percent instead of a positive .9 percent. With the exception of the 1966-1970 period, actual performance was always significantly off target from what was planned. The waste of centralized planning is self-evident.

PLANNING IN ACTION

The drafting of an annual short-term or a five-year operational plan was the end product of work by thousands of the Planning Commission agencies and offices. The Central Planning Commission derived its information from state ministries as well as from lower-level Province planning commissions. Province Planning Commissions obtained inputs from Province ministries of industry, agriculture, mining, housing, labor, energy, transportation, communication, health, education, and tourism, among others. The Province planning commissions in turn needed detailed information from district and local planning offices on recent performance, current development, and prognosis on a wide range of economic variables. District and local planning offices had to rely on field workers for data collection, which might or might not be available. And, if available, the data might or might not be reliable. The upward flow of information was assessed by Warsaw to determine whether planned targets were being met and future objectives were still achievable.

Table 2.1
Poland's Planned and Actual Net Material Product, 1966-1990 (average annual percentage change)
P=Planned; A=Actual

1966-70	1971-75	1976-80	1981-85	1986-90
P= 6.0	P= 6.7	P= 7.0	P= 0.9	P= 3.0
A= 6.0	A= 9.8	A= 1.2	A= -0.8	A= ---

Source: United Nations, 1977: 8; 1982: 134; 1988: 260.

In view of the above, production-factor availability over time needed to be evaluated. A barrage of questions had to be addressed: Were the required machines and equipment available for meeting the production target? Were the complementary inputs such as fuel, chemicals, and metals available in adequate quantity at the time and location desired? How much obsolescence of technology had taken place, and how much replacement and servicing of equipment and machinery was necessary? Could the latter be serviced and replaced from domestic sources, or must foreign currencies be earmarked to procure the same from abroad? Of that, how much equipment must be procured from the West with how much hard currency, and could the balance be secured from socialist economies? Then, to import such foreign equipment, services, raw materials, or consumer needs, how many goods and services must be exported to achieve a trade balance?

The Central Planning Commission also had to simultaneously estimate demand and supply in the labor markets--not only the number of workers needed in a given sector at a given time and place, but with the assured given levels of skill. How many people in which industry were to retire in one, two, or five years? And how many replacements were needed to be trained, upgraded, and if necessary, relocated? Plans also had to be drawn up to determine how many of school-age generation were to receive what kind and what level of education for which branch of productive activity. When youth entered the job market, would appropriate openings be available at wage rates affordable by the government and acceptable to job seekers?

When planning for labor supply, demand, and productivity, the commission would rest its hope on the unreliable assumption that not only would labor remain productive as anticipated--that is, without strikes--but also that it would produce according to plan. Given a strike, such as by coal miners, catastrophic consequences would result. Since the supply of energy in the form of domestic coal had been "planned" into the productive activities of other industries, a prolonged strike by coal miners would effectively paralyze many industries upon which many more industries depended.

As if the need for balancing material and labor spheres were not complex enough, the commission had also to achieve financial balance: the economy's aggregate income had to match its expenditure. *Expenditure* was required material inputs and wages, investments, subsidies, government services, and so on. *Income* originated from purchases made by domestic as well as foreign consumers of domestically produced goods and services. Prices and wages therefore needed to be determined. In a planned economy, where market forces do not play an active role in assessing costs and values, prices are more often than not arbitrary and distorted. Wages do not reflect marginal productivity. In Poland, the whole financial balancing act, if achieved, only helped to create unwanted surplus in some areas and shortage in others. Shortages in the supply of food, for instance, should have mandated a rise in prices, especially if purchases from abroad became necessary. But the additional expenditure was not in the plan. A price increase, on the other hand, would automatically reduce the purchasing power of the planned wages of consumers whose money income was already low. Demonstrations and riots would and did materialize. The government was thus caught in the vise of its own inflexible system, and borrowing from abroad became an alternative. Debt mounted and the plan in place had to be drastically revised in terms of production, consumption, investment, savings, trade, and other macro variables. Downward and upward communication resumed and multiplied with little prospect of restoring sectoral equilibrium for stability or growth. Planning neither fulfilled the expectations of the government nor satisfied the needs of consumers.

INDUSTRY

Poland's path of economic growth faithfully duplicated that of the Soviet Union. To consolidate its grip upon the nation, the Communist administration extolled the merits and need of rebuilding the nation's economy via consolidation of industrial enterprises. Nationalization of key industrial complexes went into effect shortly after the war ended. For enterprises in the west and southwest territories recently recovered from Germany, nationalization was accomplished without compensation to German proprietors. For enterprises owned by Polish nationals elsewhere, nationalization was with compensation in the form of government bonds. The industries nationalized were primarily of strategic importance to the nation's security or economy. Communication facilities, transport, mines, energy industries, and light industries of significance were nationalized first. But unlike in other communist countries, the Polish public was permitted the freedom of owning and operating small free enterprises with no more than fifty employees.

The first phase of industrial restructuring was accomplished uneventfully, but the Soviet experience should have alerted private entrepreneurs that the restructuring process was far from complete. The next phase quickly began in the then-mixed socialist Polish republic, where public and private enterprises coexisted. Unlike in China, where private enterprises voluntarily requested joint ownership with the state by surrendering their assets without compensation, in Poland the Communist party employed an economic squeeze on private firms first. The squeeze was completed with political manipulations, and by 1947, all private firms were required to have their enterprises registered with the state for licensing purposes. The Registration fee demanded a variable high percentage of the firm's gross income, depending upon the size of the firm in accordance with its volume of turnover and/or raw materials supplied to it (Barnett, 1988: 251-52). If such levies were uniformly imposed on both private and public firms, then the private firms would have had a chance of remaining competitive. But public-owned or state-affiliated enterprises were exempt from such taxes and fees.

Since the economy was to be guided and controlled by state planning, less individualistic behavior by the private sector meant greater flexibility and predictability by the state. To that end, private enterprises did not suit the state's preference. When the state allocated essential or strategic input to enterprises, state-owned ones received primary attention; the private sector was made to feel disadvantaged for remaining private.

The government then accelerated the industrial restructuring process by obliging private enterprises to be part of enterprise associations directed by the state. The private industrial sector was effectively brought under the sphere of government influence. "These various pressures resulted in the decline of the share of total industrial production originating in the private sector. In 1946, the share amounted to less than 9 percent of the gross value of industrial output, excluding handicrafts; by 1950, it had fallen to 5 percent; by 1953, to less than 1 percent" (Barnett, 1958: 252). The government neatly fitted this key sector of the economy into its plan and under its control, rapid industrialization process was underway. Massive state resources were poured into industries in the form of capital investment. Heavy industry was favored over light industry, light industry was favored over agricultural development, and reproducer goods were emphasized over consumer goods. It was a replica of the Soviet development model.

Rapid expansion of the industrialized sector can be seen both from the sector's contribution to the gross national product and from the increasing percentages of the labor force engaged in industries over time. In 1950, industry's contribution to Poland's national income was 24 percent. By 1970, it rose to 44 percent. Agriculture's contribution to national income for the same period fell from 60 to 23 percent (World Bank, 1987a: 3). Industrial employment increased from 1960's 3.16 million to 1970's 4.45 million (Directoriate of Intelligence, 1989: 51). The structural changes from a primarily agrarian economy to that of an industrial one were rapid.

The structural transformation within the industrial sector was patterned after the Soviet model. Capital-intensive, large, heavy industrial complexes were favored over smaller ones. Emphasis was on steel, metal, chemical, coal mining, and energy. Enterprises producing exportable goods were granted more favorable status in the state's development plan. To curry favor with the planners, smaller industrial firms had two routes: they either merged into larger ones or they associated themselves with enterprise associations. As a result, oligopolistic firms dominated a given industry, in terms of both the number of workers employed and the value product. "Socialized enterprises employing fewer than one hundred workers account for 0.8 percent of industrial employment and 0.7 percent of industrial output, while enterprises employing over one thousand workers account for 65.9 percent of industrial employment and 66.3 percent of industrial output" (World Bank, 1987b: 87).

In terms of enterprise numbers, firms employing 1,000 workers or more accounted for only 19.2 percent of the total in 1985. Not unlike the Fortune 500s, "in 1955, of the total manufacturing industry, the top 500 enterprises accounted for 40.9 percent of employment, 65.9 percent of sales, over 70 percent of export earnings, 78.3 percent of gross profits, 63.9 percent of net profits, and 49.5 percent of subsidies" (World Bank, 1987b: 88). For the government, a smaller number of larger firms meant easier direct control. In planning, the Polish industrial sector was structured oligopolistically or monopolistically with the notion that bigger was better.

By late 1950s, there was a comeback of smaller, privately owned firms, the result of promised economic reform after the 1956 Hungarian Revolution. Consequently the Polish industrial sector today is more mixed than three decades ago. The proliferation of private firms gathered momentum with the inception of the Solidarity movement. However, such firms were excluded from industries with key strategic significance. Most were small and were engaged in service-oriented industries such as commerce, handicrafts, and small scale manufacturing (World Bank, 1987b: 92). The presence of such private enterprises was not to the liking of the state, but their aggregate economic force constituted only a small portion of the total and it was tolerated.

Aside from the state enterprises and a relatively small number of private ones, since 1976 there emerged the so-called Polonia firms. Owing to economic necessity, new legislation permitted establishment of firms owned by foreign nationals, primarily investors from abroad of Polish descent (World Bank, 1987b: 92). These imported entrepreneurial establishments provided a meaningful contribution by filling voids in the market. They brought hard currency and state-of-the-art technology, they were more flexible in operations and more resourceful in identifying opportunities. These companies became a cause of discomfort to decision makers in the centralized economy. Intangible restrictions were placed on the firms, including substantial repatriation of profits in hard currencies. Tax rates on profits were also arbitrarily and exorbitantly raised, and the growth rate of Polonia firms tapered off as a result. This is one area the former administration of Tadeusz Mazowiecki worked diligently to revitalize.

MINING

Despite the relative insignificance of the mineral industry's contribution to Poland's gross national product, mining activities constituted an important facet of Poland's communist economy. Twenty percent of Poland's exports in 1986 were generated by minerals, fuels, and metals (World Bank, 1989: 245). Every five-year development plan invariably emphasized the mining industry's importance and the need for accelerating its development. The minerals having the greatest potential value were coal, copper, sulphur, lead, and zinc. The known coal deposits in Upper Silesia alone accounted for 56 billion tons, with another 100 billion tons of inferred reserve found in the general regions of Upper and Lower Silesia and Lublin (World Bank, 1987: 167ff). Copper reserves, some of the largest in Europe, were discovered in the late 1950's in Lower Silesia. Poland today still ranks fifteenth in the world's known reserves of copper, only slightly lower than Canada and Mexico. Copper production soared from 1.8 tons in 1960 to 19.7 tons in 1976 and 29.4 million tons in 1985 (Nelson, 1984: 196; World Bank, 1987: 127). The export value of Poland's copper alone amounted to a quarter of a billion dollars in 1985 (World Bank, 1987: 130). Because of the mining industry's strategic importance, no exception was made to mine owners in 1945 when nationalization of enterprises began. All mines became state owned, operated, and controlled.

The management method that the state enterprise used to control the mining industry was multipronged. Enterprise directors or managers were not the de facto decision makers within their respective firms. Early on, members of a workers council were assigned as co-custodians of the enterprise's function and performance. Decision making was a shared responsibility. Besides, as in state enterprises in the Soviet Union and in other command model economies, the party secretary in a mining enterprise had ultimate say. That included management practices, finance, accounting, investment decisions and discipline. Though in theory the party person was present in an advisory role, he or she was the one who advised, monitored, admonished, reported, and when needed, vetoed management decisions. The enterprise's director managed in a limited sense only; his or her primary responsibility was to follow state directives as per the state plan. For example, production quotas were to be met. Discipline was to be maintained. Output was to be delivered to the state. Wage guidelines were to be adhered to. The enterprise's financial plan was to be submitted and approved.

The mining enterprise was directly supervised and controlled by one of the numerous economic ministries. Besides, the Ministry of Finance, the Ministry of State Control, or the Ministry of Central Industrial Boards could all have respective influence over the firm's activities. Independent initiative or action on the part of enterprise director was not actively promoted; predictability was preferred in socialized enterprises. The parameter of flexibility for enterprise directors was narrow by design. The manager's function, therefore, was to devise ways whereby costs could be reduced, production increased, and work morale maintained so that the state plan could be implemented.

With each wave of social unrest came the promise of reform. Reform-minded activists sought enterprise self-management and financial self-accountability. Reform proposals invariably met with strong resistance from affected economic ministries, particularly those of finance, trade, state control, and planning. What the government gave in one hand, it took with the other (Obloj interview, 1990). For instance, under pressure, the government permitted the elective system for an enterprise director in place of a ministry-appointed directorship. However, giving in to pressure from within the apparatus, it exempted such elective practice from mining and other key industries. It even dismissed over 1,000 elected enterprise directors who expressed sympathy or support for Solidarity in 1982. As a whole, the structured Polish industry was based upon the formal relationship between the enterprise and the ministries, and upon the structured relationship among layers of management and labor within an enterprise. The mining enterprise was a cog in the machine that was the state.

AGRICULTURE

Rapid industrialization during the past four decades diminished the relative importance of the agricultural sector in the Polish economy. The amount of labor engaged in agricultural production was 44 percent two decades after the war ended. Fifteen years thereafter, it decreased to 29 percent. Conversely, the combined labor force of industry and service accounted for 57 percent in 1965 and 72 percent in 1980. Nevertheless, agricultural production still contributed to 16 percent of the nation's income in 1985. To an average consumer, nearly one-third of personal income had to be expended on food in the early 1970s. By 1982, owing to reduced government subsidies, the food budget rose to nearly 60 percent of household income. Thereafter, even with wage increases to compensate for inflation in general and food price increases in particular, an average Polish household still had to budget nearly 45 percent of its income for food. The implicit conclusion is that, relative to national product, productivity in the agricultural sector was low.

As in its industrial policy, the Polish government copied the Soviet model for agricultural development. The first phase of agricultural restructuring was land redistribution. Land to the west, which had been incorporated into the Polish boundaries after the war, was confiscated and given to what was later to be state farms. Land from rich landowners exceeding one hundred hectares were appropriated and distributed to landless peasants or small farms. The land redistribution program was complete.

Phase two of restructuring the farm sector was collectivization. The rationale was simple: economies of scale and specialization, and division of labor for improved productivity and higher living standards. Farmers were expected to choose the desired degree of collectivization, ranging from cooperative sharing of capital equipment to tightly organized collectives wherein producers shared all factors of production, including their lands. Unlike the strong-armed tactics employed by the Soviets during its collectivization, the approach employed by the Polish government was a combination of incentives for those who joined and economic penalties for those who desisted.   Recalling the heritage of Polish culture, it is understandable why the overwhelming majority of farm producers in Poland declined the invitation to be collectivized. Poland was the sole command-type socialist economy whose private farmers successfully resisted collectivization. As of 1985, less than one-fourth of Polish farms were in the socialized sector.

Within the socialized sector of the farm industry, there were three categories: the state farms, the collectives, and the agricultural circles. The state farms were state owned and state operated, the model for social transformation.   Their operational mode was similar to state industrial enterprises. All state farms were directly under the jurisdiction of the State Farm Ministry. Once assigned delivery quotas, the farms were charged with the task of drawing up their respective production plans geared to fulfill the assigned quotas.   The state requisitioned and allocated the factors of production. Input prices were subsidized below market price. Essential inputs, such as chemical fertilizers which were often in short supply, were allocated to the state farms first. Farm machinery likewise was allocated to state farms ahead of collectives and private farms. Despite both the tangible and nonquantifiable advantages bestowed upon such farms by the state, cost-benefits analysis revealed that state farms were only about three-fourths as efficient as smaller, privately owned farms (World Bank, 1987b: 29).

The second category of socialized farms was the collectives, which accounted for 3.7 percent of total cultivated area in Poland in 1985. Membership in collectives was supposed to be voluntary; though many smaller farms joined as a result of outright coercion or high-pressure coaxing. So that the state might have tangible control over them, collective farms were in turn joined in a Union of Collective Farms, which monitored their productive activities (Barnett, 1958: 232). As a part of the socialized farm industry, members enjoyed subsidies and related privileges from the state. Directors of collectives were elected from among their respective member farms, but guidelines and procedures were handed down from above. The decision-making process within a collective was more often than not in the hands of its party secretary, local government, and party officials.   Given the circumstances under which smaller farms became members of the collectives, work incentives were tepid at best. Many farmers contributed the assigned work hours, then expended their more productive time and energy on permitted plots. Those who had easier access to urban centers held regular part-time jobs to supplement their wage income from the collectives. Joining the collectives was not so much motivated by socialized zeal as much as to take whatever advantages the state had to offer. The farmers contributed as little effort therein as possible.

The third form of socialized farms were the agricultural circles. Loosely banded together, circle farms worked less than .5 percent of the land under cultivation. They were "cooperative organizations whose primary purpose was to provide machinery services to the small private farms" (World Bank, 1987b: 21). As early as the mid-1950s, the Polish government had already recognized that the socialized sector of the agriculture industry was less efficient than the defiant private farms. Gomulka had proposed in 1956 that members of collective farms be permitted to withdraw their memberships. Many seized the opportunity and returned to private farming. Thus over three quarters of Polish farms were under private ownership. They were more cost conscious, better managed, and more productive than state farms or collectives.

Yet for a number of reasons, the Polish agricultural sector was far from realizing its productive potential. Its per-hectare yield, even when compared with economies of the COMECON nations, was by far the lowest. Poland's 1982-1984 average per hectare yield of grains was only 66.4 percent that of Bulgaria, 63.1 percent that of Czechoslovakia, and 55.5 percent that of Hungary. Even Romania, the second lowest in per hectare yield among Eastern European nations. recorded nearly 35 percent higher yield than Poland (World Bank, 1987b: 35). One of the reasons for low agricultural productivity on private Polish farms is their size. More than 58 percent were then and still are less than 5 hectares in size. Only 16.3 percent of all farms, which included all the state farms and collectives, were 10 hectares or larger. Modernized methods of production became cost prohibitive, and the applications of yield-increasing inputs were short of desired scale. Another proximate cause of low land productivity was the inadequacy of an infrastructure. Prior to 1972, private farms were deliberately discriminated against, with the intent that they voluntarily abandon their individual holdings to join collectives or to sell to the state farm fund. Chemical fertilizer was short in supply since it was centrally allocated; state farms and collectives were the primary recipients and private farms, if granted purchase requests, had to pay inflated prices. Also, farm machinery was manufactured to suit the needs of the larger state farms. Even with the introduction of state machine centers that served the farm sector, private farmers could obtain the center's service only on specified conditions, and those conditions would bring them under some form of state control. For dairy farm producers and producers of cash crops, there was also the lack of processing facilities. More pronounced discrimination against private farms could be seen in the state's investment policy. With mainly an agrarian economy after the war, investment in the farm sector took a back seat to industry. As late as 1975, state investment in the agricultural sector was only 13.4 percent of total. In land reclamation projects, rural electrification, drainage, water supply, farm machinery, agricultural processing, and fertilizer or pesticide industries, the intent was to benefit first and foremost the socialized sector of agriculture. Over time, any trust that private farmers had in the government's helping them evaporated.

SERVICES

Health Care

Since the early days of the communist regime, health-care services were nationalized and made subject to the direct control of various levels of the government. Planning for improved health care was an integral part of the national development plan. Rules and regulations proliferated with regard to work hours and pay scales, but physicians were permitted a private practice outside the required forty hour week of service to a public institution. Medical services in general were made more available to the general public. With Gomulka's return to power in 1956, government regimentation over health-care personnel was relaxed. However, the Ministry of Health still had jurisdiction over a wide range of health-care provision and delivery systems. The ministry worked closely with the Central Planning Commission on the number of physicians and nurses to be trained during the plan period. It determined the number of hospitals and health care centers to be established, and it had control over the pharmaceutical industry and provided direction and funding for medical research. Other than health-care facilities under the jurisdiction of other government ministries--such as the military, which had its own health distribution system--all hospitals and clinics were under the jurisdiction of the Ministry of Health.

The majority of people relied on public health care provided by the government, but numbers were not indicative of consumer satisfaction. Only those who could afford higher fees frequented private clinics, where the waiting time was shorter and services more personalized. Like most consumer items in the economy, health care was heavily subsidized by the government. In 1987, total health-care and social welfare budgets were nearly 700 billion zlotys, of which the Central Ministry retained 263.1 billion. The balance was allocated among provincial administrative units. The bulk of both State and provincial health budgets was expended to subsidize the general public for hospitalization, hospital or clinic visits, prescription drugs, and extended health care in institutionalized homes or facilities. On average, a Polish citizen paid only 17 percent of health-care costs in 1970. By 1984, the patient's share decreased to only 9 percent (World Bank, 1987b: 394 ff).

Consumers of health care from private physicians were not subsidized. Prescription drugs had to be paid in full by the patient. In contrast, a patient who received care through a public facility paid only 15 percent of pharmaceutical costs. In health-care services, the role of the government was relatively less suffocating than in other spheres of economic activity.

Education

Administration of the educational system was shared by the ministries of education on various levels. For institutes of higher education, the Ministry of Science and Higher Education had responsibility for supervision and direction. But there were colleges and universities that, owing to their specific purposes, were under the direct jurisdiction of their respective ministries or government agencies.

Poland has one of the highest adult literacy rates in the world. By the mid 1970s, over 98 percent of the adult population was literate. For a nation that was predominantly agrarian a few decade ago, it is a tribute to the intensified educational programs of the government after the war. Whereas education is instrumental in the development process everywhere, it was more than a means to greater labor productivity in Poland. After the consolidation of power was complete, the Polish Communist party sought to employ the educational system as a vehicle for propagating party ideology. Beginning in 1948, from primary schools through universities, academic programs were streamlined toward that purpose. The Ministry of Education administered and directed programs embracing systems of primary, secondary, vocational, technical, and preschool education (World Bank, 1987b: 419).

Relative to other communist countries, greater latitude was accorded to school administrative rectors in Poland. University rectors were democratically elected by the faculty. The faculty was also permitted to form its own senate. University students also had independent bodies of representation. The higher education law of 1982 granted greater democratization, liberalization, and academic freedom in universities and colleges. The elected leadership in institutions of higher education thus exhibited more professional competence than ideological subserviency.

Financially, the state funded all primary and secondary schools, with the exception of a few church owned and operated ones. The state further took upon itself the total funding of college and university operations, with the exception of students living on campuses whose living expenses were "only partly" subsidized.

Transportation and Communication

With the exception of the Soviet Union, Poland has one of the best transportation systems, but one of the worst communication systems in Eastern Europe. Its communication system suffered due to planned neglect: only party offices had a communication system. In short, communication is power. Not allowing the people a functional communication system was a party method of control. Ironically, today when a new independent firm or bank wants to open, it requests an old party office building because the communication system has been in place for years.

On the other hand, the transportation system was built up rapidly after the war, owing to perceived necessity. Unfortunately, the system's design was influenced by the Soviet political agenda. Soviets permitted rails to be built on north-south routes, but prohibited development of east-west routes out of fear of the West's military. For an economy striving to develop rapidly, both systems should have been considered crucial.

The transportation sector was under the jurisdiction of the Ministry of Transport, and major forms of commercial transport included railroad freight, interprovince road freight, inland waterway and maritime transport, and car transport. Of great importance to the economy is the railway system. It ranks among the top three on the European continent, excluding the Soviet Union. The geographic spread of prime mining sites demanded that an extensive railroad freight system be established from mine heads to industrial centers, as well as to sea ports to the north. Excessive emphasis on the rapid development of heavy industry also dictated an effective north-south freight system. Being a nation of mostly plains, the cost of developing a rail system was less prohibitive than if the terrain were more mountainous. As a result, in 1987 Poland outpaced Hungary by nearly four to one in terms of millions of metric tons carried on its rail system. When contrasted with Czechoslovakia, which ranked number two in Eastern Europe in 1987, Poland carried 40.06 billion metric tons per kilometer to the former's 22.50 billion metric tons. For ocean freight, the contrast in 1987 was even more pronounced. Poland tabulated 197.0 billion metric ton per kilometer, outranking Bulgaria by nearly three to one (Nelson, 1984: 192-98).

The basic administration of the transport system was carried out by district and regional offices, as supervised by their respective central offices for rail, roads, auto transport, air, and inland shipping. The Ministry of Transport, working in conjunction with the Central Planning Commission, determined the proposed budget for various facets of ground, air, and inland shipping transports. The directives were then handed down and budgets allocated to regional and district offices through their respective central offices. A separate office, the Office of Maritime Economy, had responsibility for maritime shipping and was distinct from the Ministry of Transport, with its own budget and administrative apparatus. The purpose was to accentuate the economic importance of maritime shipping. A study conducted by a team of World Bank specialists conclusively highlighted the profitability of the maritime shipping industry in Poland: maritime enterprises had "considerable autonomy in investment and tariff decisions" not enjoyed by other enterprises

(World Bank, 1987b: 309).

The bulk of the Polish transportation system was not and did not need to be subsidized by the state. When decisions were made independently of the central office, efficiency and profitability usually were the norm. The one weak link in the system rested with air transport. The Polish Airline Lot was state owned and had a small fleet of aging planes. Operations and maintenance costs were high, especially for international flights when additional hard currencies were needed, but revenues were low owing to state subsidies for consumers. Still, transportation was one of the brighter achievements of the Communist administration.

State monopoly over the communication systems was less for economic than for security reasons. The communication system under Communist rule consisted of the postal service, telephone, telecommunication, and museums, all under the jurisdiction of the Ministry of Communication. Political factors outweighed economic considerations in operating and developing the system. In the West, data processing, speedy information flow, and information retrieval have all become pivotal to economic development. Poland has lagged far behind in all such forms of communication (Obloj interview, 1990). Investment therein was a low priority for planners.

As long as the demand for services by the government was met, demand for services from the private sector was unimportant. This was most pronounced in domestic telephone services. Having a phone in one's residence indicated status. The waiting period for a residential telephone, according to official data in 1955, was thirteen years (World Bank, 1987a: 32). Lines connecting Poland with the outside world were and still are inadequate; the waiting time to place an international call could be as long as four to six hours. Similarly, for lack of trained personnel and funding, telegram and postal services were slow. A cynical but perhaps correct explanation of inadequate investment in a communication system was that the former Office of Censorship would not have had enough manpower to monitor the phone calls or to censor the mail if the system had been more efficient.

Housing

The Ministry of Construction and the Ministry of Housing were two of the several ministries responsible for the construction industry.[1] The Ministry of Construction was concerned with erecting industrial, commercial, and other public complexes. The Ministry of Housing was responsible for building residential housing units. Similar to the waiting period for a telephone was the purchase of a residential home--approximately ten years. It was one of the numerous areas where consumers were engaged in a losing battle (Goscinski interview, 1990). To have a phone installed meant having a residence; to have a residence of one's own meant waiting a long time. Someone with an apartment of his or her own equipped with a working telephone had perhaps already reached middle age.

Polish buildings suffered severe damage during the war. After the war, Poland had one of the highest population growth rates in Europe, and housing demand outpaced supply. A cumulative undersupply led to a housing crisis.

The causes of the current housing shortage are deliberate and can be traced to inappropriate economic policies and the functioning of the planned economy. After the war, emphasis was on reconstruction and rebuilding, but the initial thrust was on restoring and repairing damaged buildings rather than constructing of new structures. After 1948, the six-year development plan committed disproportionate investment to developing heavy industry at the expense of other sectors, including housing. With increasing criticism from the public and media, Gomulka granted more funds for housing. In conjunction with the Ministry of Municipal Economy, the Ministry of Housing was able to increase subsidies for building activities--with state and cooperative housing given priority. However, the industry was routinely plagued by a shortage of building materials because the building-supply industry was not given due consideration for expansion. The housing shortage was also the party's means of control: it prevented people from relocating.

Unlike other socialist economies, the Polish government did permit private enterprise in the housing industry. But preferential treatment was granted to state and cooperative housing industries, in both credit extension and subsidies to occupants of state or cooperative dwellings. Thus, the private sector's ability to survive was constrained. After four and a half decades of Communist administrations, the private housing sector faced insurmountable obstacles.

State subsidies and the structure of the housing industry need be mentioned. There were three types of housing in Poland: state, cooperative, and private. State housing was composed of enterprise and local government housing. The former was for employees of state enterprises, one of the amenities granted to state employees, particularly in industries where worker turnover was high. Local government housing units, on the other hand, were built with state funds for low-income citizens. The combined output of enterprise and local government housing was approximately 30 percent of total annual new housing units (World Bank, 1989: 367-68).

The second category of housing was cooperative. Units of cooperative housing could be rented out, jointly owned, or owned by single families; renters could become joint owners if so desired and if financially feasible. Privileges were accorded the cooperative housing sector, however a housing unit that was cooperatively built but was subsequently sold to a single household would have privileges withdrawn and earlier benefits calculated for reimbursement to the state. This cooperative housing sector became the largest sub-sector in the housing industry; comprising approximately 50 percent of total new residential units built each year.

The third category was private housing, a luxury few could afford. These housing units were generally built in less densely populated regions of urban centers. The growth of private housing was limited, with competitiveness from state and cooperative housing, in addition to difficulties in obtaining building materials. Socialized housing was more competitive for two major reasons. First, public housing was much cheaper to rent or jointly own. State subsidies came in the form of low rent, low interest rates, and low maintenance costs--making living in cooperative or state housing units affordable. Second, the earning power of the Polish working class was such that to build and to maintain single private housing units would be financially prohibitive.

Housing subsidies came in various forms. In one form, low-income residents could qualify for occupancy at local government housing units, where the cost of building such units was borne entirely by the state. Rents were low, and residents whose income was below a certain level qualified for additional subsidies to make the rent nominal. In a second form, the cost of housing was shouldered mostly by the enterprise, and state enterprises could borrow up to 50 percent of the capital required at subsidized rates with a long amortization period. The third form offered subsidies for the cooperative housing sector: for tenants, the state granted a capital subsidy up to 50 percent. Occupants needed put forth a mere fraction of the capital requirement prior to construction, and the balance could be obtained from state banks at subsidized rates. Repayment of such bank loans was to be sixty years (World Bank, 1987b: 368-69). For single homeowner cooperatives, there was a ceiling placed on the amount of subsidized low-interest loans. The loan repayment period was also shorter. For private housing, subsidies were similar to those for cooperative single-house homeowners. The ceiling for loans and repayment periods were nearly identical. Combining all forms of housing subsidies, including the opportunity cost to the state for reduced amortization rates, the cost constitutes between 18 to 20 percent of government expenditures and between 4 to 5 percent of Poland's GNP (World Bank, 1987b: 367).

Despite such disproportionate government expenditures in the housing sector, acute housing shortage problems persisted, primarily because of the government's role in the housing market and the manner in which that role was assumed.

FINANCIAL INSTITUTIONS

Real flow brings forth the goods and services produced, whereas *financial flow* is the sum total of economic return on the factors of production. Given the relative balance between real and financial flow, there should be little evidence of disequilibrium. In Poland, as in all centralized planned economies, real flow was what mattered. Financial flow was relegated to an auxiliary role. Overproduction of some goods and severe shortage of other goods and services became common. The passive role assigned to the financial sphere may explain many of the economic crises confronting the Polish economy today.

In line with the system's propensity to plan and to control facets of economic activity, it became imperative that financial institutions be under the direct supervision of the government. At the end of World War II, the National Bank of Poland (NBP) was established as the sole authorized financial institution to issue legal tender and to play a key role in implementating the nation's development plans. Special-purpose banks, such as investment banks, state agricultural banks, central banks of the agricultural cooperative, and postal savings banks, were also either established or resurrected after the war. Private banks no longer existed. Over time, banking reforms consolidated some banks and eliminated others, with the National Bank of Poland expanding its function and authority over the banking system.

The NBP was under the direction of the Ministry of Finance. Comparable to the central banks of most nations, the NBP regulated money and credit supply. Unlike the central banks of the West, however, the NBP assumed the added responsibility of drawing up financial plans for the Ministry of Finance and the Central Planning Commission. It determined credit availability to state and cooperative enterprises, as outlined by the plan objectives. It also financed government expenditures and helped settle foreign accounts. The investment banks' function, distinct from that of the National Bank of Poland, was to finance longer-term investments by state enterprises and state-approved agencies. The state agricultural bank and special-function banks likewise extended loans to and audited their respective interest groups. To service consumers at large, the general savings bank accepted deposits and cleared checks. All banks, however, were directly or indirectly supervised by the NBP to ensure that guidelines and objectives set by the plan were heeded. Therefore, all state enterprises had to submit their respective financial plans to the NBP for approval and monitoring.

Though playing a passive role in macroeconomic activity, the banking system was faced with making things work. Unfortunately problems arose because things did not work smoothly, owing to the designated structure and function of the financial system. For instance, an objective of the plans had been rapid industrialization of the economy. Disproportionate shares of the state budget had to be invested in industry, particularly heavy industry, and the NBP financed such undertakings. Reproducer goods were produced more or less according to plan. Wage earners made demands on consumer goods and services. With inadequate investment and low productivity in the consumer-goods industries, supply fell short of aggregate demand, and inflation ensued. The NBP had no effective means of curbing inflationary pressure--it could neither allocate more credit to industries where demand for products was high, nor soak up excess money supply. Consumer preference to hold cash or keep assets liquid did not help ease inflationary pressure.

Further passivity of the financial system resided in the massive subsidy programs espoused by central planning. Since wages were fixed and workers were paid below the value they contributed, low purchasing power necessitated keeping prices of essential goods low. Since announcements of price increases, particularly those of food items, often led to strikes, demonstrations, riots, and downfalls of administrations, price subsidies remained. The NBP had little voice in correcting the misallocation of resources to achieve a consumer goods equilibrium. Where investments should have been decreased, they were not; where industries should have been granted more funding for expansion, they were not. Market distortion continued, and the NBP continued to do the bidding of the state planners.

A final example of the inefficient and ineffective financial system in Poland may be viewed from the NBP's disbursement to state enterprises according to the plan. Enterprise managers were aware of supply rigidity, particularly the supply of essential inputs. They often requested permission for greater input reserves and higher inventory for outputs. Given the guidelines of the plan, such requests were often denied. With any delay in the delivery of essential inputs, production bottlenecks developed. If what one enterprise produced was a factor of production in a forward-linked enterprise, a chain reaction of underproduction resulted. When the situation became severe--such as in the coal industry--then the plan's objectives were grossly underachieved. Yet the NBP could not come to the rescue by financing higher levels of enterprise input reserves or future output inventory, since the plans would not permit that. The financial system in Poland had been assigned a rigid structure and function that did not and could not allow meaningful participation in the efficient allocation of financial resources. The need for financial reform will be discussed in Chapter 6.

NOTE

1. Some other ministries, such as mining, energy and agriculture, and forestry, also engaged in construction, but mostly for fulfilling their respective responsibilities.

3

THE POLISH ECONOMY IN LIGHT OF PERFORMANCE CRITERIA

Few people would disagree that the economic performances of Ethiopia, Peru, or Bangladesh leave much to be desired. Fewer yet would deny the success stories of Japan, South Korea, the former West Germany, or Italy. There are objective indicators to measure success or failure in a given economy. When evaluating the performance of the Polish economy, our discussion here is limited to the economic consequences of government policy measures, since only the commonly accepted performance criteria are employed. Quantitative criteria include economic efficiency, stability, growth and development, and equity. Qualitative criteria include economic freedom and opportunity, and adaptability and progressiveness.

EFFICIENCY

In the centralized Polish economy, the decision-making processes regarding production, distribution, and consumption of goods and services were different from economies in the West. Outside of the farm sector, private enterprises made up only a small percentage of the total. Decisions for private entrepreneurs were arrived at similarly to market economy practices, however cost reduction or essential complementary inputs might not be available. The state controlled and allocated many such factors. In the farm sector, shortages of chemical fertilizers or tractor services are two ready examples. Supplies were allocated first, according to state planning, to state farms and farm cooperatives at reduced cost. In manufacturing, imported raw materials were in the hands of the state, distributed first to state enterprises for production of goods destined for export or for products high on the planned list. In either farming or manufacturing, even if the private sector was able to secure the needed factors of production through state allocation, the materials were at a cost higher than what state enterprises paid.

In a market economy, the coordinating mechanism is the marketplace.

The market allocates how much of each factor goes into the production of a given product, determined through the forces of supply and demand, and resulting in an equilibrium price for the input. All who are able and willing may procure the quantity desired at the market determined price. But in the centralized Polish economy, the Planning Commission determined who received how much of each factor to produce what the state had designated. Factor cost, which in market economies reflects resource scarcity, had little meaning; factor supply did not reflect its marginal cost. In order for state enterprises to assure fulfillment of assigned quotas, requisition of essential inputs often went beyond what was required. If they were obtained, state enterprises had little incentive to employ the factors as efficiently as possible. Their rationale was that: if there should be any surplus, requisition for the next productive cycle would have to be lowered. Efficient resource allocation was to be avoided. On the other hand, private enterprises producing the same product needed the same essential input, but the supply was either inadequate or absent, and production suffered.

A second level of inefficiency in the Polish economy came with the centralized system of distribution. Once a product had been produced, instead of permitting market forces to determine which sector of the economy was to receive how much of the product, the state's plan made the decision. For instance, even though society's real demand dictated that construction materials be used for housing projects, the materials instead went to projects mandated by the plan. The recently built city of Nowa Huta is a ready example; it was built practically from scratch.

Another illustration of inefficient distribution was how money borrowed from abroad in the 1970s was distributed among users. Market demand might suggest that the financial resources be channeled into light industry, for production of household durables and other consumer goods. However, the government decided otherwise. The money was liberally spent to acquire new heavy industrial complexes instead of updating existing ones at lower costs, and to indiscriminately purchase foreign licenses for possible future uses. In a market economy, a firm resorting to such allocative measures without calculating the costs and benefits of alternative ventures would find itself in bankruptcy court in no time. A distribution system not based on needs--as expressed by objective demand conditions--and not on real cost--as expressed by supply conditions--leads to inefficiency. By definition, *distributive efficiency* means maximum returns from minimal expenditure. Efficiency excludes waste. Efficiency rises above mediocre results. Efficiency seeks maximum return from minimum input. But the Polish economy's performance fell short on all these counts.

The third area of inefficiency was in the realm of consumption. Assuming that wages had indeed reflected the marginal productivity of labor, wage earners could then purchase goods and services according to their tastes and preferences. The value, or marginal utility, which the consumer placed on the last unit of commodity purchased and consumed, would then determine whether the consumer was willing or able to procure it. If so, then the quantity of a commodity demanded by the consumer at the equilibrium price would direct how many units of it should be supplied. That, in turn, would determine how many units of the needed factors should be allocated to production of this product.

This, however, was not the case. In 1977, the Material Supply Office of the Central Planning Commission still had jurisdiction over central allocation of nearly 1,000 essential inputs. With reform measures introduced since 1982, the centrally allocated materials were reduced to 110 in 1986 and to 64 in early 1987 (World Bank, 1987a: 118-9). These controlled materials were allocated by the state toward production of what the plan had called for, not what the consumer demanded. Many of the centrally controlled materials were foreign imports purchased with convertible currencies. And many were resources needed by private enterprises to process farm products or to produce household durables, textile products, and leather goods. Yet producers could lay no claim to such inputs, even though the end products would reflect the high value consumers placed on them. Such products, therefore, were in short supply. Expressed value for a product by the consumer was unheeded, and demand was not met with supply. Utility maximization through consumption was not achieved.

Another indication of inefficiency in consumption was the pricing system. Prices of essential consumer goods were pegged by the Central Planning Commission. Translated, this means that the prices of these commodities were below market level. Further translated, the prices were subsidized by the state. Even in market economies where farm prices are directly or indirectly subsidized, we know that such practice leads to inefficiency. In market economies, however, the prices for subsidized commodities may still fluctuate according to supply and demand. In the centralized Polish economy, fixed prices were *fixed*. Consumers who wished to purchase a given quantity at a fixed price had to obtain it from state retail outlets. The long lines were a waste of consumers' potentially productive time. When goods sold out, the demand was unfilled. Price subsidies distorted the real cost of goods and their real value to the consumer. Scarce resources were not efficiently allocated.

Other major forms of inefficiency were in the areas of investment, employment and wages, and market structure. First investment decisions in a market economy are based on the rate of return and on market share. In Poland, the guideline to follow was the wish of the state, as elaborated in the plan. Since the formation of Council for Mutual Economic Assistance (CMEA) in 1949, there have been agreements for member nations to specialize in given industries. The Polish economy was obligated to direct much of its investment into the CMEA-agreed industries, thus supply inelasticity in consumer-goods industries had on occasion forced the government to import goods that could have readily been produced domestically, wasting the much needed convertible currency. On the other hand, under agreement, Poland had to import goods that itself could have readily produced via import-substitution measures if the funds had been available. Investments made on the basis of long-term foreign obligations caused rigidity and inefficiency, hindering rather than encouraging the productive capacity of the economy. As a corollary to investment inefficiency, the structure and functioning of the financial system were inefficient. The dynamic function that could have been filled by the financial market was instead reduced to being a passive clearinghouse for the state plan.

Second, employment and wage policies in Poland found their justification in Marxism: all able bodies should work. Remuneration was "to each according to his needs." Reforms introduced prior to 1989 had loosened this rigidity, but decades of ideology had cost the economy dearly. State enterprises, which were losing money or were producing goods not much in demand, remained open for fear of creating unemployment. Workers in state enterprises that produced needed products had little incentive to be innovative or productive. Jobs were secure and wages were fixed. Sick leaves were taken whenever workers could find friend-physicians who would sign the certificates. Since wages were not a function of value productivity, and since real wages were not sufficient to purchase needed goods and services, many workers who moonlighted gave more of their productive efforts to their second job, where wages were a greater function of productivity. Also, a university professor, most respected in Polish society and culture, was paid less than a coal miner or a shipyard worker, as determined by the budget plan (Johann interview, 1990). The incentive to be better educated, to be creative, to be resourceful, and to be truly productive was subdued by monetary considerations. Creative minds were wasted in the machine of state planning, and decreased productivity was inevitable.

And third, market structure in the centralized Polish industry was inefficient. The tens of thousands of private enterprises that had existed in 1944 had been squeezed out of the market by calculated policy measures. Both large and medium firms were nationalized--only small private enterprises were permitted, effectively reducing the competitive forces in the marketplace. In 1947, employment in the state-controlled sector accounted for 86.8 percent of total employment in Poland; in cooperatives, 4.1 percent; and in private enterprises, 9.1 percent. In 1949, these were, respectively; 89.3 percent, 6.1 percent, and 4.6 percent (Landau, 1985: 199).

Private firms were small. They were deprived of ready access to raw materials; and, on top of higher input costs, they had to pay higher taxes than state and cooperative enterprises. Economies of scale became irrelevant for firms with expansion potential. While the prices private firms charged for their products had to reflect the real cost of production, state and cooperative costs were subsidized and their prices were fixed below cost. The monopolistic power of the state and of the giant state enterprises effectively choked the vitality and efficiency of competitiveness. Allocative efficiency of the factors of production and products produced was no longer realizable.

STABILITY

In the process of economic growth, undesirable consequences may occur. Some of them are avoidable, but some attach themselves tenaciously to growth as an unavoidable by-product. In a market economy, problems arise with respect to unemployment, inflation, oligopolistic or monopolistic power, less inequitable distribution of income, and unethical business practices. In the centralized Polish economy, a number of these problems seemed to be less severe. Unemployment was not supposed to exist. Income was to be equitably distributed, and prices were planned to be stable. On closer scrutiny, however, the evidence shows the same problems existed, except that they had been swept under the rug.

Price Stability

Stability may be described as the ability to avoid disruptive cyclical disturbances; *disturbances* are significant fluctuations in the economic indicators. In terms of the Polish economy, a major disturbance was inflation, with the consequent economic results. Disturbance, or the absence of stability, could also include economically induced social and political unrest, which adversely affected Poland's economic performance.

Inflation is feared by governments more than unemployment. Though the Phillips' curve is no longer an iron-clad doctrine, decision makers are more ready to trade higher unemployment for lower inflation. In the planned Polish economy, when price controls were rigidly enforced and when consumers offered no great resistance to consumer-goods shortages, the lid was kept on inflation. According to a World Bank report, "the rate of increase of retail prices rose from 2.5 percent per annum in the first half of the 1970's, to 6.8 percent in the second. The United Nation's report indicated inflation rates of 21 percent, 101 percent, 22 percent, 15 percent, and 18 percent, respectively, for the years 1981 through 1986" (World Bank, 1987a: 12, 13). The World Bank cites an average annual inflation rate of 31.2 percent between 1981 and 1986 (1988: 223). Both sets of data on Polish inflation were low; the rates were on open inflation only. If hidden inflation had been duly quantified via shadow pricing and incorporated into the calculation, the figures would have been staggering. If the state's subsidies had been removed and black market prices inputed, aggregated, and incorporated, then a three-digit inflation rate in recent years would not have been far-fetched. Polish consumers may more readily agree with this estimation than with the official double-digit rates.

To grasp the magnitude of price instability in the planned Polish economy, one need only apply the official Polish rates of inflation to the United States scene: The housing industry would collapse. There would be daily devaluation of the dollar. Commodity prices would soar. Interest rate changes would tick like a clock. Persons on fixed incomes would become destitute. Investors in government bonds would go bankrupt. Investing would become cost-prohibitive. Buying sprees to hoard commodities would be daily exercises. The velocity of money would accelerate and confidence in its value plummet. The financial system would be thrown for a loop, and productive activities would come to a screeching halt.

Some of these consequences did not take place in Poland, for the simple reason that its economy was centralized, or controlled. But the fact that turmoil did not break out in no way implies that inflation was not there. The causes and effects of price instability in Poland have been variously discussed in earlier sections; the fact is that there was no meaningful price stability in the planned Polish economy.

Employment Stability

Persistent high inflation in a market economy can bring down an administration--so can sustained high unemployment. Economic stability is a cherished value. The more developed an economy, the greater is the consumer's fear of losing predictable income. Consumers become more security conscious, and economic entities become more conservative financially. In the planned Polish economy, the appearance of employment security and stability was misleading, and it merits closer examination.

Poland, under Communist rule, experienced high labor turnovers, while many working-age people knowingly declined to be part of the mainstream work force. Outside of the Soviet Union, Poland has had the highest population growth rate among CMEA member nations during the past two decades. The baby boom children after the war reached middle age and themselves became parents of working-age children. Poland's working-age population grew by 2.7 million from 1970 to 1980, while the labor force for the same period grew by only 1.36 million people. Therefore, by 1980, 1.34 million Poles who could have joined the labor force did not. Many continued their professional education. Many women married and began to have children. (World Bank, 1987a: 151, Table 6). The drop-out rate for the 1980-1985 period was even higher. From 1980 through 1985, the working-age population grew by 2.57 million people, but the increase in the number of people employed by 1985 was only .146 million. That is, within five years another 2.42 million of the employable population took themselves out of the mainstream work force.[1] For a total work force of 17.92 million people in 1985, those unaccounted for numbered 1.34 million plus 2,424 million within a fifteen-year period. There was a serious problem with employment.

By definition, Poland under communism did not have an unemployment problem. Unemployment occurs when, at prevailing wages, those who wish to be gainfully employed cannot. Poland had no such problem. Poland had a labor shortage, not unemployment, and the labor shortage was so acute that "the government had also introduced laws against *work evasion* or parasitism, requiring persons without jobs to register at unemployment exchanges, with apparently little success in reducing the number of persons in this group" (World Bank, 1987a: 151).

This *employment* situation in Poland created other problems, such as pervasive disguised unemployment and underemployment. Similar to the iron rice bowl practice in China of the recent past, workers who were on the state payroll did not get off the payroll unless they relinquished their jobs. More productive and enterprising individuals tended to seek employment in rewarding private settings or to emigrate (Sterniczuk interview, 1990); the less venturesome continued in their posts. Since wages reflected no measure of productivity, there was no reason to perform according to ability, and the genuinely productive potential of workers hibernated. State enterprises, therefore, operated with an oversized labor force that could have been significantly reduced if workers performed according to their ability. But under this layer of nearly 18 million fully employed persons, there was a deeper layer of disguised unemployment. Also, in the private sector where wages were generally higher, there was underemployment: a greater number of able and willing people than jobs available. This was another layer of untapped productivity.

Further evidence of unexploited labor productivity was the fact that employed persons were in the habit of calling in sick. According to the World Bank "Absenteeism is extremely high--an annual average of 222 hours per worker. Reducing absenteeism by 25 percent would be equivalent to increasing employment by 875,000." A director in the Ministry of Labor reported in 1986 that nearly 1.5 million workers were absent from work daily in socialized enterprises (World Bank, 1987a: 152). Discontent with their work situation was evident in an average annual work turnover rate of 19.0 percent in 1980 and 19.0 percent in 1985.

There was apathy toward work, but real zeal for political action, and economic instability manifested itself beyond the boundaries of economic activity. Dissatisfaction with the system was at the heart of the political ferment of 1955, in the Poznan riots of 1956, in the student demonstrations of 1968, in the Baltic region worker strikes of 1970, in the June Events of 1976, in the emergence of Workers Solidarity, in the origins of the Student Solidarity Committee in 1979, in the formation of Rural Solidarity in 1981, in the imposition of martial law in December 1981, and in recurrent street demonstrations in the late 1980s. Poland under communism was plagued not only by high inflation and unstable employment but also by more serious social and political disturbances. The latter were an external expression of deep tension beyond the realm of price and employment. They reflected the issues of trade imbalances, foreign debts, fluctuating labor and capital productivity, consumer goods shortages, black-markets activity, and housing shortages. There was no real economic stability under Poland's centralized system.

GROWTH AND DEVELOPMENT

The loss of lives and property sustained by Poland during World War II ranked among the highest in the world. After its enclosure in the Soviet camp upon the signing of the Yalta agreement, Poland was forcibly drawn to the Soviet Union politically, militarily, and economically. Centralized control over prices, wages, employment, and investment was aimed at squeezing the economy to finance industrialization and rapid economic growth. This strategy made Poland "one of the world's 12 most industrialized nations" (Nelson, 1984: 165).

Beginning in the 1940s, large investments were made in heavy industry at the expense of agriculture, light industry, and consumer goods. Domestic consumption was kept low by design, so that forced savings could be funneled toward more rapid growth. Table 3.1 provides an overview of three and a half decades of investment, net national income-NNI, and structural change.

Table 3.1
Selected Economic Indicators of Development, 1950-1986

	Gross Investment as Percent of NI Distributed	Index of Net NI Produced (Net Material Product), 1950=100
1950	20	100
1960	24	207
1970	27	374
1975	36	596
1980	20	633
1986	18	644

Source: World Bank, 1987a: 3.

Table 3.2
Average Annual Growth Rate of Real Gross National Products of United States, GDR, West Germany, and Poland, 1961-1987

	U.S.	GDR	West Germany	Poland
1961-1965	4.8	3.0	4.9	4.5
1966-1970	2.8	3.1	4.2	4.0
1971-1975	2.3	3.5	2.1	6.5
1976-1980	3.3	2.0	3.4	.7
1981-1985	3.0	1.9	1.3	.6
1986	3.0	1.5	2.4	2.8
1987	2.9	2.2	1.7	-2.5

Source: Directorate of Intelligence, 1989: 33.

From 1950 on, gross investment consistently surpassed 20 percent of the national income, with 1986's 18 percent the only exception. The 1955-1960 Five-Year Plan earmarked nearly one-fourth the national income for investment. By 1975, as a result of heavy borrowing from abroad, more than one-third of the national income was allocated to investment. This trend of increasing share of the national income for investment brought rapid increases in NNI. From 1950 to 1960, it more than doubled; from 1960 to 1970, it grew by another 82.7 percent. From 1970 to 1975, NNI grew by nearly 60 percent.

Then came the realization that mismanaged investments of borrowed money had sown the seeds of macroeconomic problems. For the decade following 1975, belt-tightening measures resulted in slow growth, as evidenced in Table 3.2. Poland's gross national product-GNP growth from 1961 through 1975 was comparable with the United States and the German republics. Growth during the 1970-1975 period was particularly rapid, and rapid structural changes took place as well. Thereafter, the Polish economy began to stall. In 1987, growth was negative. The erratic growth both in investments (Table

Table 3.3
Average Annual Growth Rate of Real Per Capita Incomes of United States, GDR, West Germany, and Poland, 1961-1980

	U.S.	GDR	West Germany	Poland
1961-1965	3.2	3.0	3.8	3.2
1966-1970	2.1	3.4	3.4	3.3
1971-1975	1.5	4.7	1.7	5.5
1976-1980	4.1	2.0	4.1	0.5

Source: Directorate of Intelligence, 1986: 40.

3.1) and in resulting GNP (Table 3.2) suggests the absence of economic rationality in the plans.

Taking population growth into consideration, Table 3.3 presents a similar pattern. Until 1970, the per capita GNP growth was respectable relative to other economies. The comparison begins to falter from 1976 to the present. On the aggregate, the Polish economy grew rapidly following the war, but from 1970 onward its performance was erratic.

Table 3.4 also depicts rapid structural transformation in the Polish economy. The percentage of agriculture's contribution to the national income decreased consistently from 1945 on. In three decades (1945-1975), Poland's economy was transformed from agrarian to industrial. Industrial contributions to the national income doubled, from the 1950s' 24 percent to 1975's 48 percent; construction's contribution rose by 75 percent for the corresponding period. The most rapid increase in industry's contribution to the national income, however, came from state enterprises, with minimal private participation, the result of force-feeding by the state. Industry's increasing contribution to national income did not correspond to an increase in consumer well-being, either. Many consumer essentials were short in supply. Major exceptions were the Fiat-licensed automobiles and some household durables that did become more available. The disproportionate emphasis on industrial growth was also reflected in the relatively unimportant contribution made by the service sector. As is true in industrialized market economies, structural changes in an economy are normally accompanied by more rapid growth in the service sector. Rapid economic growth in Poland between 1945 and 1975 was not accompanied by such a change. For decades there was economic growth in Poland, but there was no commensurate economic development. *Growth* measures the increase in value or material productivity. *Development* is more inclusive and extensive--it also takes into account welfare indicators such as housing, health, education, price stability, income equity, job satisfaction, the environment, consumer goods supply, welfare in general, and even leisure. Some of these will be discussed in a later chapter. Here, the topics of environment and leisure are briefly mentioned to illustrate consumer

Table 3.4
Percentage Contribution to National Income Produced, 1950-1986

	Industry	Construction	Agriculture
1950	24	8	60
1960	34	10	34
1970	44	12	23
1975	48	14	15
1980	51	10	13
1986	48	11	13

Source: World Bank, 1987a: 3.

neglect.

Environmental issues have come to the fore only recently. Blackened palaces, castles, and bastions in major cities of Poland testify to the government's neglect of consumer well-being. A major producer and exporter of hard and brown coal, Poland has relied heavily on coal as a major source of energy. Processing lead-free gasoline was costly, therefore motorists used leaded gasoline. With rapid industrialization, the level of chemical pollutants emitted into the air, spilled onto the ground, and discharged into waterways kept rising. It then became obvious that cutting corners could no longer be tolerated. The fifth five-year plan allocated approximately 3.5 percent of public investment on environmental protection. That amount was doubled in the sixth five-year plan of 1981-1985, totaling more than 7 percent of investment (United Nations, 1988: 263). The last five-year plan increased the amount to 8 percent, but the efforts came too late and were too little. The best hope was a deceleration in environmental deterioration. Meanwhile, life expectancy in Poland was slowly decreasing. Consumers today may expect poor air quality for years to come, especially in industrial centers like Warsaw, Nowa Huta, Gdansk, Katowice, Poznan, Lodz, Wroclaw, and Szczecin. A steep price is being paid for past mistakes.

As for leisure time, instead of the regular six-day work week a recent law reduced work hours on Saturdays and now a worker needs only to work on alternate Saturdays. The Poles are a people of culture and the arts. Creative thinking and creative entertainment, including reading, are important aspects of life. Cultural activities are a valuable source of entertainment. For those financially better off, vacations are zestfully planned and taken. With the most recent relaxation of passport ownership, everybody applied and received a passport. But the constraint now is financial and the options of enjoying one's leisure time are limited. The Polish economy grew for decades under Communist administrations, but for the majority of consumers, development was lacking.

EQUITY

The fourth quantitative measure of an economy's performance is equitable distribution of income. *Equity* is the fairness with which the national product is distributed. It differs from *equality* or *equalness*. Some economists equate the two as if more equal distribution of income is a desideratum, and that, *equity* and equality in income distribution should not be too far apart. In practice, equality contributes to disincentives: it provides incentives to not be productive or innovative and neutralizes incentives to be dynamic and venturesome. The performance criterion here is equity, or fairness, in income distribution, not equality.

Data on income distribution in Poland were not readily available. The general belief has been that income in centralized socialist economies is more equal--not necessarily more equitable--than in market-oriented economies. There was no wealthy class in Poland, at least not in the open. Even if a household inherited some old money from before the war, there was no investment opportunity in a centralized planned system, and the wealthy could not become much wealthier. Conversely, there was no abject poverty in Poland, either; there were no panhandlers or homeless persons in sight.

With no wealth, income came either from wages, pensions, or transfer payments. In 1968, an agricultural worker in the socialized sector received a monthly salary of 1,752 zlotys--it was the lowest salary among working groups. In the same year, a transport worker's monthly salary was 2,155 zlotys and a miner's 3,032 zlotys--the miner was the highest paid among the five groupings listed. Wage differentials among various groups were modest. In 1984, monthly salaries for workers in the agriculture, transport, and mining industries, respectively, were 16,782, 16,412, and 33,153 zlotys. The transport worker's earning position declined slightly over the sixteen-year period relative to a farm worker, and that of the miner's gained slightly. Still, the income differentials were moderate, especially since strike-resulted income increases were politically rather than economically induced.

No one was well off. No one was unduly poor in relation to others. Within the manufacturing sector, the income differential was even less. In 1974, the lowest paid worker was in apparel manufacturing; his or her monthly wage was 2,469 zlotys. The highest paid was a worker in iron and steel manufacturing; his or her monthly wage was 4,101 zlotys. A decade later, the lowest paid worker was in furniture manufacturing, at 15,311 zlotys a month. The highest paid worker was still in iron and steel manufacturing, with 22,272 zlotys. If there was an income differential in 1974, then the gap was being narrowed over the decade. In 1974, the lowest paid worker received 60 percent that of the highest paid. In 1984, the gap had been whittled down to 31 percent (World Bank, 1987a: 211).

This equal distribution of national income had caused muted discontent among those who felt that their productivity was higher than that of mine workers, and yet their income was equal to or lower. The near-equal incomes of a miner and a university professor is an example. The academician gave up years of potential earnings to pursue an advanced degree. He or she incurred considerable opportunity cost by preparing to be more productive. Yet upon appointment to an academic position, the salary as a beginner was lower than that of a novice miner. The incomes were equal; they were not equitable. Those who felt unfairly treated by the state, therefore, could not be expected to apply themselves to be as productive as they otherwise would. Similarly, a worker whose income was not much different from his co-worker's, even though he worked more conscientiously and applied his innovativeness and industriousness to the productive process, was not expected to work as diligently on a sustained basis. Equality meant unfairness. It impeded the actualization of society's productive potential.

More equal distribution of income in Poland was practiced from 1944 through 1982, and motivation was being actively curtailed by disincentives. Enterprising individuals, whose private investment initiatives could have effectively provided the missing links in the planned system and could have helped ease the supply-side bottlenecks, were constrained from effecting their dreams. Subtle obstacles were placed in their way so that their capitalistic tendency could more easily be contained and kept from polluting those in the state enterprises. Enterprise permits, tax burdens, credit availability, and supply of essential inputs were some of the controlling mechanisms. As a consequence, expansion of the private sector was curtailed and income differential among various sectors of the economy was kept in check. Reforms initiated in 1982 made progress toward the removal of such disincentives in favor of less equal but more equitable distribution of income. Instead of the slogan "to each according to his need and from each according to his ability," there was the motto that promised "to each according to his ability." In plain parlance, the change permitted a worker's wage to be more of a function of his or her marginal value productivity. Though the increase in wages and bonuses was not quite commensurate with the increase in one's productivity, it was a step in the right direction. Therefore, even during the waning years of Communist administration in Poland, there was the beginning of a less equal but more equitable distribution of national income.

ECONOMIC FREEDOM

The extent to which a factor of production is free to move from one producing activity to another so as to realize its productive potential, is a measure of economic freedom and opportunity. Absenting from the ideological conviction that the state knows what is best for society, this criterion is evaluated on the basis of economic consideration alone. Here, we make simple comparison between Poland's practices during Communist administrations and those of a market economy's such as the United States. In a market economy, a high school graduate may decide to be an electrician, an auto mechanic, a truck driver, or an engineer. He or she makes the decision based on aptitude or preference and the prospect of satisfaction to be derived from a chosen profession. Satisfaction may include monetary rewards as well as intellectual or aptitudinal. Subjective weight is given to various values the individual espouses, and decision may take into account base salary, prestige, knowledge, and professional advancement. For example, a college entrant sets out to be an engineer. Upon graduation, he or she lands a job with a firm at an acceptable location. If the job situation, pay, and professional advancement satisfy him or her in general, he or she remains with the firm. On the other hand, if the person is disillusioned, is dissatisfied, or is offered a better opportunity, he or she decides whether to change jobs. The government does not and cannot impede an individual from freely making her own decision in search of the best opportunity for oneself.

The reality of incurring high opportunity cost by being too mobile or not mobile enough is always a decisive factor in the decision-making process. At least theoretically, wages reflect one's potential value productivity. Seeking higher pay also implies a forthcoming increase in value productivity. The individual gains in income and in actualization of potential; society gains in value and material productivity. Aggregated, this means that granting economic freedom to the factors of production to search for their respective highest productive usages means the economy moves forward. In general, factors are engaged in the most productive usages possible under given conditions, including technology, or supply and demand conditions. This applies not only to labor but to free mobility of material inputs as factors of production.

The economic model the Polish government adopted in 1944 was that of the centralized command type. Freedom of choice by producers and consumers alike was reduced or eliminated by design. Private Polish farmers were the only ones in CMEA nations who successfully resisted being collectivized. But they paid the price by being discriminated against in terms of input supply shortages, higher input prices, higher taxes, and compulsory delivery of output, among others. With the exception of farm labor in the private sector, there was no input factor mobility. The state controlled and allocated production factors at fixed prices and in accordance with planned schedules. In the manufacturing sector, the disappearance of private enterprises was sufficiently telling that free or non-state coordinated productive activities were anathema.

Though no internal passport was required, as it was in the Soviet Union, labor mobility was discouraged for fear of disrupting production schedules and objectives (Pacuski interview, 1990). College graduates who received free tuition and subsidies while in school were assigned to designated posts for specified years of service. With an extensive state-coordinated control mechanism in place, factors of production--whether labor or material inputs-- had no economic freedom and therefore no opportunity to actualize their respective productive potentials. Economic opportunities were lost in order to enforce uniform execution of the state plan. College graduates could not obtain jobs best suited to their talents. Material inputs could not flow to producing units best suited for the production of the goods and services most valued by society. It was similar to not permitting water to seek its own level. At great expense or opportunity lost, the energy was channelled to where it did not belong or was less suited.

The low level of economic freedom and opportunity in Poland was also evident in the absence of a dynamic financial system. Savings were forced, and yet they were used mostly for state-designated purposes instead of more productive investments. Individuals with resources could not direct or move their financial resources to where they belonged, or to where society or the consumer needed them the most.

ADAPTABILITY AND PROGRESSIVENESS

An economy grows and develops from the economic dynamism within. A dynamic economy is capable of adapting to changing economic conditions, domestically and internationally. An economy performs well when it can weather adverse economic conditions and take advantage of favorable ones. It adapts, adjusts, and keeps moving forward. Japan, in recent decades, is such an economy. It first imitated, copied, and then improved upon foreign products. Then it began to invent, continuously adapting to changing market conditions abroad. From the ruins of war, it progressed to second largest economy in the world. For the Polish economy to be dynamic under the centralized system, it would have been essential to adapt to exogenous conditions. The ability to adapt requires flexibility, resilience, and recognition of economic forces. Adaptability to the end-product market requires an ability to adjust to changes in the production-factor market. Only constant adjustments to changing economic conditions assure efficiency in input employment and product mix.

Owing to detailed central planning, Poland's economic structure until 1989 did not allow flexibility or adaptability. With a tight delivery schedule from input producer to output manufacturer, a breakdown in a key industry could render the forward-linked industries immobile. As mentioned earlier, a prolonged coal miners' strike could paralyze an economy's manufacturing industry or rail transport. In a market economy, the coal users could pay a higher price for alternative energy to continue their operation. But in Poland, all essential supplies were centrally allocated. There were no alternative sources or alternate supplies. Thus, bottlenecks multiplied, and the centralized economy kept suffering setbacks, having no recourse to adjustment mechanisms except to revise the plan objective downward for the following period.

Reforms had been introduced, and the last reform effort under the Communist regime moved in the right direction. The Jaruzelski administration at least manifested its willingness to accommodate and adapt. It permitted decentralization of the planning mechanism, reduced the scope of centralized allocation of input factors and products, and downplayed the state's role in centralized purchasing. The state also permitted the private sector to grow in manufacturing and service. It provided incentives for establishment of Polania firms and sanctioned joint ventures between state enterprises and foreign investors. The state also decreased the number of items on its list of regulated prices, and finally, under economic and political pressure, relegalized Solidarity. In brief, Poland's Communist regime of the late 1980s did take steps toward greater economic adaptability and freedom. But the steps came too late and were not sufficient. The economy came close to being bankrupt. By September 1989, the difficult task of rescuing the economy was shifted onto the shoulders of Tadeusz Mazowiecki's new government.

PAST REFORMS AND FAILURES

Poland was partitioned by foreign powers, but regrouped. Foreign governments sought to eradicate Polish culture and even its language, but its people withstood the test. Poland lost 6 million of its population in World War II, but the country recovered. The tasks ahead are arduous, but if reform measures are appropiate, timely, realistic, and implemented in an orderly manner, the historical opportunity can be seized.

Governments form economic policies, and they change those policies when faced with changing needs or circumstances. Gorbachev has admitted mistakes in restructuring the Soviet economy. China has admitted some of its mistakes and has experienced measurable successes. Now that Poland is free from Soviet intervention and Communist rule, it is attempting national reconciliation. Not since 1944 have adjustments and reforms been more feasible. But let some failures of past reform attempts be discussed first.

The First Reform Attempt

In April 1987, the Party Congress reaffirmed the reform legislation passed by the Sejm in 1981-1982. That it had already been approved in 1981 by the ninth Party Congress and the Sejm should make one wonder what happened in between and why there was any need for reaffirmation. The 1987 legislation was not the first reform attempt in Poland since 1944. It was the fifth--the third major--reform attempt.

It became evident in the early 1950s that the economic system imposed upon Poland by Stalin was not working. Intellectuals had already expressed concerns through open criticism, but during the Communist decades the only triggering mechanism for economic reform came through street demonstrations, strikes, riots, confrontations, imprisonments, and deaths. Without these public protests there would have been no attempts at reform.

The first major reform attempt was made in 1956, after Wladyslaw Gomulka succeeded Boleslaw Bierut as party secretary. The second major reform effort came after Gomulka was replaced by Edward Gierek in 1970. And the third reform attempt was initiated after Wojciech Jaruzelski replaced Stanislaw Kania in 1981, who had replaced Gierek in 1980. In between, there had been minor reform attempts in 1964 and 1973 (Marer and Siwinski, 1988: 65). Each of the reform attempts came in the wake of announced price increases and their immediate rescinding.   But thirty years after the first reform movement, a central issue had still not been resolved: should the pricing mechanism function within the system?

More than thirty years ago, a group of eminent Polish economists on the Economic Council had outlined the fundamentals of economic reform in Poland. The recommendations are still valid today, but in between are thirty-two years of lost time and missed opportunities.   The basic problems remained, with the added burden of a crunching foreign debt.   These economists had not proposed changes in the political system, nor did they urge abolition of the Central Planning Commission.   Rather, they called for the smoother functioning of market forces within the framework of government planning and supervision.

The basic features of the proposal were greater autonomy for enterprise operations, profit as a guiding force for enterprise decisions, wages as a function of productivity, worker participation in enterprise management, and competitiveness among producers via meaningful pricing mechanisms that reflect the real value to consumers and the costs to producers.   The state would provide long-term indicative-type planning to coordinate enterprises and market activities via instruments such as "pricing policy, credit policy, taxation, interest charges, and amortization rates" (Flakierski, 1986: 5-6). Such measures would have safeguarded investments and ensured production decisions based on efficiency and progressiveness.   Market-determined successes and failures would have corrected judgmental errors along the way. The Polish economy could then have avoided much of its cumulative waste and could have more effectively employed its resources to maintain equilibrium and reach balanced growth.   But the proposals appeared too radical and too threatening to decision makers.   Officials with interests in maintaining the status quo overruled the proposals.

Instead, the 1956 reform was mere window dressing.   In industry, enterprises were permitted to form workers councils as an aid toward self-management within the plants.   In place of central boards, industrial associations were formed along product lines.   These changes were supposed to increase worker participation in enterprise operations and facilitate product planning with the industrial associations, but even such limited experimentatation with economic democratization was short-lived.

Although some of the changes introduced after 1956 proved persistent, the reconstruction of the so-called Polish Economic Model was checked and certain fields even regressed in the 1960's. Above all, the degree of worker influence over management and the central role of elected administrative bodies decreased in favor of organs appointed by upper levels of administration. The independence of enterprises was also gradually limited. (Landau, 1985: 251)

Reform measures pertaining to agriculture were political moves unaccompanied by economic aids. Private farmers were permitted to remain uncollectivized, and those in socialized farming could return to private farming if they desired. The state farms were supposed to sell a prescribed amount of land to those who chose to leave, but minor bureaucrats placed impediments in the way. In fact, attempts to purchase land from state farms were thwarted wherever possible along every step of the petition process.

On a more positive note, the reforms recognized the importance of the agricultural sector, and an additional agricultural investment was budgeted. Yet most of the investments were made in the socialized sector, which accounted for less than 20 percent of total farm production. In the late 1950s, investments made by private farmers even declined slightly. Gomulka's reform of 1956 was more cosmetic surgery than an attempt to address the real farm problems. Many of the promises were never delivered. Some economic historians concluded that Gomulka, who was conservative by nature, not only prohibited the Polish economy from propelling forward but "returned to the policy of centralized planning, pursuing the goal of rapid industrialization and increasingly focusing on capital goods production" (Nelson, 1984: 83). Reform of economic structure, practices, and policies did not materialize. Instead Gomulka crystalized the modus operandi, making future reforms more costly and difficult.

The problem of disequilibrium persisted. Reform had failed. Consumer dissatisfaction mounted, morale was low, and incentives were absent. Tempers flared. The bloody riots in Gdansk and other Baltic seaports brought down Gomulka's administration. The riots had erupted because of announced price increases, particularly in food items. 56 percent of a household's budget went to food (Schopflin, 1979: 57). Subsidized prices were necessary because the successive five-year plans did not peg wage increases to increased productivity. Wage increases were not a function of productivity because the state's policy was to curtail aggregate demand, so that more money could be deployed for investment in capital goods. Nominal income could not cope with price increase of consumer goods without a corresponding decrease in real income. Thus, the riots were an expression of a long-suppressed social discontent with the economy's performance. And the economy's poor performance was the result of defects in the economic system. Unless fundamental issues were addressed squarely and the problems resolved, there would be no long-term stability or progress.

The Second Reform Attempt

When Gierek replaced Gomulka in 1970, another reform movement was initiated. Bowing to pressure, Gierek's first order of business was to annul the intended price increases. To show concern for the general public, high government officials were sent to visit factories to listen to complaints. But no steps were taken to liberalize the economy--neither structural nor functional changes were made. To avoid social unrest, real wages for industrial workers were increased by 18 to 20 percent for the fourth five-year plan, 1971-1975 (Landau, 1985: 291). The basic thrust of economic direction continued to be on rapid industrial growth.

The socialized sector of agriculture once again was chief beneficiary of state investment in farming, accounting for 70 percent of the farm investment budget. Real wages of farm producers decreased relative to their industrial counterparts, however, and there was significant farm-to-industry migration in search of jobs. To support the accelerated industrial expansion plan, Gierek needed to create new jobs for displaced farm workers as well as for new entrants into the job market, and following increased real wages for industrial workers, he needed to increase imports of consumer goods. Gierek turned to the West for assistance. Foreign credits were secured to finance the patchwork "reform" policies while promises were made to hold subsidized commodity prices constant for three years (United Nations, 1974: 80). As a concession to the private farmer, the compulsory produce delivery system was abolished. Also, there was an increase in procurement prices for selected farm products and a decrease in the land tax and in industrial-supplied factor prices (United Nations, 1972: 65).

Wielka Organizacja Gospodarcza WOG reform, or Enterprise Association reform gave greater autonomy to large state enterprises on issues pertaining to employment limits, wage funds, and production operations (Landau, 1985: 299). But following the general trend in CMEA economies at the time, management restructuring or recentralization in 1974 began (United Nations, 1975: 71). By 1975, economic conditions had deteriorated. The improvements in living standards, built upon borrowed money, could not be sustained. Partly owing to a worldwide recession, the intended growth in exports did not materialize. Also, the desired results from both the agricultural and the industrial sectors did not materialize. "The announced reform of the Polish economic system, thought inevitable by economists, was washed away. The changes introduced were only partial, and the system resulting from them was inconsistent" (Landau, 1985: 300). By then, the Polish economy was faced with imminent disaster. State attention was directed to coping with the mounting trade imbalances. The reform movement dwindled to sporadic and piecemeal policy directives in an effort to stem the tide of impending bankruptcy.

The Third Reform Attempt

The food crisis of 1976 prompted the Polish government to announce food price increases. Just as in 1970, riots broke out. Even though the government immediately cancelled the intended price increases, avoiding the spread of social unrest, the public's confidence in the government and the system sank to a new low. The situation in the late 1970s is capsulized by Jacek Kuron,--a leading dissident--in an essay, in which he expressed the sentiment that "the country was close to explosion. Price rises were now inevitable, the mood of society was close to anarchy, respect for the state administration had vanished, and the authorities continued to behave as if everything was normal" (Schopflin, 1979: 13). Price increases were announced in the summer of 1980. Again, the public took to the streets, and Gierek's ten-year tenure came to an end. Kania first, and then Jaruzelski, came on the scene, and the third major reform began in 1982.

That the two previous reform attempts failed came as no surprise. Prominent Polish economists had long warned of the need for meaningful reforms. By holding onto short-sighted approaches, the decision makers of the 1980s felt comfortable with keeping more of the same than taking surgical measures. Drastic changes were rejected, either out of ideological bigotry or fear of eroding their own power. The basic method of reform was still control, with some temporary and superficial flexibility measures thrown in. Problems were postponed, not resolved, consequently, they became more serious. As discussed earlier, some tangible reform measures were implemented during Jaruzelski's administration, but the changes were not sufficient to head off mounting social discontent. The third reform attempt was a stillbirth.

Reform in the agricultural sector failed this third time because the government neglected the private farmers who constituted more than four-fifths of Polish agriculture. Though the socialized sector consistently received the bulk of state investments plus favorable allocation of essential inputs and services, it was less efficient and less productive than the private sector. This was easy to understand: extra contributions by public farmers netted no additional remuneration, whereas minimized effort reaped the same benefits and pay.

As for private-sector agriculture, because of discrimination by state policy, there was no ready access to needed inputs, including credit. Compulsory delivery of produce at regulated prices dampened the incentives for intensive cultivation of land. Real income was not adequate, inducing many to work at a second job in the city. Though private farms were more efficient and productive than their public-sector counterparts, the opportunity cost of committing all their productive capacity to the farm was high. With more than four-fifths of farm producers diverting part of their labor to nonfarm production, there was a resulting chronic shortage of farm products, particularly meat and poultry. Even when the obligatory delivery system was removed and purchase prices were increased, real wages remained low relative to the nonfarm sector. The younger generation left the farm rather than seek yield-increasing farm techniques or expand (Bylinski interview, 1990). And with an increased nonfarm population and increased demand by the younger generation, supply often fell short of demand.

The expected development and growth of the farm sector failed to materialize. The equimarginal principle of state investment was made sacrificial lamb to the ideologue. Economies of scale were not capitalized upon; input prices still did not reflect the cost of production; product prices did not reflect real value. A straitjacket remained on the planning, supervision, control, and allocation processes, beclouding the minds of those in power. Just as machine parts react to human commands, the reactions of subordinates were equated with assured results. They lost touch with human wants and needs, and apathetic attitudes and low labor morale resulted. The policies failed. The Reform attempts failed.

The third Reform attempt in the industrial sector failed in a somewhat different way. Unlike agriculture, industry had always been the crown jewel and "favorite son" of Communist administrators. Though farm prices were to be raised in 1956, 1970, 1976 and thereafter, prices of industrial products remained unscathed. When Gierek raised the real wages of industrial workers, farmers were left out in the cold, although the latter were granted a place in the pension plan. When workers took to the streets or locked themselves inside their work places, the government paid attention. Yet despite excessive investment in industry, and in spite of favorite son status, reforms in the industrial sector also failed.

The reasons for failure were basic. Reform measures were "reactive" in nature, and politicians lacked the political will to overhaul the economy's inefficient structure. To placate rioting workers, announced price increases were nullified. To give the workers a sense of independence, self-management was promoted, in the form of a workers council and abolishment of the mid-level ministerial bureaucratic apparatus. But the role of the workers council in employment, wages, investment, production, and other enterprise decisions was short-lived. Industrial associations were formed to reintroduce tangible control over enterprise operations, and the promised transformation of the system never materialized. No substantive changes were made. No fundamental questions were addressed. No structural changes were considered. It was a live-and-let-live arrangement that traded short-term social calm for ultimate problem resolution.

To answer the question of input shortages, the state should have probed for the underlying causes and resolved them. To avoid demonstrations over price increases, it needed to address the matter of real costs of production and real value of products. To deal with widespread discontent, the state had to come to grips with equitable real wages, gainful employment, demand for consumer goods, economic freedom, job satisfaction, and higher living standards. However, continued centralized planning and management perpetuated wasteful investment, promoted low work morale, created supply bottlenecks, built inflationary pressure, and mounted internal as well as external imbalances. Reform attempts were a mere exercise in rhetoric to appease the public. The officials who engineered or personified past failures somehow always managed to resurface as behind-the-scenes administrators.

As a whole, these major reforms failed for six reasons: (1) attempts at reform aimed only at symptoms, not causes; (2) decision makers either failed or were unwilling to ask the right questions and pursue the correct answers; (3) the state failed to heed the sound proposals of eminent Polish economists, because of either ideological frigidity or anxiety over loss of personal influence and power; (4) there was an inability or unwillingness to distance the country from long-term agreements with other CMEA members; (5) the cause of many problems was systemic and structural deficiencies inherent in agriculture and industry; and, (6) the financial system continued to be passive. A general approach to economic reform begins with a statement of objectives. Thereafter, obstacles that contributed to past failures are removed. Then, policies aimed at specified targets are formulated and concrete steps are spelled out. The next chapter presents the major legacies of the Communist administrations--some of which are obstacles to be removed so policy changes can proceed.

NOTE

1. During the 1986-1990 planning period, another 350,000 people were expected to reach working age (United Nations, 1988: 261).

4

THE MAIN LEGACIES
FROM THE PAST

For forty-five years, the Communist administrations in Poland subjected the economy to a planned, centralized command system. There was more of a human face to the system in Poland than in some other parts of the world. Nevertheless, the system created a contorted structure that could neither function nor achieve the nation's potential. The die had been cast. It adversely affected the economy then, and it left rigidities and imbalances that are difficult to correct now.

INVESTMENT: POLICIES AND PRACTICES

Despite impressive gains in net national material output, particularly in heavy industries, the command system created many white elephants in the industrial sector that contribute to the current economic crisis. From the first six-year plan on, agriculture was relegated to the back seat. Rapid industrialization was the measure of success. The intent was to collectivize farms and to monopolize industrial enterprises so that all major economic activity could be planned, regulated, supervised, and monitored to achieve planned objectives. In the farm sector, the state's inability to mobilize the farm owners to cooperative production led to calculated and intense persecution of capitalist-minded individuals. A compulsory delivery system was introduced. The grain quota was periodically raised. Yield-increasing inputs, when available, were diverted to state and cooperative farms and provided at subsidized prices. Prices of farm products were kept low by design. Private farmers, though operating efficiently within the framework of their constraints, were deprived of meaningful investment opportunities. The state's farm-investment priority was the socialized farms and cooperatives. But the original intent of milking the farm sector, particularly private farms, to finance industrial expansion did not lead to desired results. The Polish agricultural sector was still underdeveloped more than a decade after the war. Investment in farm machinery had been in production of large tractors suited for large-scale state and cooperative farms. By 1957, three-fourths of the nonhuman energy used on farms was still derived from draft animals (Barnett, 1958: 241).

On the other hand, the government was successful in nationalizing major industrial enterprises. The decreasing number of small private enterprises were forced into state-controlled associations. Through external controls imposed by various ministries and by the party and state-controlled unions, industrial enterprises were expeditiously brought under state planning and control. The initial phase of centralized planning, input distribution, centralized product purchasing, and product distribution was accomplished under the tutelage of Soviet "experts," and this tied the Polish industrial sector closely to Soviet needs. During the six-year plan of 1949-1955, there was accelerated investment in heavy industries. Poland became dependent on the Soviet Union for the product market. Steel, iron ore, mechanical engineering, reproducer goods, coal, and chemical products were among the chief exports. Investments were made in industries not geared to expanded trade with the West.

Unbalanced industrial growth came at the expense of agriculture and the consumer-goods industry. Even with a respite caused by Hungarian Revolution of 1956, the trend in heavy industry investments continued, and consumer welfare housing, foodstuffs, household durables, and services-- continued to suffer. Under the rationale of a full employment policy, investments were increased again and again. In 1956, indexed industrial production was 100; it grew to 134.6 in 1960, 184.2 in 1964, 233.3 in 1967, and 285.5 in 1970 (Landau, 1985: 254).

To further lock Poland's industrial structure into heavy industry, agreements among COMECON nations obliged Poland to commit its scarce investment resources to metallurgy engineering, metal works, and energy. As a result, annual growth in metallurgy in 1968 was 14.7 percent; thereafter, growth was 7.9 percent, 11.6 percent, and 7.3 percent for 1969, 1970, and 1971, respectively. Growth in engineering and metal works was even speedier. For the same four-year period, the annual growth was 17.1 percent, 14.9 percent, 15.7 percent, and 15.8 percent, respectively (United Nations, 1972: 72).

The riots of 1968 and 1970 forced Gomulka out of office, but the disastrous economic policy of the early 1970s began thereafter. Poland borrowed heavily from the West to finance unprecedented expansion. This time, consumer welfare was heeded, although consumers' long-term interests were not important. "The grand gesture, prestigious projects such as the Katowice steel works, the growth of motorization from 453,000 private cars in 1971 to 2,219,000 by 1980, Western cigarettes and consumer durables, all provided the veneer of success disguising from view the underlying crisis and the failure of strategy" (Kolankiewicz, 1988: 104). The investment frenzy fed on borrowed hard currency.

Instead of using borrowed capital to modernize or expand existing enterprises, Polish politicians were intent on starting new projects. The new investments neither contributed to modernizing agricultural methods nor strengthened the forward or backward link in industry. Gomulka admitted as early as November 1968 that "we have not mastered modern methods of control of structural changes on a large scale" (Landau, 1985: 259). But Gierek's investment policies of 1970 plunged Poland deeper into the abyss of a distorted structure. The new projects were undertaken on the basis of newness of buildings and largeness of plants. Politicians lobbied to have new projects located in areas of interest to them. With promises of low cost and high productivity, estimates for these new projects were knowingly kept low. Once the projects began, cost overruns became easier to justify and continued funding easier to secure. There were too many investment commitments, made too soon. The need for essential inputs, including technical experts and managerial ability, was greater than the country's ability to supply. Therefore, materials and human resources had to be imported from the West, further draining the nation's borrowed capital.

Actual investment during the 1970-1975 period went 31 percent beyond the five-year plan itself (Landau, 1985: 292). The aggregate effect of this spending spree became obvious by 1975, even to carefree central decision makers. There followed a "belt tightening" period when many projects were left unfinished and many purchased foreign licenses were never applied or used.

In a market economy, entrepreneurs are guided by the profit motive: careful calculation of construction and operating costs and of long-term returns takes place. Basic economic concepts such as opportunity costs, incremental capital-output ratios, expected rates of return, and anticipated dynamic changes in the marketplace, all are taken into account before an investment is made. But Polish decision makers disregarded the likely economic consequences of billion-dollar investments. They sought grandeur or temporary relief from social and political tensions: borrowed money was spent to buy time. Unfortunately, trade deficits ensued and debts came due. The government-appointed state Commission "froze or abandoned some 1500 projects with a value well in excess of 1,000 billion zlotys--$8.8 billion--in 1984 prices" (World Bank, 1987a: 40).

The haphazard manner in which the borrowed hard currency was committed to overly ambitious, grossly miscalculated, poorly coordinated, and sadly managed investment ventures in the early 1970s may be seen from a number of perspectives. First, as shown in Table 4.1, the average annual growth in gross fixed capital formation for 1971-1975 was a high 17.1 percent. No other COMECON economy came close to it. Romania, which had the second

Table 4.1

<u>Planned and Actual Gross Fixed Capital Formation and Investment Ratios, 1971-1982</u>

		Average Annual Percentage Change	Ratio of Gross Fixed Capital Formation to NMP
	1971-1975	17.1	34.3
Planned	1976-1980	0.2	31.5
Actual	1976-1980	-0.4	35.9
Planned	1981-1985	---	---
Actual	1979	-7.9	35.8
Actual	1980	-12.3	33.3
Planned	1981	-16.8	27.0
Actual	1981	-25.0	28.7
Planned	1982	-0.7	28.2

Source: United Nations, 1982: 239.

highest annual growth rate within the COMECON bloc, recorded 10.7 percent. Even the Soviet Union had only a 6.8 percent annual growth rate. As can be expected, such rapid growth cannot be sustained. The planned annual growth rate for the 1976-1980 five-year plan period was a meager 0.2 percent. Even that objective was overly ambitious, since it implied maintaining the investment level at the 1970-1975 period. The actual annual growth rate for the 1976-1980 period was -0.4 percent. Since many projects underway had already exhausted substantial amounts of borrowed capital, it would have been better if the decline had been more drastic. And since repayment was already a problem, many of the unfinished projects were not likely to be completed. Therefore, those projects not likely to be ever completed should have been discontinued, instead of being allowed to continue longer, further draining financial resources. Successive years of changes in average annual growth rates--1979 through 1981--were more reasonable. But by then, much of the capital spent on the eventually unfinished projects had already been wasted.

A further indication that decision makers were not resolute enough to resort to an investment retrenchment policy can be seen in the difference between 1981's planned and actual decline in fixed capital formation. Since the handwriting was on the wall by the mid-1970s, planners and politicians should have taken realistic and drastic measures to lower fixed capital formation for subsequent years. Yet the planned decrease for 1981 was a "mere" -16.8 percent. Reality set in to lower it to -25.0 percent. Also, Table 4.1 shows the magnitude of change in the ratios of gross fixed capital formation to net material product (NMP) for the decade 1971-1981. Although the actual ratio of gross fixed capital formation to net material product (NMP) in the 1976-1980 period was higher than in 1971-1975s--35.9 percent for 1976-1980 as compared to 34.3 percent for 1971-1975s--the NMPs for the 1976-1980 period were lower. A more telling comparison of the erratic investment measures during that period may be seen by contrasting the 1971-1975 period's 34.3 percent to 1981's 28.7 percent. The 1971-1975 period was one of investment expansion, yet capital efficiency was low relative to the 1980s. Thus, ex-post evidence suggests irrationality in Poland's investment policy during the early 1970s.

Table 4.2 shows annual percentage changes in total gross investment from 1970 to 1988. Prior to 1971, Poland's investment schedule was modest, if not conservative. In 1970, growth in total gross investment over the previous year was a mere 4.0 percent: Poland had the lowest growth rate in that category among COMECON nations. Czechoslovakia, which had the second lowest growth rate among Eastern European nations, recorded a 5.8 percent increase that year--a 45 percent faster rate than Poland. And other COMECON economies were growing between 75 percent to 325 percent faster than

Table 4.2

Total Gross Investment, 1970-1988 (annual percentage change)

	Total	Material Sphere	Nonmaterial Sphere
1970	4.0	3.0	8.0
1971	7.4	9.6	1.4
1972	23.0	26.0	16.0
1973	25.4	26.5	19.9
1974	22.3	23.3	19.8
1975	10.7	16.1	7.4
1976	1.0	0.2	4.1
1977	3.1	1.6	8.6
1978	2.1	-0.1	9.7
1979	-7.9	-11.2	2.3
1980	-12.3	-12.8	-11.0
1981	-22.3	-23.5	-19.9
1982	-12.1	-15.3	-5.7
1983	9.4	8.2	11.4
1984	11.4	11.8	7.2
1985	6.0	6.7	4.6
1986	5.1	5.8	3.7
1987	4.2	4.2	4.3
1988	5.4	5.6	5.1

Source: United Nations, 1988: 338; 1989: 393.

Poland.[1] Also notable is the differential in growth rates between material and nonmaterial spheres for 1970. The material sphere, including construction, mining, machinery, and equipment, had a growth rate of 3 percent. The nonmaterial sphere, including education and health, had an 8 percent growth rate. At the beginning of the 1971-1976 Five-Year Plan, the emphasis was reversed. Investment in the material sphere, particularly in the industrial sector, was growing nearly six times more rapidly than investments in the nonmaterial. Then came the investment spree in 1972 and the years thereafter. Poland's 1972 growth in total gross investment was 23.0 percent, more than twice as fast as the nearest competitor--Romania--which had a growth rate of 10.4 percent. And it was 284 percent that of the Soviet Union's 8.1 percent.

The trend started in 1972 continued several years, but by the mid- 1970s, growth in gross investment came to an abrupt halt: A new trend of negative growth began in 1979. A reversal came again only in 1983, when Poland recorded a positive growth rate of 9.4 percent--after Poland obtained a line of new credit from the Soviet Union in 1982, totaling U.S. $2.2 billion. This 9.4 percent positive growth in 1983 was not significant, for there had been a nearly 40 percent cumulative decrease in gross investment between 1978 and 1982. Nevertheless, after the feast-or-famine fiasco between 1971 and 1975, 1983 marked the beginning of a new stabilizing period. With past mistakes bearing down hard on the Polish economy, however, particularly in the realm of investment blunders and mounting foreign debt, Poland's centralized system was to bequeath economic obstacles for the 1990s.

PRODUCTIVITY: RELATIVE EFFICIENCY

The concepts of productivity and efficiency carry slightly different connotations when evaluating the Polish economy under the Communist system. The measure of success in a centralized economy is meeting planned objectives, physical production, and physical efficiency, not monetary or market gains.

Where appropriate, data on Poland's productivity and efficiency are compared with that of the former German Democratic Republic (GDR). The former GDR is selected as a reference point because it had one of the most rapid increases in productivity and achieved the fastest growth in consumer real income within the COMECON bloc. In Table 4.3, the period between 1950 and 1969 casts a favorable light on Poland's economy. In the Value Added Output column, Poland's average annual growth rates in agriculture were comparable with GDR's. This was achieved despite GDR's more rapid increases in Fixed Capital Stock (column 2). More significant increases for GDR were its Fixed Capital Per Person Employed (column 5). This rose

Table 4.3

Employment and Factor Productivity in Industry, Agriculture, and Service for Poland and GDR, 1950-1969 (annual percentage compound rates of growth)

	Employment		Fixed Capital Stock		Value Added Output		Output Per Person Employed		Fixed Capital Per Person Employed		Output Per Unit of Fixed Capital	
	Poland	GDR	Poland	GDR	Poland	GDR	Poland	GDR	Poland	GDR	Poland	GDR
Agriculture (Forestry & Fishing Included)												
1950-1952 to 1958-1960	2.2	2.3	-0.1	-2.6	1.8	3.2	2.3	5.0	1.9	6.0	0.4	-0.9
1958-1960 to 1967-1969	1.6	1.7	0.0	-2.3	3.0	6.4	1.6	4.1	3.0	8.9	-1.4	-4.4
Industry (Mining, Utilities, & Manufacturing)												
1950-1952 to 1958-1960	9.4	10.1	4.0	1.3	3.1	3.6	5.2	8.7	-0.9	2.3	6.1	6.3
1958-1960 to 1967-1969	8.3	5.2	3.5	0.1	7.0	5.9	4.6	5.3	3.5	5.8	1.2	-0.5
Services (Construction Included)												
1950-1952 to 1958-1960	6.4	5.1	3.1	1.9	2.8	1.1	3.2	3.1	-0.3	-0.8	3.5	4.0
1958-1960 to 1967-1969	5.8	4.0	3.3	1.3	3.0	2.2	2.4	2.7	-0.1	0.9	2.5	1.8

Source: United Nations, 1972: 18.

Note: Service here includes construction, material, and nonmaterial service-related activities.

faster in GDR than in Poland, owing to more rapid upward movement in its fixed capital stock as well as more rapid decrease in persons engaged in agricultural production (column 1). Output Per Person Employed (column 4) in GDR was more than in Poland for the period under consideration. Labor productivity on farms in GDR was higher than in Poland, owing to more intensive application of inputs such as farm machinery and irrigation. Indeed, these figures demonstrate the inefficiency of capital employment in GDR relative to Poland (column 6).

Lower output per person in Poland may be attributed to low capitalization. Taking into account both the proportionately high Fixed Capital Per Person Employed (column 5) and the relatively low Output Per Unit of Fixed Capital in GDR (column 6), in addition to comparable growth rates in Value Added Output (column 3), for the two economies, it is clear that farm employment in Poland was more efficient than in GDR for 1950-1969. This relative success in turn may be ascribed to the fact that 80 percent of the farms in Poland were privately owned and operated.

The figures on productivity in the industrial sector, however, paint a less attractive picture. Also in Table 4.3, the growth rates in industrial employment in Poland exceeded that of GDR during both periods by far. Fixed Capital Per Person Employed (column 5) decreased in Poland for the 1950-1960 period, yet the increase in Output Per Unit of Fixed Capital (column 6) was nearly identical in the two economies. The evidence suggests that Fixed Capital Per Person Employed (column 5) for 1950-1960 was significantly higher in GDR than in Poland. It points to one reality: industrial labor productivity in Poland was measurably lower than in GDR. Since industries in both economies were socialized, the further implication is that Poland's labor force was less motivated by or was more resistant to a centralized system. That both economies scored significant gains in output per person employed is less an issue, since rapid capitalization and industrialization were the objectives for both economies' development plans. Data for the 1958-1969 period point to the same conclusion: industrial labor was less efficient in Poland than in GDR. Output Per Unit of Fixed Capital grew by 1.2 percent annually in Poland (column 6); in GDR, it decreased by .5 percent annually. Yet Output Per Person Employed (column 4) increased more rapidly in GDR than in Poland. Simply stated, labor was more efficient and productive in GDR than in Poland.

The service sector data suggest that structural changes were taking place faster in Poland than in GDR during that period. Growth in service-oriented employment, as in industry, was faster in Poland than in GDR. This was in part due to the more rapid population increase in Poland after the war, and in part to Poland's rapid off-farm migration.[2] The growth rate in Fixed Capital Stock (column 2) in the service sector was higher in Poland than in GDR. Fixed Capital Per Person Employed (column 5), however, declined in three out of four instances. Growth in Output Per Person Employed (column 4) was respectable for both countries. A comparison of labor productivity in the service sector yielded no significant difference between Poland and GDR. In short, other than low labor productivity in the industrial sector, Poland compared favorably with GDR in factor efficiency for the period 1950-1969.

Table 4.4 presents the aggregate productivity of labor and capital in the two economies. There was a sudden surge in annual labor productivity in Poland for the 1971-1975 period. Though data on capital productivity for the same period was not available, the rapid increase in labor productivity can be attributed to massive investments in industries in the early 1970s. Poland's growth in annual labor productivity nearly doubled, from 1958-1969's 4 percent to 1971-1975's 7.8 percent. However, a drastic decline followed immediately thereafter. The annual growth rate decreased from 1971-1975's 7.8 percent to 1976-1980's 1.2 percent. The increase in GDR's labor productivity also declined for the corresponding periods, but the decline was not drastic.

In Poland, as discussed earlier, the period 1976 to 1980 was indeed a time of severe cutbacks in investment. But the restive atmosphere among workers at that time must also have contributed negatively to labor productivity. This trend in declining labor productivity continued, with the period 1981 to 1985 recording a 0.1 percent annual decrease. That negative growth in labor productivity materialized despite heavy investments made just one decade ago. If massive increases in fixed assets had not taken place between 1970 and

Table 4.4
Labor and Capital Productivity, Poland and GDR, 1971-1989 (average annual percentage change)

	Poland		GDR	
	Labor Productivity	Capital Productivity	Labor Productivity	Capital Productivity
	(output per person employed)			
1950-1952 to 1958-1960	4.4	3.4	6.4	5.1
1958-1960 to 1967-1969	4	1.9	4.4	0.9
1971-1975	7.8	---	5.3	---
1976-1980	1.2	5.4	3.7	-1.3
1981-1985	-0.1	-3.4	4.3	0.2
1986	4.6	2.7	4.5	0.1
1987	1.9	-1.2	3.6	-0.2
1988	6.4	2.2	3	-1.2
1989	5	---	2.8	---
1986-1989	4.5	---	3.5	---

Source: United Nations, 1972: 6, 16; 1978: 19; 1988: 220.

1975, the decrease in labor productivity for the 1981-1985 period would have been even more pronounced. The most severe decline in labor productivity came immediately before and after imposition of martial law in 1981. There was improvement in labor productivity by 1983, 1984, and 1985.[3] Therefore, the average annual -0.1 percent decrease for the five-year period was related more to low work morale than to labor inefficiency. This is further evidenced by the even speedier decrease in capital productivity for the corresponding period: from 1976-1980's 5.4 percent annual increase to 1981-1985's -3.4 percent annual decrease.

Another perspective on capital efficiency may be gained from the data on incremental capital-output ratios (ICOR). Poland then was a seller's market. No objective measure of the value productivity of goods and services was available, but the ICOR data in Table 4.5 could help shed some light on capital efficiency. ICOR measures the ratio between additional output produced and additional capitalization required. A high ICOR value indicates a greater proportion of increased investment leading to a smaller percentage of increased output. The lower the ICOR value, the greater the efficiency of additional investment. For investment ratios, a small ICOR value indicates greater capital productivity and efficiency. By definition, investment ratios measure gross fixed capital formation as a percentage of gross domestic product GDP. The investment ratios and ICORs in Table 4.5 thus portray a picture of decreasing capital efficiency and productivity for both Poland and GDR. The investment ratios for both economies suggest that GDR's capital was still more productive when compared to that of Poland's. However, although GDR's investment ratios were consistently lower than that of Poland's, the investment ratios for both countries were increasing rapidly over time. The sudden increase in Poland's investment ratios from 1960-1969's

Table 4.5
Investment Ratios and ICOR, 1950-1980

	Investment Ratios[A]	Poland ICOR	Investment Ratios[A]	GDR ICOR
1950-1959	16.9	2.4	13.8	1.6
1960-1969	21.2[B]	3.6	18.7B	4.6
1971-1975	36.4	3.7	28.7	5.3
1976-1980	----	4.9	----	7.6

Source: United Nations, 1970: 16; 1977: 10; 1982: 138.

Note: [A] Investment ratios measure gross fixed capital formation as percentages of gross domestic product.
   [B] Investment ratios were for 1960-1968 period.

21.2 to 1971-1975's 36.4 was the result of investment sprees in the early 1970s. Poland's investment ratio between 1969 and 1975 rose by 71.7 percent; in GDR, it was 57.7 percent (World Bank, 1987a: 84).

Fixed capital formation was increasing more rapidly in Poland than in GDR. This may be confirmed by examining the ICOR values over time. GDR's ICOR for the 1950-1959 period was 1.6, lowest among COMECON nations. That is, for the decade of the 1950s, capital investment in GDR had been the most productive and efficient within the COMECON group. Poland fared moderately well on that score, too. Its 2.4 ICOR was much lower than that of Hungary's 3.5 but higher than Bulgaria's and Romania's 1.9 for the same period. As time progressed, however, the ICOR values increased in both Poland and GDR, signifying decreasing capital efficiency and productivity. For Poland, despite the rapid investment expansion during Gierek's term in the early 1970s, the ICOR rose only slightly from 1960-1969's 3.6 to 1971-1975's 3.7. With investment retrenchment during the 1976-1980 period, the number of not-completed industrial projects rose, and the ICOR value for the Polish economy as a whole rose to 4.9. Capital in Poland was becoming less efficient and less productive over time. While ICOR values for the decade of 1980's are not available, investment ratios for both Poland and GDR declined significantly from 1980 on. It was encouraging. However, the ratios were still significantly higher in 1989 than during the 1960-1969 period, indicating lower capital efficiency in the late 1980s than in the two decades earlier.

Table 4.6
Productivity and Changes in Standard of Living for Poland and GDR,* 1975-1987 (1970=100)

	1975	1980	1985	1986	1987
POLAND					
Productivity	143.5	147.7	143.7	149.8	152.3
Real Wages	155.4	172.7	140.0	143.8	138.1
Real Incomes	152.5	175.9	161.3	164.0	-----
Retail Trade	156.6	178.9	161.5	169.2	175.2
GDR					
Productivity*	127.3	150.2	182.9	190.8	197.6
Real Wages	119.9	137.0	151.9	156.9	-----
Real Incomes	131.9	162.4	199.6	209.7	219.3
Retail Trade	131.1	160.4	182.3	189.9	196.6

Source: United Nations, 1989: 186.
*NMP Per Worker.

In Table 4.6, productivity for both Poland and GDR have been indexed at 100 for 1970. Polish productivity on average was increasing at a considerably faster pace than that of GDR's, owing to Poland's expansion in fixed capital formation between 1971 and 1975. By 1980, the trend in increasing productivity was reversed for the two economies. GDR was gaining at about the same pace between 1970 and 1975 and between 1975 and 1980. Between 1980 and 1987, GDR steadily gained ground on productivity over Poland. Poland, on the other hand, either regressed or was crawling forward with difficulty.

In brief, labor and capital productivity for Poland fared relatively well for the period 1950-1969, but it suffered during the period 1970-1987. Erroneous economic policies, particularly heavy borrowing from abroad and subsequent wasteful investments, may account for much of the deteriorating productivity during that period.

THE CONSUMER GOODS SHORTAGE

The sales pitch of communist philosophy was to build a workers' paradise. There would be equality and abundance. Worker-consumers would benefit from their communal effort. After forty-five years, the young generation that entered the labor market after the war had reached retirement age, but the paradise had not been built. It was not even in sight. There had been improvements since the Communists came to power, but those improvements had been achieved decades earlier in the noncentralized economies of the West.

While its Western neighbors were concentrating on speedier development and higher living standards, the Polish Communists were still grappling with the basic issue of meeting the consumers' generic needs. The divergence in results between the West and Poland is due in part to the different points of departure. In market economies, the economic policy is oriented to satisfying consumer needs and wants. It is a buyer's market. Assured of adequate goods and services, the consumer works to earn purchasing power based on individual ability. Entrepreneurs and investors play their roles to assure adequate supply. Investments are made and the factors of production are employed in light of market conditions. Equilibrium is achieved and maintained through the market mechanism: no surpluses or shortages exist for an extended period of time.

Under Communism, on the other hand, Poland relied heavily on centralized direction. Production and distribution were planned. To achieve objectives quickly, the centralized system emphasized production. It was a seller's market. Market pricing was replaced by the state's determination as to what constituted value. Production took precedence over consumption. To produce the state's desired goods and services, investments were channeled according to the plan. To meet investment needs, forced savings through shortages in consumer goods became part of the plan. Consumers were to be motivated by revoluntary zeal rather than the lure of consumer goods; state-espoused ideology was intended to be the motivating force. Personal sacrifices were extolled. Meanwhile, officials luxuriated in privileges and perks. Work morale was low, and the planned production of goods and services suffered in quality and, at times, in quantity. The following discussion traces the state's planned policy of control over consumer well-being.

In place of market coordination, the tension between the supply and demand (for factors of production as well as end products) became the responsibility of the state's Planning Commission. Wages were controlled; prices of consumer goods were pegged high relative to income, so as to curtail aggregate consumption. Private farmers, who resisted collectivization in the late 1940s and early 1950s, fared relatively well, but the standard of living for industrial and service workers fell from 1947 through 1956 under Boleslaw Bierut. By the end of the five-year plan of 1950-1955, social discontent began to assume more violent expressions. After the Poznan riots in 1956, Gomulka succeeded Bierut as the party's first secretary. Gomulka recognized the root cause of social unrest, and he promised an adequate supply of consumer goods. But by then it was already too difficult to convert the complexes of fixed assets from industrial to consumer goods production. Also, the COMECON had already been formed and commercial agreements obliged Poland to continue along its current path of product development. Consumer needs were given only occasional attention by planners, depending on the immediacy and frequency of riots or revolts. Consumer prices were kept under control; so were wages. Real wages inched up at a snail's pace. The market was still short of many consumer items, and rationing of essential goods was the rule rather than the exception. Sporadic and periodic unrest marred Gomulka's administration. Though sympathetic to the Polish cause, Gomulka succeeded little in meeting the needs and wants of consumers. Social tension, built up by economic deprivation, erupted in 1968 and 1970. Students demanded freedom and reform, while workers struck over announced price increases. Demonstrations and strikes led to many violent deaths in 1970. They were just symptoms of deeper social, political, and economic malaises.

The Polish people, cultured and brought up to feel free and independent, found it offensive to be directed in every important sphere of living. The state planned, and it wanted the plan implemented by the people. But what it wanted went unheeded. When the economy failed owing to the system's innate deficiencies, those who labored for the state's objectives suffered the consequences. The announcement of 1970s price increases, thereby lowering consumer purchasing power, was the straw that broke the camel's back.

Gierek replaced Gomulka as the party secretary--consumer needs and welfare could no longer be blatantly ignored.

But political freedom was not in the cards, and essential state controls remained while inefficiency persisted. To provide a semblance of adequate consumer goods, foreign imports at state-subsidized prices began to appear in the marketplace. Rapid wage increases were also granted to pacify social discontent. But this temporary social calm was bought with money borrowed from the West. The state's deep-rooted unwillingness to promote the growth of private enterprise doomed Poland to continued dependence on foreign imports in order to meet an increasing appetite for domestic products. Ironically, foreign imports included agricultural produce, which domestic producers could have readily supplied if given appropriate economic incentives.

Poland's political decisions were not based on economic reasoning. The symptoms have temporarily been relieved with high dosages of foreign borrowing, but the root cause of the problem--stagnant supplies of domestically produced consumer goods--remained.   The contrived improvement in consumer welfare was short-lived, however. Mounting evidence of Poland's inability to repay its foreign debt prompted an austerity program. Investment retrenchment was coupled with curtailment of aggregate consumption. By June 1976, in order to reduce consumer purchasing power, new price increases were announced. Civil disturbances immediately followed. Once again, Gierek's administration rescinded its intention to raise prices on essential commodities.

Both consumers and the government were perched on the horns of a dilemma. There was no prospect of a long-term solution to Poland's economic problems. Out of necessity, the government caved in to people's demands, but it continued to be constrained by a systemic inflexibility of its own weaving. Then consumer dissatisfaction widened into political dissent: "General dissatisfaction with the slow pace of improvement in living standards during the last decade was the basic cause of the social unrest, which came to the surface toward the end of 1970" (United Nations, 1971: 130). The Committee for the Defense of Workers was formed in 1976. A year later, the Movement for the Defense of Human and Civil Rights was established to combat what was perceived as the administration's oppressive policies. Students, on their part, formed the Student Solidarity Committee across campuses. Other opposition groups banded together to form the Confederation of Independent Poland (Schopflin, 1979: 10-12). The only quasi-ally the government had was the Roman Catholic hierarchy, which played the roles of a moderate as well as mediator between the government and its opposition.

Meanwhile, consumer needs were not being better met. Economic stagnation and political stalemate helped ferment dissent. Workers became more militant. When meat price increases were announced in the summer of

1980, people took to the streets again. Stanislaw Kania replaced Gierek in September 1980. Kania, in turn, was replaced by General Wojciech Jaruzelski a year later. Changes of administration were effectuated mostly through public discontent in the form of strikes or demonstrations; and such demonstrations were mostly triggered by economic issues. Economic issues evolved into political demands by late 1976.

It was a blessing in disguise that no meaningful economic adjustments were feasible without political reform. A Commission for Economic Reform was appointed in late 1980, producing a report that placed the blame squarely on the centralized system of planning. The commission recommended drastic changes. Even with a modified version of the report, attempts were made by vested interests within the party to delay implementation of reform measures. Reform acts were passed by the Sejm, but the economic and political crises had been brewing too long. Societal concerns and consumer interest, as embodied in Solidarity's increasingly more militant expressions, could no longer be addressed with patchwork reform proposals. Then martial law was imposed in December 1981. The opposition, spearheaded by Solidarity, was silenced by force. But consumer needs were no better met than before; instead, Poland's economy plunged into near bankruptcy. Foreign debt kept mounting, and domestic production and productivity fell two years in succession. Prices rose, real wages fell, and the standard of living slid back to 1970 level. Only with the blessing of clement weather in 1983 and 1984 was the agricultural sector able to give consumers a respite in food shortages. Consumer well-being slowly edged upward in subsequent years, but not to a level acceptable to consumers. The relegalization of Solidarity in April 1989, and the agreement signed between the Communist government and Solidarity, ushered in a new era of the Polish economy.

Tables 4.7 and 4.8 provide an overview of aggregate consumer well-being since the late 1950. As mentioned earlier, initial investment was in heavy industry, and neglect of agriculture and consumer goods led to severe shortages early on. The only reason prices of essential commodities did not rise more rapidly in the 1950s and 1960s was because of price controls.

As can be seen in Table 4.7, prices rose very slowly in the late 1960s. Announced price increases would have caused widespread unrest, so from 1960 through 1970, price increases were moderate. But price control did not mean adequate supplies. Many consumer goods had to be rationed, and consumers could secure only what was supplied at given prices. Anything beyond that had to be obtained on the black market. Though there might have been disposable income, it was not of use because the financial flow was not accompanied by a real flow. Forced savings bid up prices on the black market; the currency represented no real value. Then the disturbances of 1968 and 1970 led to more rapid increases in real wages. Whereas wage increases in Poland were much slower than in GDR in the late 1960s, they

Table 4.7
Consumer Price Index for United States, GDR, and Poland, 1960-1988 (1980=100)

United States	GDR	Poland	
1960	36	79	39
1970	47	89	50
1975	66	91	64
1980	100	100	100
1983	121	104	285
1984	126	106	330
1985	131	109	386
1986	133	111	417
1987	138	112	600
1988	144	113	1020

Source: Directorate of Intelligence, 1989: 39.

escalated for six consecutive years from 1971 onward and surpassed that of GDR. At the same time, the Polish consumer price index showed only modest increases between 1970 and 1975--a brief reprieve for Polish consumers. But this condition also sowed the seed of numerous macro dislocations to come. The false sense of consumer well-being was built upon false premises: there were no sound internal adjustments to achieve equilibrium with growth. On the surface, the Polish economy fared better than the United States in terms of inflation. From 1970 to 1975, the United States experienced a cumulative 40 percent inflation rate, primarily caused by the energy crisis. Poland, on the other hand, experienced only a 28 percent increase in prices for the same five-year period. But the price the Polish consumer had to pay came shortly thereafter: real income increased by 15.4 percent in 1975 but dropped by 2.4 percent in 1978 and by 24.9 percent in 1982. Unlike real wage changes in GDR, which were consistently positive and relatively stable, the Polish wage earner went from feast to famine. The contrast is even more glaring when data in Tables 4.7 and 4.8 are compared. The inflation rates may be inferred from Table 4.8. They suggest stable prices in GDR from 1975 through 1987. As for the United States, inflation was rapid between 1975 and 1982, but it began to taper off satisfactorily from 1983 onward. It was a different picture for Poland. Prices doubled in 1982 alone (World Bank, 1987a: 12), reflected not only in Table 4.7's rapid price increase from 1980's indexed 100 to 1983's 285, but also manifest in Table 4.8's change in real wages for 1982. To this day, the Polish consumer has not as yet recovered lost purchasing power. Wage increases since 1983 have been effectively neutralized by hyperinflation; consumer confidence has eroded while the value of zlotys kept sliding. Inflation has not only rendered debt servicing increasingly problematic but also negatively affected work morale in the Workers' Paradise.

INFLATION: CAUSES AND CONSEQUENCES

In Poland, as in other centrally planned economies, inflation was customarily written off by planning mechanisms, including stabilizing prices. The practice did not eliminate shortages, however. In Poland, the situation was unique, in that inflation was compounded by the inflexibility of the planned system as well as by supply inelasticity and a staggering foreign debt.

The inflation rate in Poland between 1960 and 1970 averaged a mere 2.82 percent. From 1970 through 1975, it rose to an annual rate of 5 to 6 percent. Then it climbed to 11.2 percent per year between 1975 and 1980. The year 1980 was also the beginning of a new wave of social unrest. With the founding of Solidarity and subsequent martial law, productivity and production fell precipitously. As a result, inflation between 1980 and 1983 rocketed to 61.7 percent annually. Thereafter, annual inflation rates were 15.7, 10.9, 20.9, and 28.5 percent, respectively,[4] for 1984 through 1987. For 1988, the rate of inflation was 70 percent. Despite the government's promises and pronouncements that inflation would be reduced to single digit by 1987, it kept rising--and at an alarmingly accelerated rate. Confidence in the financial system and in the currency was more than eroded; it was destroyed. Private savings in zlotys made no economic sense, since the value of the zloty could no longer be what it said it was worth. This helped to fuel inflationary pressure over time.

The effects of inflation in Poland were obvious. There was no desire to save zlotys. Yet consumer goods were short in supply, and demand placed added pressure on commodity prices. Time was wasted queuing up for a limited supply of goods. Pressure for wage increases mounted. Government expenditures, fueled by adjusted prices, exceeded revenues. The value of the zloty kept decreasing relative to hard currencies. The ability to import the much-needed industrial goods was curtailed, and the nation's ability to secure foreign loans kept declining. Social unrest became more widespread and increasingly frequent. Poland lost ground in trade with other countries. While its neighbors to the West kept prospering, the Polish economy stagnated, faced with collapse.

The inflationary causes in Poland came in varied shapes and forms. The first major cause of inflation was the perennial budget deficit. From 1980 through 1986, the government's expenditures consistently exceeded its revenues. The year 1985 was an exception when there was a perfect balance. But 1986 saw a deficit totaling U.S. $233 million (World Bank, 1989: 223 and 267). This deficit would have been acceptable if it had been incurred as a result of expanded domestic investment for growth. The deficit would also have been more manageable if the economy had not been sustaining significant foreign exchange losses. But the losses were due to the decreasing value of the zloty relative to foreign currencies, and were borne by the government but

Table 4.8
Real Wages and Per Capita Real Incomes for GDR and Poland, 1956-1986
(annual percentage change)

	GDR		Poland	
	Real Wages	Real Incomes	Real Wages	Real Incomes
1956	---	---	11.6	---
1957	---	---	8.3	---
1958	---	---	3.5	---
1959	---	---	5.1	---
1960	---	---	-1.5	---
1961	---	---	2.6	---
1962	---	---	0.4	---
1963	---	---	2.4	---
1964	---	---	2.1	---
1965	---	---	0.0	---
1966	---	---	3.3	---
1967	2.2	---	2.5	---
1968	4.4	---	1.3	---
1969	4.5	---	1.7	---
1970	4.7	3.3	1.6	4.0
1971	3.6	4.2	5.7	8.7
1972	4.2	6.7	6.4	11.8
1973	3.9	6.3	8.7	9.7
1974	3.4	6.3	6.6	5.0
1975	3.4	4.8	19.9	9.0
1976	3.5	5.0	4.5	5.6
1977	3.0	6.1	2.4	6.2
1978	3.3	4.2	-2.2	-0.5
1979	2.7	3.4	2.2	2.5
1980	1.1	2.8	3.9	0.8
1981	2.2	4.4	2.4	3.3
1982	1.9	4.1	-24.9	-18.0
1983	1.3	2.4	1.2	0.3
1984	2.0	5.1	0.5	1.8
1985	2.6	5.2	3.8	6.0
1986	3.5	5.7	2.7	1.7
1987	5.4	4.6	-3.5	0.8
1988	2.9	4.1	14.4	13.2
1989	1.6	---	9.1	---

Source: United Nations, 1971: 125; 1988: 336; 1990:391; Landau, 1985: 295.

did not appear in its expenditure column. The government's overspent money was competing for, and chasing after, a relatively constant supply of commodities. Prices rose, while the expectation of future price increases was

Table 4.9
Monthly Nominal Wages, Total Gross Investment and Gross Industrial Production 1970-1989

	Monthly Nominal Wages (zlotys)	Total Gross Investment		Gross Industrial Production (annual avg. change)
		Material Sphere	Non-Material Sphere (annual avg. change)	
1970	2,235	3.0	8.0	8.1
1971	2,358	9.6	1.4	7.9
1972	2,539	26.0	16.0	10.7
1973	2,798	26.5	19.9	11.2
1974	3,185	23.3	19.8	11.4
1975	3,783	16.1	7.4	10.9
1976	4,116	0.2	4.1	9.3
1977	4,415	1.6	8.6	6.9
1978	4,686	-0.1	9.7	4.9
1979	5,100	-11.2	2.3	2.7
1980	6,040	-12.8	-11.0	---
1981	7,689	-23.5	-19.9	-10.8
1982	11,631	-15.3	-5.7	-2.1
1983	14,475	8.2	11.6	6.4
1984	16,838	13.8	7.2	5.2
1985	20,005	6.7	4.6	3.7
1986	24,095	5.8	3.7	4.7
1987	29,184	4.2	4.3	3.4
1988	53,090	5.6	5.1	5.3
1989	205,000	---	---	-2.0

Source: United Nations, 1988: 335ff.

built into consumers' psychology. Further, owing to its deteriorating currency, a greater percentage of future government expenditures needed to be earmarked for foreign debt service, lessening the state's ability to fulfill domestic obligations. If the government had wished to borrow from the public to meet its domestic obligations, the interest rates would have to be inflated drastically to entice the savers to part with surplus zlotys. But higher interest rates would have significantly reduced incentives for investment, especially by the private sector, thus retarding growth over time. It was a losing proposition.

The second major cause of inflation centered on the expenditure side of the government's budget. While a detailed expenditure structure is not available, Table 4.9 may shed light on general characteristics. Nominal monthly wages doubled from 1970 to 1977; they nearly doubled again, from 1981's 7,689 to 1984's 16,838 zlotys, a three-year doubling. Since most wage earners were employed in the socialized sector, wage increases had to come from government expenditures. Meanwhile, government revenues did not rise as much. Also note the column Total Gross Investment. Rapid increases in investment in the early 1970s were made with excessive borrowing from abroad. Toward the end of the 1970s, both material and nonmaterial sphere investments not only declined but declined at an alarming rate. This is reflected in part by the resulting gross industrial production figures for the early 1980s. The government also had to shift expenditures from investments to higher nominal wages. On the other hand, labor productivity did not rise as a result of wage increases: productivity increases for 1981-1985 were only 0.1 percent per year, while capital productivity for the corresponding period was -3 percent per year (United Nations, 1988: 220). Total gross industrial production declined by 10.8 percent in 1981. It declined by another 2.1 percent the year after. Even though production for 1983 rose by 6.4 percent, it came on the heels of a combined loss of 12.9 percent for the two previous years. By the end of 1984, the total industrial production level was still below the level of 1980. Since nominal wages had more than tripled by the beginning of 1985, while gross industrial product remained nearly constant, it is easy to appreciate the cause as well as the magnitude of Poland's inflation problems.[5]

A third cause of the inflationary spiral in Poland was the excessive burden that the government had taken on to subsidize various sectors of the economy. Subsidizing food prices, for instance, in effect lowered the price of food items to consumers. In accordance, demand increased, partly owing to lowered prices and partly to increased purchasing power. Another instance was the subsidies for housing industry. The central government granted below-market interest rates for construction of housing units sponsored by local governments or housing cooperatives. As inflation kept up, the value of the currency decreased but the rate of interest remained constant. Subsidies kept bleeding the state budget, and the deficit rose while some programs got cut. Subsidies, particularly when faced with inflation, led to greater shortages in the longer run and intensified the inflationary pressure. The rigid fiscal structure through central planning could not cope with a fluid economic reality.[6]

A fourth major cause of persistent inflation was that "government expenditures were inflexible while tax revenues relied heavily on sales, profit, and wages which were sensitive to the declining level of economic activity. As a result of this contradiction, a budget deficit appeared" (Jozefiak interview, 1990). In 1985, the combined contributions from these sources amounted to 66.2 percent of government revenue. In 1986, it increased to 67.4 percent--in short, two-thirds of government revenue had to be derived from these sources (World Bank, 1987a: 179). This would have been fine if the Polish economy had enjoyed an uneventful pattern of growth. But as had been seen earlier in Table 4.9, wage increases from 1979 onward had been skyrocketing. Wage-tax increases, which accounted for 9.3 percent of total revenue for both 1985 and 1986, did not keep pace. More important, while the average annual inflation rate between 1980 through 1986 was 31.2 percent (World Development Report, 1988: 223), government revenue from sales and profits were increasing at an annual rate of only 10 percent. Government expenditures had to rise with inflation, but government revenue kept falling further behind. The budget could not be balanced for lack of an effective means to increase revenue.

The fifth and final major cause of inflation to be discussed here was Poland's rising foreign debt and its weakening trade position with the West. Debt servicing requires foreign earnings, and foreign earnings come mainly from exports. Foreign debt had reached a critical high, but the Polish government was unable to meet its debt obligations because earnings from exports had not risen appreciably. Investments in export-oriented industries required additional hard currency, but the source of additional borrowing had dried up. Both the government and the private sector needed foreign currency for different reasons, bidding up the prices of foreign currencies and depreciating the zloty. Value and confidence in the zloty kept eroding, and consumers sought to dump zlotys as fast as they were received. The velocity of money accelerated, further fueling inflation and further eroding the zloty's position relative to foreign currencies.[7] That led to an increase in the minimum amount of money needed for debt servicing and industries wanting imported goods for production. In a chain reaction, the real value of the zloty was driven down, fueling the inflationary flames of expectation. In summary, the inflation that plagued the Polish economy had its roots in the fundamental structure and functioning of the economic system. With a built-in mechanism for indexed subsidies, wage increases, and other government expenditures, without commensurate means of increasing government revenues, inflation was unavoidable.

TRADE: IMBALANCE AND WEAKENED POSITION

Many economies have taken advantage of international trade to achieve rapid growth. Japan, Taiwan, South Korea, Singapore, Italy, and West Germany are a few such economies whose rapid growth has been fueled by successful foreign trade. This section discusses Poland's foreign trade under the following administration: (1) Wladyslaw Gomulka (1945-1948) and Boleslaw Bierut (1948-1956); (2) Gomulka (1956-1970); (3) Edward Gierek (1970-1980); and (4) Stanislaw Kania (1980-1981) and Wojciech Jaruzelski (1981-1989).

The Gomulka and Bierut Administrations (1945-1956)

Gomulka was a believer in communism. He was Poland's first postwar premier and party secretary. He was a nationalist, believing in a Polish road to socialism rather than a Sovietization of the Polish economy. His resistance to Stalinist pressure caused him to be ousted in 1948, replaced by Bierut, who was a close ally of the Soviet Union. Gomulka's primary task after the war was to reestablish the Polish nation and to rebuild it from the extensive destruction. External trade was not yet high on the priority list. The transportation system to ferry exportable items was not adequate. For exportable items, there were primarily mineral products, raw materials, and farm produce. Total value traded in 1945 was only U.S. $39 million, of which U.S. $35 million was exported to the Soviet Union and only U.S. $1 million to other Eastern European nations. Similarly, U.S. $34 million worth of imports were recorded for the year, and most of them came from the Soviet Union as well. Total trade with the West in 1945 was a meager U.S. $3 million. An observable pattern between 1945 and 1948 was the rapid increase in value traded, much to the credit of investments made in the transportation system (Landau, 1985: 207, 236).

Poland needed capital-intensive reproducer goods from both the East and the West, so trade with other European nations became more active. Poland's exports to Eastern European nations, excluding the Soviet Union, climbed from 1945's 3 percent to 1946's 32.9 percent, 1947's 34.8 percent, and 1948's 52.8 percent (Landau, 1985: 207).[8] Trade imbalances and unfavorable export-import ratios in 1946 and 1947 were the result of Poland's need to import heavy industrial equipment for re-construction, while all it could export were relatively cheap raw materials.

By 1948, Gomulka's sympathy toward Yugoslavia's Marshal Tito, in the latter's dispute with Stalin, made him unacceptable to the Kremlin, and he was replaced by Bierut. A year later, the COMECON was formed in Moscow, which closely tied Poland's exports to the CMEA nations. Because of long-

Table 4.10
Foreign Trade, 1945 - 1956 (Million U.S. $)

	1945	1946	1947	1948	1949	1950	1951	1952	1953	1954	1955	1956
CMEA Members Export To:	36	76	109	235	281	361	434	505	569	602	578	580
Other Nations	3	51	137	296	338	273	327	270	262	267	341	405
Export Total	39	127	246	531	619	634	761	775	831	869	919	985
CMEA Members Import From:	31	114	111	245	269	408	535	563	556	641	605	677
Other Nations	3	32	209	271	363	260	389	280	218	262	327	344
Import Total:	34	148	320	516	632	668	924	843	774	893	932	1021
Balance	5	-21	-74	15	-13	-34	-163	-68	57	-24	-13	-36
Export/Import Ratio	1.15	.86	.77	1.03	.98	.99	.82	.92	1.07	.97	.99	.96

Source: Landau, 1981: 207, 236.

term contracts with CMEA members, Poland's export industry committed more of its long-term investments to production of goods demanded by CMEA members. Trading activities with the West decreased proportionately. The Ministry of Foreign Trade's needs were met by credit from the Soviet Union, and this money enabled Poland to import significantly more than it was able to export during Bierut's administration. Capital equipment and fuel constituted two of the most important imports, while Poland continued to rely heavily on raw materials, particularly coal, and agricultural products for export earnings. As can be seen in Table 4.10, trade deficits incurred during the 1949-1956 period were mostly from the Eastern bloc nations. Export-import ratios during these years indicated a general trend of slightly less than one. However, owing to growth in value traded, cumulative trade imbalances placed greater pressure on increasing exports. Although Poland was able to export more of its machinery equipment abroad by the mid-1950s, its market in the West was curtailed by the cold war. That necessitated debt forgiveness by the Soviet Union: "Remission of debts, on the score of credits granted to Poland by the Soviet Union in the past years, as on November 1, 1956, releases us from an obligation to repay an amount of more than 2 billion roubles (more than U.S. $500 million) in the years 1957-1965" (Landau, 1985: 239). Bierut was cautious enough to achieve a relative trade balance with the West, since hard currency was an exceptionally scarce financial resource that Poland sorely needed to accumulate. In short, the Polish trade sector developed rather smoothly during Bierut's years of administration.

The Gomulka Administration (1956-1970)

When riots forced Bierut out of office, Gomulka was recalled to lead the nation for the next fourteen years. By then, however, Gomulka had little choice but to honor the trade agreements with CMEA nations. Much of the trade during his second tenure as prime minister had been locked in via long-term CMEA agreements. Taking inflation into account, trade volume nearly trebled, from 1956's U.S. $985 million for exports and U.S. $1,021 million for imports, to 1970s U.S. $3,548 million and U.S. $3,607 million for exports and imports, respectively. With the exception of 1964 and 1968, Poland experienced trade deficits for twelve of Gomulka's fourteen-year tenure as the premier (Landau, 1985: 276, 277).

With the CMEA economies, Poland consistently imported more than it exported for all these years, with 1964 and 1968 as the only exceptions. That posed little problem, since Polish exports could more readily find buyers in the East than in the West. Besides, there had been structural changes in the composition of Polish exports to CMEA nations during that fourteen-year period. The percentage machinery exports had seen a steady rise, whereas exports of raw materials and farm products had declined. A trade imbalance with the West during that period, however, became more of a problem. Poland consistently imported more from the West than it was able to export. Poland's growing ability to produce capital-intensive products such as automobiles, ships, and machinery did not enable it to capitalize on the growing Western markets. The West had fully recovered from the war and was able to produce its own high-quality industrialized products. Likewise, Polish exports of industrial products were not in high demand.

The recurrent trade imbalance with the West meant a loss in value for the zloty. More Polish goods and services were required in exchange for Poland's imports from the West. Combining trade deficits from the East and West, and aggregating the trade deficits from 1945 through 1970 minus the equivalent of U.S. $500 million forgiven by the Soviet Union--Poland's trade deficit posed a staggering problem. In only five out of twenty-five years was Poland able to achieve a trade surplus. And of those five years--1945, 1948, 1953, 1964, and 1968--three came in early, with a combined value of only U.S. $77 million at current prices. The fourth (1964) and fifth (1968) year's surpluses were an insignificant U.S. $25 million and $4 million, respectively. Still, no belt-tightening measures were taken to correct the trade imbalance. (Landau, 1985: 205-209)

The Gierek Administration (1970-1980)

The absence of a reasonable trade policy during Gierek's administration sowed the seeds for much of the current debt problem. According to a U.N. report, "Poland planned in 1970 to achieve a balance on trade account and aimed at a faster increase in exports than in imports; in fact, it envisaged a bigger fall in the rate of growth of imports than of exports." (1971: 141) That, however, was on paper. Owing to Poland's need for industrial expansion but its inability to supply needed parts and raw material domestically, imports could not and did not decline. Gierek, who replaced Gomulka, envisioned rapid industrial expansion by way of heavy borrowing and purchases from abroad. As has been pointed out earlier, poor planning and poorer coordination of investments led to extensive waste in imported machinery equipments and licenses.

Every year during the decade of 1970-1980 saw a trade deficit, but the complications came on two major fronts. First, the deficits were no longer in the two-digit $U.S. million ranges. The deficit more than doubled from 1970's U.S. $59 million to 1971's U.S. $166 million; it more than redoubled in 1972 to U.S. $402 million and to 1973's U.S. $1.42 billion (Landau, 1985: 312). Poland's exports did grow rapidly during that period as well, but not fast enough relative to the much faster growth in imports. The second major complication of perennial trade deficits came from the fact that the trade imbalance was almost exclusively a result of Poland's trade with the West. Since imports were being financed through credits from the West, the problem of debt service had long been noted by economists. But the warnings were not heeded by policymakers. "In 1971 debt service costs accounted for about 17 percent of the total export receipts, in 1973 for 14 percent, in 1976 for 34 percent, and in 1980 for 82 percent." (Landau, 1985: 111) The problem reached nearly insurmountable proportions. Since growth in exports to CMEA nations nearly matched growth in imports therefrom, debt repayment to the West had to be exclusively in hard currency. At the same time, Poland was unable to make inroads into Western markets to earn that needed hard currency. Poland did find markets abroad for machine tools, metallurgy, and electrochemical products, but mostly in developing and CMEA economies only. The decade's feasting on borrowed money and on foreign imports was over.

The Kania (1980-1981) and Jaruzelski (1981-1989) Administrations

The most recent period to be considered is from 1981 through 1987. Kania replaced Gierek in September 1980, and Jaruzelski replaced Kania as party secretary in October 1981. Martial law was declared in December 1981. Though open opposition to the regime was suppressed, the economy faced a crisis beyond telling. Strikes were forbidden. Low morale adversely affected work incentives and labor productivity. Production fell by 5.2 percent in 1980; it fell by another 11.9 percent in 1981, and yet another 1.6 percent in 1982 (United Nations, 1984; 107). On the other front, capital productivity fell by 7.0 percent in 1980, dropped by another 15.8 percent in 1981, and grew by a meager 0.7 percent in 1982. (United Nations, 1984; 107) By the end of 1983, both labor and capital productivity were still below 1978 levels. This woeful plight was compounded by economic sanctions imposed on Poland by Western nations after imposition of martial law. Western governments also discontinued negotiations for debt rescheduling. In 1981 alone, Polish exports fell by 19 percent (United Nations, 1984; 219), but the nation was unable to obtain additional credit from the West. Poland was in need of equipment, supplies, parts and services from the West for its machinery imported earlier. Production bottlenecks appeared; even exports to CMEA nations suffered as a result.

As part of the austerity measures, imports were drastically trimmed. They fell by 17 percent in 1981 and by another 14 percent in 1982. In the new five-year plan, exports were programmed to grow faster than imports, yet performance more often than not fell short of the target. By the early 1980s the government made an extra effort to convince foreign creditors and potential lenders of its intent to achieve trade surpluses as well as to honor debts.

Table 4.11 presents the results of the belt-tightening policy on trade. Recovery in the trade sector came from 1983 onward. For the first time since 1945, the Polish economy was able to show a meaningful trade surplus of U.S. $695 million. As noted earlier, there was a trade surplus of $5 million in 1945, $15 million in 1948, $57 million in 1953, $25 million in 1964, and $4 million in 1968. Thereafter, for nearly fifteen consecutive years Poland suffered from trade deficits amounting to hundreds of millions and later billions of dollars each year. The year 1983 therefore was a landmark period in Polish foreign trade. The amount of surplus in 1983 was significant. More important, Poland proved to foreign nations that it was intent on reversing the trend and was able to accomplish that. Poland has been able to achieve sizeable trade surpluses ever since.

A few observations can be made from trade data in Table 4.11. First, Poland's trade balance with CMEA economies showed initial deficits for the years 1983 through 1985. But surpluses of U.S. $466 and $330 million were achieved for 1986 and 1987, respectively. CMEA member countries' demand for Polish fuel, metallurgy, and especially engineering products was and has been firm. The trend is expected to continue. Second, Poland's trade surpluses for the five-year period of 1983-1987 came mostly from its trade with the West and with developing economies. Exports of engineering products, food, construction, chemicals, and agricultural products were finding

Table 4.11
Foreign Trade, 1957-1970 (Million U.S.)

	1957	1958	1959	1960	1961	1962	1963	1964	1965	1966	1967	1968	1969	1970
Export to:														
CMEA	578	620	682	830	939	1034	1123	1351	1409	1400	1611	1878	2064	2266
Others	397	439	463	495	564	612	647	746	819	872	915	979	1078	1282
Export total:	975	1059	1145	1325	1503	1646	1770	2097	2228	2272	2526	2857	3142	3548
Import from:														
CMEA	778	714	923	949	1054	1246	1326	1306	1548	1604	1737	1838	2144	2473
Others	437	512	497	546	633	639	653	766	793	890	908	1015	1096	1134
Import total:	1215	1226	1420	1495	1687	1885	1979	2072	2341	2494	2645	2853	3210	3607
Balance	-240	-167	-275	-170	-184	-239	-209	25	-113	-222	-119	4	-68	-5.9
Export/Import Ratio	0.80	0.86	0.81	0.89	0.89	0.88	0.89	1.01	0.95	0.91	0.95	1.00	0.98	0.98

Source: Landau, 1985: 276-7.

readier markets than before. That was translated to an inflow of modest but much needed convertible currencies to meet import needs as well as for debt servicing. And, third, despite its need to import Western raw materials and machinery, Poland's aggregate growth in imports has been on the decline since 1984. Even a negative growth of -3.5 percent was achieved in 1987. The trend in trade deficits has been altered in favor of Poland. With the democratization of society and the liberalization of its economy, the relevant concern now is how to substantially increase the trade surplus in order to meet forthcoming debt obligations.

FOREIGN DEBT AND CREDITWORTHINESS

By 1989, Poland was struck with an economic crisis unprecedented in its postwar history. Of its most severe problems, mounting foreign debt ranked high. Two decades ago, Poland's total external debt was slightly over half a billion dollars. By 1986, it soared to U.S. $36.6 billion--the equivalent of 47.6 percent of Poland's 1986 gross national product (World Bank, 1988: 253). The situation would have been more manageable if the debt incurred was for well-planned industrial expansion for manufacturing exports. But most of the foreign debt was in convertible currencies owed to the West, and a substantial portion was expended on domestic consumption and on poorly planned and coordinated projects. The foreign debt has become the burden of the new government working for a new economic order.

The foreign debt problem began in 1970. Social discontent was widespread and the atmosphere was ripe for riots. Gomulka was replaced by Gierek. The latter promised decentralization and liberalization, and also to improve living conditions. Thus a borrowing binge began. The original reasoning was correct--that investments made with borrowed money could increase the number of exportable goods for repayment of the debt. "From 1972 to 1976, Poland's hard currency loans grew at an average annual rate of 60 percent, and in 1976, when the external hard currency debt reached U.S. $11.5 billion, the debt service ratio had risen to 30 percent; but repayments in 1979 amounted to 92 percent of hard currency exports, the ratio rose to 101 percent in 1980" (Nelson, 1984: 220). From 1972 through 1981, imports exceeded exports by tens of billions of U.S. dollars. By 1980, foreign debt rose to $29.3 billion. And by 1989, it was a staggering $41 billion. It became increasingly obvious that Poland could not possibly meet its obligations, and it requested negotiation with foreign governments, banks, and institutions for re-scheduling.

Throughout, given the proud nature of the Polish people, the country never intended to deny its responsibility for repayment. Since there was much goodwill toward the Polish people, negotiations were held. Many of the official loans from foreign governments were rescheduled, with terms favorable to Poland. Foreign banks, likewise, signed agreements in 1981 to have 95 percent of the debts rescheduled (Nelson, 1984: 221). However, repayments on principal and interest were due in four years to foreign banks and eight years to foreign governments. Although the trade balance began to shift in favor of Poland starting in 1982, the surplus was not sufficient to meet these obligations.[9] The only redeeming feature was that nearly two-thirds of the debt was due to foreign governments, with the balance to foreign banks. As of 1988, total payments due for 1988 through 1995 were as follows: $3.23 billion for 1988; $2.16 billion for 1989; $4.18 billion for 1990; and $4.52, $3.47, $2.99, $2.53, and $2.50 billion for 1991, 1992, 1993, 1994, and 1995, respectively. Delayed principal and interest payments, together with later years' payments, added up to $3.83 billion (World Bank, 1987a: 94). Poland was in no position to meet its obligations.

The country's trade position had been favorable until 1971, and then a number of things went awry. First, a rapid increase in exports of electrochemical products, which accounted for 40.3 percent of total exports by the end of the 1970s was not destined primarily for Western economies (Landau, 1985: 314). Second, the value of coal exports began to decline toward the second half of the decade, and earnings fell short of plan. And third, farm produce exported to the West decreased around the same time. The expected rise in export earnings failed to materialize. Aside from that, there were sustained imports of machine parts from the West. The trade deficit kept mounting while repayments came due. Because of rapid borrowing and importation of machinery or intermediate goods and purchases of high-tech licenses, imports consistently exceeded exports beginning in 1972. It was planned as a short-term phenomenon, since export-oriented investments made in the early 1970s were expected to pay off in the near future.

Numerous investments, which could have yielded dividends in time, were never completed. First, as Poland's inability to meet its debts became obvious to lenders, credit began to dry up. The needed additional short-term credit was not granted, leaving many projects incomplete for lack of new and replacement parts. According to Professor Michael Dobro of Warsaw University, more than 1,500 major investment projects were not completed but could have been if additional money from the West had been secured (Marer and Siwinski, 1988: 179-80). Thus, while awaiting assistance from foreign creditors, these potentially productive investments could not make a meaningful contribution to the export column on the balance sheet. Second, the labor force was such that qualified workers and managers for the suddenly expanded industrial projects were not forthcoming. Further, of the 428 industrial licenses obtained from abroad, only 70 percent were used (Marer and Siwinski, 1988: 28). And third, the accelerated investment programs were ill conceived, poorly managed, and inefficiently coordinated. When martial law was declared in December 1981, productivity plummeted and the economic crisis came to a head, worsening Poland's debt servicing ability. Poland's credit worthiness has been called into question ever since.

NOTES

1. The former German Democratic Republic and Hungary had 7.0 percent and 6.9 percent growth rates, respectively (United Nations, 1988: 338).

2. As had been noted earlier, when the state failed to organize private farms into cooperatives, the plan deliberately discriminated against Polish farmers. Disenchanted with low farm income, the Polish farmer needed and sought nonfarm income, either by leaving the farm or by obtaining a second job in an urban center.

3. The annual percentage changes in labor productivity for 1983 through 1987 were 6.9, 5.9, 2.9, 4.6, and 2.5, respectively. The annual percentage changes in capital productivity for the same period were 3.4, 2.8, 0.3, 2.7, and -0.5, respectively. Therefore, the .1 percent annual decrease in labor productivity and the 3.2 percent annual decrease in capital productivty were exclusively due to the phenomenal decreases in both labor and capital productivty for the 1981-1982 period (United Nations, 1988: 121).

4. Inflation rates were calculated from Consumer Price Index of the Directorate of Intelligence, *Handbook of Economic Statistics.*

5. For the 1981-1985 period, the net material product actually decreased at an average of 1.1 percent annually. For the same time period, the annual change in gross social product was -.2 percent, gross investment was -7.4 percent, labor productivity was -0.1 percent, and capital productivity was - 3.4 percent (United Nations, 1988: 260).

6. For instance, subsidies for foodstuffs increased from 1985's 310 to 1986's 401 million zlotys. Similarly, the combined subsidies for state and cooperative housing, not counting reduced interest rates extended to cooperatives for fifty to sixty years, increased from 1985's 194 to 1986's 240 million zlotys (World Bank, 1987a: 183).

7. Expenditures related to the velocity of money for Poland surged from 1981's 3.2 to 4.6 in 1982, decreased to 4.5 in 1983, then increased again to 4.8 and 4.9, respectively for the next year and 1985 (World Bank, 1987a: 173).

8. Author's calculations.

9. Poland had a trade surplus of U.S. $358 million in 1982; $1,262 in 1984, $1,162 in 1985, and $1,035 in 1986 (World Bank, 1987a: 89).

5

THE POLISH ECONOMY IN TRANSITION, 1987–1989

This chapter bridges the two final years of Communist administration with the democratic new government of 1989. It provides a perspective on economic reform efforts by General Jaruzelski. And given the prevailing economic structure and conditions in Poland, this chapter also outlines the policies, plus the pace, needed for an orderly transition to take place. The chapters thereafter will analyze the current reform in progress, together with its positive and negative ramifications.

Amid an economy confronted by mounting pressures from within and from outside, the Polish government and Communist party attempted to induce involvement and participation from below. Early 1987 saw the dissemination of 174 Theses on the Second Stage of Economic Reform (Gabrisch, 1989: 180).[1] The intent was to have the general public discuss the logic, or lack thereof, of these theses, with the results taken into account by policymakers. The final version of this Second Stage was then to be voted upon by the Sejm and by the voters in the form of a general referendum. All these steps were to take place in 1987. In essence, the Second Stage of Reform was a variation on the ideas proposed in the wake of Gomulka's 1956 and Jaruzelski's 1981 reforms. Issues such as decentralizing the Planning Commission and the Ministry of Economics, greater enterprise autonomy, increased reliance on market function, and financial adaptability, were recurrent themes. The implication was that past efforts lacked enunciated objectives.

The Second Stage of Reform was less an attempt to introduce new measures than to acknowledge past failures. Emphasis in the second stage was on action: time was running out. And the 174 theses did cover all salient aspects of the problems facing the Polish economy. The fabric of state control over enterprise was to be trimmed or discarded. For production, greater enterprise autonomy--both organizationally and financially--was stressed. With the exception of those in key industries such as energy and transport, enterprises were to determine their own level and direction of investment based on market conditions. Production and product mix were to be market tested, no longer to be determined from above. Hiring and firing decisions were to be made by management representing the will and interest of workers. State monopolies were to be dismantled. Enterprises could enter into contractual agreements with other domestic or foreign economic entities, without obtaining prior government approval. These agreements were to include subcontracting, joint ventures, partnerships, and direct foreign investment. Production efficiency, entrepreneurship, and invention were to be promoted. Earnings in the form of profits would lead to enterprise growth via plowbacked investments, not growth in consumption. Competitive forces would be fostered, with inefficient enterprises liquidated and unemployment permitted to rise. Worker performance would be reflected in wages, however wage increases would still be monitored and controlled so as to avoid fueling inflation.

While promoting reform policies to increase productivity and production, the proposed reform measures also sought to stem growth in consumption. The most salient measure announced was the reduction of perennial subsidies for basic consumer goods. By July 1989, the farm sector was to be deregulated and subsidies of farm products were to begin phase-out, so that prices could gradually rise to reflect supply and demand conditions. It was a calculated move to gradually reduce government expenditures on the one hand and to discourage consumption on the other. This two-pronged subsidy reduction was to be applied to other essential consumer items such as energy and housing as well.

To accomplish production expansion and consumption curtailment, the proposed reform measures also included a redefinition of the functions and organization of the financial system. Apart from the National Bank of Poland, all other banks in the provinces were to be operated as profit-oriented enterprises. Credit was to be extended on the merits of the requisition. The duration of loans and consideration of risk factors were to be taken into account. Interest rates would be a function of money-market conditions. Passive allocation of credit according to the plan was to be discontinued. Subsidies of state enterprises in the form of fixed low interest rates were to be phased out. To further activate the financial dynamics, reform measures called for supervision of an enterprise's performance by competing banks instead of state-appointed ministries. In theory, investments were to be made where value product held the highest promise. In the long run, where demand was greatest, supply would be forthcoming, since consumers would be willing to pay for market-valued products. The problem of shortages in consumer goods would then be remedied in time, and rationing and the black market would disappear.

Reform measures also called for a price system that would reflect the real cost of production, while value produced for export would be synchronized with world market conditions. To encourage local entrepreneurial ventures, export permits would be easier to obtain and export tax incentives provided. To finance export-oriented enterprises, both private and state owned, convertible currencies could be purchased from and sold to Polish banks at realistic exchange rates. In the long run, this would align domestic prices with those in the world market. In the short run, exports would expand significantly because exportable items commanded higher prices abroad than domestically. Domestic prices would then rise under pressure on their own accord, an objective the regime had long fancied but had failed to pursue for fear of social unrest. Expanded export industry, if successful, could also increase foreign earnings to assist debt servicing and help finance the required imports. In the process, quality products as well as state-of-the-art technology could emerge, bringing the Polish economy more in line with the developed economies in the west.

The elements of these proposed reform measures were not significantly different from the earlier stages of reform or phases of adjustment. The measures were intended to render the economy more efficient, but keep it within the institutionalized framework of a centralized model. If fully implemented, there could be significant and orderly progress over time. It would be futile to speculate as to how far Jaruzelski, at that time, had intended to carry the reform beyond the 1987 proposals. But the second stage of reform did hold theoretical promise for a structural and functional transformation of the system.

With the winds of change gathering force in the Soviet Union, the Communist government in Poland agreed to discussions with Solidarity. The discussions were followed by quasi-democratic elections in which, as General Jaruzelski later remarked, "Our defeat is total." With blessings from Gorbachev, who on July 4, 1989, stated that "we could deal with the new government [in Poland]," the process of political reform was begun and completed in less than a year. With opposition represented in the Sejm, and with the newly created Senate dominated by Solidarity representatives 99 to 1, economic transformation now had to move forward.

Under the skillful management of former Prime Minister Tadeusz Mazowiecki, the political transformation was smoothly accomplished. The Communist apparatus simply faded away from the national scene. But the heritage of Communist administrations, though in existance less than half a century, could not be as readily eradicated from Poland's economic scenario. Given the sad economic situation in the late 1980s, the margin for error was narrow. Major miscalculations or blunders by policymakers in the new administration could mean a much longer and more painful transformation. The concrete approach taken by the Mazowiecki administration will be presented in later chapters. The remainder of this chapter is given to outlining the general preconditions, caveats, direction, and policies conducive and necessary for economic transformation in Poland in the 1990s.

THE STRUCTURE OF REFORM

Reform means reformulating policy measures or approaches where they have proved ineffective. *Adjustment* applies to when the basic premise might be correct but different circumstances dictate that either the scope, the pace, or the arrangement be revised in accordance with economic reality. Some economists recommend prescriptive measures, advocating comprehensive marketization of the economy with little or no attention paid to the essential and indispensable preconditions for fostering operational institutions.

The people of Poland know what profit is. But how to make a profit is a different issue. They have been entrepreneurial, but the activity was practiced within the planned, centralized system. Being entrepreneurial under the communist system does not automatically qualify them to be entrepreneurs in the new system, however. Economic reform entails more than a people's willingness to work toward an objective--it *presupposes* that willingness and is built on the ability to achieve it. Reform is a superstructure that requires an infrastructure not only conducive to change but also functional. Most people are trapped--some are even fossilized--in old ways of thinking and going about their work. Introducing a new game with new rules--forcing people to play competitively without due preparation--can lead to social and economic chaos, which Poland's weakened economy can ill afford. To consider reform or reformulation of the relationships among economic agents, we need to take into consideration what was inherited from the past. To build for the future, it is imperative to acknowledge what is presently lacking. Only when corrective measures are appropriately and timely implemented can a structure for the future be built.   To render the Polish economic reform effective and meaningful, there has to be active participation by all potentially productive economic agents. The government has a positive role to play: that of macroeconomic-coordination, of national budgeting, of providing and nurturing a stabilizing environment, and of service to the people. The government cannot *make* an economy develop; development has to be the aggregate of constructive activities by the people. Therefore, the primary role of government is to provide framework that encourages individuals to actively participate in the process.

The function of government is to enact laws, particularly economic laws that protect and promote the interests of those who engage in constructive economic activities. Poland sorely needs economic laws that will foster the emergence of a leading class of entrepreneurs, who will in turn oil the machinery of economic growth. These entrepreneurs can come in varied hues and from diverse social and economic strata. The laws to encourage them need to offer rewards in tangible, measurable terms to those who efficiently mobilize and organize productive resources, who innovate and adapt, who take risks, and who in essence serve the needs of consumers and society. Conversely, there should also be laws to specify penalties, or the absence of rewards, meted out to those who are able but not willing to contribute to economic transformation, or to those who act contrary to the interests of society and the economy. Such laws--or rules of the game--need to be thoroughly promulgated so that everyone is well acquainted with the system. Insofar as such laws are reasonable, equitable, clear, and beneficial to participants, constructive entrepreneurship can germinate and yield fruit.

Policymakers also need to recognize that institutional changes are imperative to salvage the ravaged economy. Such institutional changes include property ownership, profit motive, a pricing system based on market mechanisms, a positive work attitude, consumerism, and competitiveness. The spirit of venturesomeness, entrepreneurship, acquisitiveness, and innovation; the values of pride, self-respect, and individuality; and material progress and economic freedom are key ingredients in the reform program. These ingredients do not materialize out of thin air or automatically follow from reform measures. Changing the institutional ways of doing things takes time and the results of these changes also take time. Reform measures aimed at establishing new institutional values and practices need to be supplemented with aids and inducements. But given the unique strength of the Polish economy inherited from the centralized system, surgical procedures over time would be less traumatic and more beneficial.

CAVEATS FOR REFORM

Proven economic policies effective in the market system can be beneficial to Poland if the less quantifiable yet vital institutions remain in sufficient numbers and strength. Such less prominent institutions often are, but should not be, taken for granted in attempts to transform an economy. What works effectively for an economy in an advanced stage of development may not work effectively in one less developed. Consequently, decision makers must determine which institutions need first to be either modified, strengthened, removed, or initiated. Only when these rough spots are smoothed over can reform measures be introduced and meaningfully implemented. A number of caveats, therefore, are in order.

First, given the proven failure of the centralized system, the temptation is to dismantle all existing mechanisms of the system and discontinue all past practices. Yielding to such temptation is to court chaos. National energy would then need to be directed toward coping with one crisis after another, with little ability to work toward perceived objectives, or to achieve a systematic and orderly transformation.

Second, given Poland's disproportionately heavy investment in nonconsumer goods industries, the temptation is to apply the brakes and shift into reverse. For instance, threatening to shut down shipyards and coal mines because they have been inefficient or not cost-effective can cause uncertainty far beyond the confines of those shipyards and coal mines. This is not to suggest that inefficiency should be perpetuated, or that state resources should continue to be channeled into such enterprises indefinitely; rather, consideration needs to be given to the degree and cause of inefficiency, the magnitude of the state subsidy, and the cost and feasibility of restructuring or reorganization--compare to the alternative of instant mass unemployment. State transfer payments to displaced labor have to be made; capital equipment depreciates while it sits idle. In other words, the opportunity cost of continued operation should be compared to the short- or medium-term zero productivity of tens of thousands of otherwise productive individuals. Minimizing both economic as well as social costs should be the rule. Only when the economy is at the point of expansion, and is able to absorb surplus labor, should these inefficient state enterprises be gradually and painlessly phased out.

Third, other than the agricultural sector and a limited number of private enterprises, the Polish economy had for more than four decades been directed and managed by central authority. The fashionable line of thought is immediate decentralization of all economic activity, thus placing unqualified confidence in the market system. The decentralization process needs to be gradual, orchestrated, synchronized, and flexibly coordinated by central authority. For example, which major state enterprises need to be scaled down, which ones need to be merged to achieve economies of scale, and which ones need to be phased out are not decisions to be left to the provincial governments or to enterprise managers. Decision therein makers have no training, experience, or tradition along this line.

Fourth, essential commodities to consumers have always enjoyed state subsidies. Food, dairy products, gasoline, construction materials, public transportation, housing, and medical care are only a few of the subsidized goods and services. If price subsidies are abruptly withdrawn, purchasing power is reduced to subsistence level or lower, and extreme hardship and prolonged frustration can lead to social unrest and political instability. It is a phenomenon the young and tender democratic society of Poland can ill afford. A more rational approach to eventual elimination of state subsidies is the often-practiced multi tiered pricing system. Immediate deregulation of prices can apply to products more or less in adequate supply but with relatively weak demand. Continued price regulation can apply to essential commodities, often in shorter supply but constantly in demand. As the economy stabilizes and slowly grows, selective commodities can gradually be phased into the next price tier, with increasingly lower subsidies.

Fifth, the market system is new in Poland. It is known to have been operating in the West, but how it specifically works may still be alien to the majority of Polish people. New rules and legal institutions compatible with economic well-being, therefore, need be established, nurtured, and promulgated. The reason for appropriate legal institutions is simple. Investors, politicians, and private citizens all have the propensity to push to the limit of what is legally permissible in their endeavors. Investors wish to minimize loss and maximize profit. Politicians wish to maximize political mileage. And citizens wish to maximize utility. Profiteering, corner cutting and gaining an upper hand are characteristics of human beings, not only of a capitalistic system. But the negative results often lead to social and economic harm. Clearly, laws need be instituted and enforced with respect to property rights, contract agreements, exchange activities, advertising, product liability, patents, and market procedures, to name a few. Likewise, economic laws need be promulgated and enforced. Only then can the risk factors of new business ventures be mitigated and confidence in rational business decisions fostered.

Sixth, public servants--at least a good percentage of them--need to undertake an attitudinal change. Their function now should be to assist, to facilitate, to coordinate, to serve, and to inform--all in the spirit of national interest. But right now, they are relics from the past. Instead of being overlords, they now need to service and promote the common good. They are the catalysts that can encourage economic growth, providing information, facilitating social well-being, and ensuring economic efficiency. Only when the public's perception of officials as dedicated public servants is firmly established can their services be more meaningfully translated into constructive results.

And finally, introducing systemic transformation needs sensitivity and patience. In implementing policies conducive for economic growth, here mean not just general fiscal, monetary, investment, or trade policies. They refer also to the less tangible but more permeating values, beliefs, and practices of a social, cultural, and political milieu, wherein the productive potential of society can function unimpeded in a legal and orderly fashion. Guarantees of rights, privileges, opportunities, and remuneration are to be inculcated in the subconscious of the masses. Thus, with confidence and trust, growth ideas may be more readily translated into concrete results.

The intangible social institutions that need be introduced and strengthened by governmental policy should aim to convince all persons that the economic revolution belongs to and involves all segments of society. The people need to recognize and believe that they are active and meaningful participants in this revolutionary process. Unless and until society believes in an attainable promised land, there will be resistance to change. In attempting to transform an economic entity composed of 38 million nerve endings, caution must be exercised that social, economic, and cultural traumas are minimized. Those less adept at surviving in this new environment need to be given the time and opportunity to adjust. All potentially promising elements of Polish society economy need be given due nurturing regard.

The above is not to advocate the creation of a new welfare state. Nor is it a vote for quasi continuation of the old. Rather, given the history and cultural traits of the Polish people, it is a generalized caveat. The frustration suppressed in the past may readily be transferred to the present.

THE BEGINNING OF CHANGE

Given the present situation, it is imperative to realize that the most productive segments operate in the tradition of a centralized economic system. The leading role in the near term rests on government, not on free economic agents. Laws need continuous monitoring and timely updating. With changing economic relationships, well-designed laws and institutions can assist individuals or entities in realizing their potential. In due time, entrepreneurship matures, useful capital accumulation materializes, market forces become more operational, bottlenecks diminish, linkages strengthen, investment increases, and confidence and trust in the future grow. More and more responsibility for productive coordination and economic adjustment will pass from government to economic decision makers. Development will ultimately be built on a foundation of orderly and healthy systemic transformation.

The democratically elected government in Poland has inherited a society whose population has experienced democracy for only a short period. A high percentage of the Polish people, at least subconsciously, are still looking for cues from their decision makers. The transition from having been told what to do and how to do it for nearly half a century to deciding by and for themselves cannot be automatic. Taking economic initiatives, assuming risks, venturing into unknown territories are new ideas. They do not become commonplace by government decree. The new Polish leader must guide the economy in the correct direction while at the same time providing social, economic, and legal institutions that minimize trauma while instilling hope and confidence in the future. It is a tall order for a bankrupt economy with a new crew.

On October 6, 1989, Poland's new government announced plans for a market economy. On December 17, 1989, the prime minister introduced economic reform legislation with the immediate goal of curbing inflation. On December 28, 1989, the legislation was approved by the lower House; the following day, it was ratified by the Senate. On December 30, 1989, the

Parliament approved the economic reform measures. Thus, January 1, 1990, marked the beginning of the most radical economic reform effort by any of the Eastern European economies.

The central goal of the reform was to replace the planned and centralized system with a market system--almost immediately. Reliance on market forces was in vogue. Relative to December 1988, retail prices had risen by 70 percent, food prices by 75 percent, nonfood items by 60 percent, and services by 210 percent (Warsaw Voice, 1990: 2-18, 3-18). Compared to December 1988, the price of pit coal increased by 700 percent, electricity by 300 percent, gas by 250 percent, oil and road transportation rose by an average of 200 percent, telecommunication services by 100 percent, postal services by 150 percent, and fuel by between 90 to 100 percent (Warsaw Voice, 1990: 1-14). Meanwhile, wholesale food prices remained low while prices for essential inputs as well as consumer goods were permitted to rise freely. Food production fell by 41.69 percent between January 1989 and January 1990 (Warsaw Voice, 1990: 2-18). At the same time, exports fell. Demand for farm machinery and yield-increasing inputs fell. In protest, farm producers held back food supplies.

In March 1990, a Polish Airlines ticket from Warsaw to New York cost U.S. $1,232. The same ticket, with one-year validity, cost less than $800 if bought from Pan American Airlines. A phone call from the United States to Poland cost between $0.75 and $1.50 per minute, depending on the time of day. A call from Poland to the United States cost approximately $2.50 per minute (Warsaw Voice, 1990: 3-11). Free pricing seems to have been interpreted to mean whatever price the seller fancied--not fully aware that market pricing is radically different from arbitrary price setting.

The perennial long lines for consumer goods disappeared overnight, not because supply had increased but because prices had skyrocketed. Since goods were available, provided the consumers were able and willing to pay the higher prices, the market system had eliminated shortages overnight. Throwing the centrally planned and administered system out and overnight replacing it with a market system meant that the Polish economy had no system in the concrete.

Ever since, the energy of the legislature and the administration has been focused on price stabilization, on foreign investments and joint ventures, on balancing the budget, on privatization of the 7,000 largest state enterprises, on the rescheduling and servicing the mounting foreign debt, and on politics. Little attention has been paid to whether the new policies will work and how they might work.

The democratically elected government of Poland inherited a complex of institutions that artificially supported the superstructure that was communistic centralism. The superstructure has been dismantled, but the infrastructure, to a large extent remains. Its functions in a brand-new economic system have not undergone significant change commensurate with need. To explain, the infrastructure made up of individuals; these individuals are, in turn, unique entities with beliefs, values, attitudes, and behaviors. They have new aspirations and hopes. But attaining them, in large measure, is on a totally different plane for most. They did not believe in a centralized system. Neither can they be convinced that the new market system will work. Their attitudes were passive then, and their attitudes are still passive: wait-and-see. Active responsiveness to prospective economic opportunities does not seem realizable for most individuals. Fear of losing one's job motivates an individual more than active optimism of working for a future. And the actions taken, either by an individual or an economic entity, often are tainted with uncertainty and apprehension. Now the decision-making process has been made more complex by introduction of more unknown or previously uncommon variables. The structure is new. The mechanism is new. The processes are new or unfamiliar. In brief, the people are not prepared. At the same time, new legislative proposals are being introduced, discussed, modified and passed. And new administrative policies and political compromises are being made. All have been on the macroeconomic level. The small producer, investor, consumer, or supplier on the micro level, on the average, does not know how to promptly and correctly respond to this rapidly changing milieu.

To make the market system in Poland work, as anywhere else, the macro policy needs to be validated and supported by responsive micro economic units. To date, productive forces have not been responsive to economic liberalization, largely because they are not able to respond. The infrastructure conducive to a freer economic system is absent. Effective incentives are not present. Inertia and the lack of knowledge and experience in market competitiveness work in conjunction to the detriment of macro policies.

The question is how to begin building the institutions to support a market system. How does Poland rise from ruin and begin building a new economic design? Poland has the semblance of a market system but lacks the institutions to render it a market economy. The following chapters present the new economic policies pertaining to macro variables. Analysis and evaluation of the same provide a fairly clear map of where the new Polish economic order is headed. Recommendations and their respective rationale are presented thereafter.

NOTE

1. Scholars were not clear as to when or what the first stage of economic reform was. The 1987 action probably refers to Jaruzelski's second attempt at reform.

6

FISCAL AND MONETARY POLICIES

The main objective of current economic reform in Poland is to replace the centralized planned economy with a free-market one, for economic efficiency and for economic development. The Central Planning Commission was eliminated, replaced by the Central Planning Office. The function of the latter is planning only--the days of centralized distribution, purchasing, and management are over. Investment, production, distribution and consumption are the exclusive domain of market mechanisms. But past fiscal irresponsibility has left the new democratic administration with budget deficit of nearly U.S. $4 billion, incurred during the first six months of 1989. In addition, there is a U.S. $42 billion foreign debt, also bequeathed to the new government by the past Communist administration.

When the current reforms were instituted, the structure of the economy was inflexible. Inflationary recession was on its way. The economy was in a deep crisis. There was the need for an immediate moratorium on debt obligations. Creditors, however, demanded that negotiations for debt rescheduling be preceded by reform proposals, approved by the International Monetary Fund (IMF) and the World Bank. No reform specifics had been suggested or demanded by the creditors, however. The choices left to the Mazowiecki administration, therefore, were to propose an orderly and systematic transformation, with desired results to materialize in a more distant future, or to introduce radical reform measures. The proposals of deputy prime minister Leszek Balcerowicz prevailed: shock therapy, with the blessing of the Council of Ministers, the IMF, and the World Bank. The "therapy" was administered with little waste of time, to the shock of Polish producers and consumers alike.

FISCAL POLICY

Owing to the anticipated acceleration of inflation, an extremely tight fiscal policy was introduced by late 1989 and held sway throughout 1990. The brakes were applied to the growing budget deficit for the remainder of fiscal year 1989, and a balanced budget was to be achieved for fiscal year 1990. While the budgetary law for 1990 was still being drafted, the Mazowiecki government quickly applied a two-proned approach of expenditure reduction and revenue enhancement. Aggregate demand was to be reduced. Food prices were to be liberated--subsidies on food items were drastically reduced and government expenditures for food subsidies were quickly slashed. Prices of other commodities were also permitted to seek their respective natural level in the marketplace (Goscinski interview, 1990). To further alleviate government's subsidy burden, prices of public transportation, industrial hard coal, electricity, and communications, among others, were permitted to begin their upward climb. By the beginning of 1990, government subsidies to suppliers of these goods and services were reduced by nearly 80 percent (Bossak, 1990: 60). Subsidies for meats, dairy products, bread, and other agricultural products were completely eliminated by the end of 1989 and the beginning of 1990. The plan was to remove all government subsidies, including subsidies for energy and housing, by the end of fiscal year 1990.

On another front, in order to reverse the trend of excessive investment in heavy industry and to reduce expenditures, government investments in state-owned enterprises declined. It was hoped that the market pricing mechanism would then replace the former role of government, to more efficiently allocate investment and production resources. The role of government in economic activity could thus be quickly reduced to macroeconomic planning and coordination.

Other than subsidy removal and cuts in investments, the Mazowiecki administration moved to lower defense expenditures by retiring or laying off nonessential public servants in the censorship office and the internal security bureau. Reduced government spending necessarily led to decreased aggregate demand, not only in the public sector but also in that segment of the economy which depended on government purchases and employment. As had been planned, the gross national product took a nosedive.

In the private sector, hyperinflation combined with extremely tight wages, and low income led to a significant decrease in consumption. The state enterprises, confronted with loss of subsidies and reduced aggregate demand, were forced to adjust their budget outlays. Investment declined. Plant closings, plus forced reduction in work hours owing to sluggish demand, combined to induce a recessionary trend. Thus, the planned reduction in government spending produced its desired effects. The budget deficit as a percentage point of expenditure for the first six months of 1989 was 44.7.

For the second six months, the deficit was a modest 6.3 percent (World Economy Research, 1990: 30). As of August 1990, there was a balanced budget for the first time in decades. In fact, even though transfer payments had increased and the revenue base had narrowed owing to plant closings, there was a temporary but modest budget surplus by March 1990. A balanced budget continues to be a major fiscal-policy objective.

On the revenue side, taxes on corporate income were increased, export tax exemption privileges were revoked, and tax relief for failing state enterprises was reduced. Eventual abolishment of remaining subsidies and reliefs is being drafted into new tax laws. Measures were also taken to eliminate the loopholes in tax collection procedures. In the new tax law for 1991, a personal income tax was introduced. For 1989, revenue increased from 4,588 billion zlotys for the first six months to 15,057 billion zlotys for the second half of the year (World Economy Research, 1990: 30).

Increased government revenue meant decreased purchasing power for the private sector. Since government spending was at the same time being tightly controlled, aggregate demand decreased. With it, the monthly rate of inflation tumbled from August 1989's 39.5 percent to December's 17.7 percent. Inflation rebounded to 78.6 percent in January 1990, however, owing to planned deregulation of prices for most goods and services. Inflation quickly stabilized again by March 1990, with a rate of a mere 4.7 percent. Nevertheless, the problem of inflation in Poland is not over. Inelastic supply and investment retrenchment will not permit prices to move downward for some time to come. But a tight fiscal policy, in conjunction with an equally tight income policy, should be able to keep hyperinflation at a safe distance.

Although there were no personal income taxes in 1990, the prohibitive tax on wage increases beyond a permissible level was in effect a personal income tax (Jozefiak interview, 1990). Since, owing to hyperinflation, real income had been eroded by 40 percent in less than a year, the government's threat of high taxes on wage increases beyond a sanctioned level was aimed at consumers who were already poor. Their marginal propensity to save being low and to consume being high, the measure effectively reduced aggregate demand and therefore relieved inflationary pressure.

On the other hand, the increase in corporate income tax effectively reduced the investment ability of enterprises. And the decrease in demand helped to contain the rise in inflation. However, the investment retrenchment was not as damaging as it might appear, owing to excessive investments by state enterprises during the Communist administrations. The demand condition, for now, does not warrant increases in aggregate investments. The increased corporate income tax, therefore, has forced a leaner enterprise-investment schedule. Investments now must be efficient and reasonable--while more taxes go into the state treasury, wasteful investment is reduced. On yet another front, elimination of export tax exemptions helped enhance the state's coffers but it put a damper on investments in export activities.

As for drastically and suddenly reduced government spending, there have been merits and demerits. Three perspectives are readily discernable. First, the reduction in internal security forces, the phasing out of the censorship bureau, and the cuts in defense spending are positive. The former two are socially counterproductive to begin with, and the latter is neutral in the sense that, whether a threat should come from the East or from the West, even drastically increased defense spending would do little good. With the vastly improved East-West relations, expenditures on military hardware are being trimmed. With regard to reduced subsidies to enterprises and consumers, it is a judgment call. Distinctions should be made among enterprises in industries where subsidies are being reduced by how much and how soon. Admittedly, the administrative cost of differentiating among enterprises within a given industry could be high, and objectivity might not always prevail. Yet at least in theory, some selective differentiation should be applied. First, there are state enterprises that should not have been established to begin with, yet financially they have been a burden. A number of enterprises in heavy industries have served no economic purpose, and their absence would not have much negative impact on the Polish economy. The simultaneous withdrawal of state subsidies and the increase in corporate income taxes therefore can hasten their natural demise. Jobs are indeed lost, and suffering of the unemployed is a social as well as economic factor to be reckoned with. Unemployment is a high price to pay for the mistakes of former administrations. Nevertheless, the price needs to be paid--and the cost borne by society as a whole. Appropriate social and economic programs should be readied to cushion the loss.

Second, there are enterprises that have been inefficient but that do serve economic and social purposes. A sudden subsidy reduction or elimination, as has been implemented, might be inappropriate. Subsidies should be reduced in accordance with a predetermined schedule, so internal adjustments could then be made by the affected enterprises. The enterprises would be forced to be less wasteful, leaner, more efficient, and more market oriented. The disguised unemployed could be laid off, but at least plant closings need not be widespread. The government would then have the lead time to organize job-training programs to absorb the displaced labor.

Economic efficiency and price stability are indeed two of the major objectives for economic development, but so are full employment and economic stability. It would be incorrect for decision makers in Poland to assume that an unemployment rate of 6 percent or more is acceptable and manageable, as in the West. In highly developed economies, there are support systems for the unemployed. In Poland, there are practically none. Also, capitalist acumen takes time to develop and mature. If the vise of fiscal authority is tightened in measured dosages, enterprises faced with financial hardship, and workers with possible unemployment, can have time to restructure and retrain. As it is, however, those salvageable enterprises that have since gone under, and those potentially productive workers who have since been laid off, have become more of a burden on society than a savings.

The last perspective on reductions on government expenditures concerns socialized firms that have consistently been efficient. Speedier subsidy reduction or elimination is economically justifiable and desirable. However, both reductions in subsidies and increases in corporate income tax also represent higher costs of production. Two scenarios may result. First, if products from these firms find their market mostly on the domestic scene, then domestic prices will increase--it represents a decrease in consumer surplus. But the justifiable price increase resulting from an increased cost of production is less offensive than a price increase because of speculative activities. The second scenario occurs if an enterprise's product is destined for foreign markets. A subsidy reduction and income tax increase will lead to a higher-priced product abroad. The commodity becomes less competitive on the international market, and lower sales means reduced foreign earnings. In light of the need for a growing trade surplus, reduced government expenditures via subsidy reductions or higher export taxes may not be productive in the longer run. It is worthwhile to recall how some of the developed economies, by design, have resorted to tax and spending policies to starve industries serving the domestic market while feeding the export sector. Blanket policy is effective, but it is also blunt. A policy framework with fine tuning and differentiation is more difficult to design and administer, yet more sound and rewarding in the long run. Long-term market positioning should not be sacrificed for short-term objectives of balancing the budget to a tee.

Withdrawing subsidies from state enterprises affects the survival or competitiveness of those enterprises directly, and the market supply of goods and services indirectly. Withdrawing subsidies from consumers via the elimination of subsidies to key industries negatively impacts the consumer's real income--instantly. Products such as engineering equipment, industrial chemicals, or steel are not in the consumer's market basket, but price increases in such goods affect consumers indirectly. The elasticity of demand for such products tends to be significant. However, goods and services such as food items, medical care, electricity and natural gas, housing, rentals, and public transportation are chief consumer expenditures. The fact that people could survive on low income before was due to subsidies for suppliers of these goods and services. Real income in terms of goods and services consumed was measurably higher than nominal wages received. In its effort to balance the budget and curtail inflation, the new policy of practically freezing wages while removing subsidies for basic essentials has left the average consumer in a bind. The consumer is poorer now as a result of higher prices and meager wage increases. The hardship is severe; the noose was tightened.

The government's so-called stabilization policy, or shock therapy, caused widespread destabilization. It was successful in combating inflation, but it failed in its ultimate objective of economic reform. The same results could have been realized gradually, with the negative impact distributed over an extended period of time. The reform package received the approval of the IMF and the World Bank, but even experts abroad deemed it too drastic and too ambitious. So far we have dealt with how the budget deficit could otherwise be reduced if an austere fiscal policy had not been implemented. Herewith, a few suggestions.

Attempting to achieve a balanced budget right after taking over the helm was unrealistic. Experts from the IMF and the World Bank would or should have so realized. The letter of intent demanded by Poland's foreign creditors would have been satisfactory, or at least acceptable, to members of the London and Paris clubs if the reform schedule was to be rational, orderly, and promising. The letter of intent approved by the IMF and the World Bank tried to give greater assurance to foreign creditors that the debt equity was worth more than feared, but the consequent social and economic cost to Poland has been too steep. Besides, the end result may fall measurably short of expectations. If the reform program had been carefully and logically crafted for the creditors to see, foreign creditors as well as the IMF and the World Bank would have acceded to the proposal. In other words, so long as the direction of reform was correct and the pace reasonable, belt-tightening measures could have been taken in stages. Once the foreign creditors had been given assurance, focus could then be turned to determining a suitably tight fiscal policy for eventual balance of the budget.

On the side of revenue-enhancing measures, improved tax collection procedures--as were in place--already had led to increased revenues. An increase from the first six months' 4.588 billion zlotys in 1989 to the second half-year's 15.057 billion zlotys is ample proof. In addition, other approaches to revenue enhancement have not been implemented, although some are being contemplated. Others not yet under discussion by policymakers have merit and may be worth considering.

For example, a second approach to raising revenue is to issue long- or medium- term government securities or bonds. To alleviate any fear of erosion of value owing to mild inflation, the earnings from such government-issued notes could be made adjustable, so that at maturity they are in real terms at a predetermined rate. If the rate offered is attractive, it effectively soaks up excess money to dampen inflation. Also, since equity held by consumers represents deferred consumption, a feeling of security and wealth can replace that of loss as a result of hyperinflation and increased taxes. On the part of the government, internal borrowing can be judiciously allocated to finance the deficit. Understood herein is that public borrowing will decrease over time as subsidies are gradually withdrawn.

Another way to assure savers that the real value of their principal and the associated earnings of government securities will be maintained is to peg the purchase value at a given major foreign currency. Since internal convertibility of the zloty was one of the main features of the stabilization package, it would be easy to convert zlotys back and forth against this particular foreign currency for purchase and redemption. Institutional investors and private savers who have been hoarding hard currency would then find it attractive to make their idle resources productive.

A third form of raising revenue is through sales taxes on finished products. The turnover tax has already been raised from 15 to 20 percent, therefore a sales tax could be low. Whereas income taxes, whether corporate or personal, make the taxed party feel poorer, a sales tax is levied only on consumers who choose to make the purchase. The sales tax is translated into a higher price, yet psychologically it is a matter of free choice.

A fourth approach to raising revenue is a gradual rise in rates for public utilities. This is different from subsidy withdrawal, in that it can painlessly lead to decreased consumption. It also means less energy needs be produced. Therefore, when subsidies are gradually withdrawn, it is less painful to producers, since fewer financial resources are required to meet the reduced level of need. This chain reaction could lead backwards to other industries such as coal and natural gas, whose needs for subsidies could likewise be proportionately reduced in the process. This not only represents a savings to the state treasury but also is a measure of resource conservation.

A fifth avenue to raising revenue is the sale of government properties. Housing units that are government owned can be sold to current tenants. To the buyers, this is ownership of real estate, not common in Poland as of yet. To the government, this is revenue as well as genuine privatization of assets most tangible to consumers. Land owned by the government can be sold for housing developments or new business premises. And with an orderly transfer of real estate from the public to the private sector, there is also a transfer of purchasing power from private to public. Over time, not only will government revenues increase, thereby reducing public debt, but aggregate demand will correspondingly alleviate inflation.

The other side of deficit reduction is reduced government spending. Reductions could be planned, programmed, and gradually implemented, but in order to maintain social and economic stability, Poland's initial ability to reduce government spending is limited. Nevertheless, some cuts could be made. First, unlike other entities in the 1990 budget law, the Defense Ministry has practically no income. On the expenditure side, the amount allotted is still approximately U.S. $1.18 billion. In contrast, the subsidy for 1990 to dairy farmers, who have been subjected to extreme hardship owing to manifold price increases in feed and associated inputs, is a meager U.S. $73,700. Although the U.S. $1.18 billion is modest relative to the defense expenditures of the West, it is one branch of government where spending can be trimmed for significant savings. The need for a strong defense no longer exists.

Second, there can be gradual reduction in subsidies to housing units. If combined with privatization of rental housing properties, expenditures for housing subsidies will decrease over time. Rent increases need to be announced in advance, lest consumers be caught unaware and refuse to pay, as happened in Hungary. At the same time, sales of rental units to current occupants can be initiated so that mortgage payments are within reach of buyers, yet measurably higher than the current monthly rent. As soon as the title is signed over, the owner's housing subsidy ceases. Government savings could be significant, while the monthly mortgage payments represent steady income.

Third, state control over some educational and health care systems can be privatized over time, reducing the need of government spending in these two extensively subsidized service networks. The budget for the Ministry of Education in 1990 was 3.882 trillion zlotys, or approximately U.S. $487 million. And the 1990 budget for the Ministry of Health and Social Welfare was 7.612 trillion zlotys, or U.S. $800 million.[1] Given the Polish population of nearly 38 million in 1989, per capita expenditures for education, health, and welfare are nothing when compared to the West. Yet the projected incomes to the two respective ministries for 1990 was only 519.8 and 123.06 million zlotys, respectively, or U.S. $54,000 and U.S. $13,000. The extent of subsidies is obvious. Public education and health care are indispensable. But that does not mean that all institutions need to be publicly owned and operated. A portion can be privatized to suit consumer needs, and a portion of the subsidies therefore reduced.

Fourth, gradual withdrawal of state subsidies to enterprises can result in reduced government spending. The subsidy reduction in a *graduated* manner represents a smaller savings to the state budget than if subsidies were withdrawn altogether, however it is a reduction nonetheless. For the reasons given earlier, a sudden and nearly total subsidy withdrawal leads to mass unemployment and social unrest. But planned subsidy withdrawal schedule-- for carefully selected industries--means smaller reductions in government spending but correspondingly less social cost. It also means slower growth in unemployment and less in welfare payments.

In summary, the 1990 fiscal policy was too tight for comfort. A decently paced progression toward marketization should and would have been acceptable to the IMF and the World Bank. And a reasonably acceptable budget deficit would have sufficed to allay the fears of foreign creditors. The harsh measures taken resulted in excessive suffering of the masses and could have been mitigated. Certain taxes could have been selectively raised without tearing the fabric of social and economic stability. And some subsidies could have been gradually withdrawn according to a well-publicized schedule. Public borrowing with government guarantees and an attractive rate of return would have cushioned the deficit in a constructive manner. Economic restructuring would then have been more stable and surer.

EVOLVING FINANCIAL INSTITUTIONS

Similar to other CMEA nations, Poland had no financial institutions other than the state-owned banks or indirectly owned cooperative banks.[2] There were no money or capital markets, since they represented the vilest manifestation of capitalist greed. Banks were at the service of the state, and money played a passive role in the planned Polish economy. As a result, the banking system in Poland is a problem for the new administration: the bank cannot as yet adequately cope with its new functions. Banking reform was intended as early as 1982, with demonopolizing the National Bank of Poland (NBP) as the objective, but no action was taken until the new banking law of January 31, 1989. The banking network now consists of fifteen state-owned banks, thirty-five commercial banks, and an assortment of cooperative banks. The majority of the commercial banks are owned by private shareholders (Baka interview, 1990).

The National Bank of Poland (NBP), as in market economies, is the bank of banks. It functions as a central bank like that of the Federal Reserve Bank in the United States. It is the sole issuer of bank notes, and it participates in the formulation of monetary and credit policies, supervises the operation and practices of member banks, determines the rate and level of foreign exchange, maintains foreign reserves, sets the reserves for member banks--currently at 15 percent of holdings--represents the government in its dealings with foreign financial institutions, adjusts the discount rate and finance, issues treasury bills and government bonds, and promotes the circulations of money through the new two-tier banking system (Baka interview, 1990). In accordance with the new banking law, the National Bank of Poland is an entity independent of government control. Unlike the past, when the deficit was financed by printing more money, the new law explicitly forbids this. In case of need, a government budget deficit can be financed only through transactions of regional, commercial, or foreign banks.

The commercial banks in Poland today function as do their counterparts in the West. They accept deposits, extend credit, settle accounts, issue bank guarantees, and deal in bonds. They are under the supervision of the NBP and must abide by the new banking law code. To compete with each other, commercial banks must attract customers by way of quality banking service and competitive interest rates. Given their legal status, they are free to engage in all lawful economic activities, including the issuance of equity shares and financial transactions with foreign legal entities.

Among the commercial banks are nine regional banks and several special-purpose banks. The special-purpose banks include, among others, the Food Economy Bank, Export Development Bank, and the State Credit Bank. The Food Economy Bank, for instance, was created as a joint stock cooperative bank with its origin in 1,600 rural cooperative banks. Unlike before, none of these commercial and cooperative banks is directly dependent on or dictated by the NBP. If the market exists for them to enter the housing or construction industry, they are free to engage in business therein. They are also free to engage in activities deemed most beneficial to them and to their stockholders.

Enterprises, whether state-owned or private, are also free to choose whichever bank they wish to patronize. Interbank competition has become the norm. The new government intends to privatize more of the presently state-controlled or state-owned banks to inject even greater competitiveness into the system. The expectation is that more special-purpose banks will materialize as needs arise.

The existing state-owned banks also witness continuous structural changes. Professor Wladyslaw Baka, president of the National Bank of Poland, met with the presidents of twenty groups of Western banks in July 1990, inviting them to participate in the transformation of state bank ownership. Depending on the success of economic reform, foreign capital is expected to join Poland's domestic financial resources to privatize the current state-owned banks. Eight foreign banks--Deutsche Bank AG, Dresdner Bank AG, Mitteleuropeische Handelsbank AG, all from the Federal Republic of Germany; Centro Internationale Handelsbank of Vienna; the French Societe Generale; Banca Commerciale Italiana; Banque Nationale de Paris; and the Private Banken of Copenhagen--have already established offices in Warsaw (Stupnicki, 1990: 80). To date, these foreign banks have not rendered banking services--they are probably waiting for concrete signs of successful economic reform. The hope is that foreign banks will assume a more active role in Poland's financial activities. If this happens soon, then they will indeed be extending a helping hand in restructuring the Polish banking industry.

The demonopolization of the banking system should promote competitive forces in the market system, measure the real flow of the economy with realistic financial flow, stimulate private enterprises in investment ventures, and make the financial system an effective instrument for implementation of monetary policy. Banking reform has accomplished much in a relatively short period of time but it is still constrained by infrastructural deficiencies. For example, there is an acute shortage of trained bank personnel. To remedy the situation, preparation is underway to establish an international school of banking in Poland (Pacuski interview, 1990). Foreign capital, professors, and technology will be involved in this effort, and among the participants will be the French and U.S. governments.

There is also no modern telecommunication systems or wire transmission equipment (Obloj interview, 1990). To improve on this front, the president of the National Bank of Poland has signed an agreement with the Minister of Telecommunication to install a separate and modern teletransmission system on both regional and international levels. There are also no financial institutions such as mutual funds, pension funds, insurance companies, commodity exchanges, mortgage banks, or savings and loans institutions to make the banking system more effective in oiling the mechanism of a monetized free economy.

To move the economic transformation forward in Poland, a well- developed financial system--with new financial instruments, new markets, and special-function institutions--must exist to coordinate the real and the financial aspects of economic activity. Within five years, banking services in Poland are likely to be vastly improved--the process has just begun (Baka, 1990). The future success of Poland's economic reform will depend heavily on a successful transformation of the banking system and the development of associated financial institutions. In a very real sense, the transformed banking system is the hub on which the spokes of other economic reforms must be centered.

MONETARY POLICY

In a developed market economy, provided the control mechanisms are in place and the money and capital markets are developed, monetary policy can be a potent tool for regulating the money supply. Since money accompanies and directs the real flow of goods and services, an appropriate monetary policy often leads to predicted and desired objectives. In the present Polish economy, money and capital markets are not yet operational. The National Bank of Poland has indeed been demonopolized, but the number of member banks is small. Foreign banks have established offices, but they have not provided services yet. The National Bank of Poland does establish discount rates and determine reserve requirements, but the extent of its influence over the money supply ceases there--member banks are now independent and exercise their discretion and formulate their own banking policies. Other than the reserve requirement and setting discount rates, the only effective monetary control mechanism at the disposal of the NBP is leadership in setting interest rates and credit policy.

In tandem with a tight fiscal policy, the government introduced a tight monetary policy designed to reduce the money supply. The rationale for this tight monetary policy is obvious from Poland's recent inflationary trends. For example, the January 1989 inflation rate was 11 percent. February of the same year had an inflation rate of 7.9 percent. March brought 8.1, and April, 9.8. Thereafter, May, June, and July had rates of 7.2, 6.1, and 9.5 percent, respectively. By August, a hyperinflationary rate of 39.5 percent was quickly followed by another 34.4 percent in September, 54.8 in October, 22.4 in November, and 17.7 in December. With more extensive price deregulation beginning January 1, 1990, the inflation rate for January soared to 78.6 percent. Relative to April 1989, the rate of inflation by April 1990 was 1,302.7 percent (Ministry of Finance, 1990: 2).

The inflation had been present prior to August 1989, but it was tolerable because there was partial wage indexing along the way. A major cause of inflation then was the budget deficit, and the deficit was financed by borrowing from the National Bank of Poland--money was printed faster than the rate of real growth. After August 1990, the hyperinflation was caused almost exclusively by the liberalization of prices. Food prices were the first permitted to rise, then nearly all remaining goods and services were permitted to seek their natural level in the marketplace. It was the pull of demand and the push of cost--demand pulled because supplies were inadequate while the money supply was loose, and cost pushed because the lid on production costs had been lifted. The only exception was wages. Market forces were permitted to determine prices for products as well as other factors of production, but wages were controlled to curb inflation. This inconsistency in policy resulted in extensive hardship for consumers.

The hardships unleashed on Polish society could have been mitigated if price deregulation, as discussed earlier, was gradual. Hyperinflation after August 1989 was avoidable, but price deregulation could have begun with fewer essential consumer goods and services. It could have been implemented in a graduated fashion to provide producers with time to respond. Given time, entrepreneurship and management skills could have been developed to match the dynamism of economic restructuring.

Inflation could also have been milder if price deregulation was accomplished industry-by-industry, or even by one essential commodity after another. Appropriate fiscal and credit policies could have been applied to industries that were most essential to consumer well-being and that produced goods in short supply. When supplies become more elastic over time, graduated price increases could then be permitted. If a policy schedule had been well articulated beforehand, enterprises would have been better prepared to face market forces, while consumer well-being would have been safeguarded. But shock therapy was administered and rampant inflation ensued. A tight monetary policy had to be applied to stop the inflationary spiral.

Table 6.1 presents more recent data on money supply. Because of inflation in the first half of 1989, consumers chose to keep their savings liquid. The second half of 1989 was plagued by hyperinflation, and the supply of nominal money soared. July 1989's 19,307.3 billion zlotys grew by nearly 283 percent to December's 73,881.4 billion. In terms of the real money supply, a generally

Table 6.1

Monthly Total Money Supply, January 1989-April 1990 (in billions of zlotys)

	Nominal		Real	
	1989	1990	1989	1990
January	12086.2	98041.4	10888.5	7422.22
February	12900.2	103756	10768.1	6339.2
March	13799.9	112879	10664.5	6587.0
April	16195.8		11397.5	
May	17853.4		11722.5	
June	18679.1		11558.8	
July	19307.3		10901.9	
August	22680.6		9182.4	
September	29922.4		9023.6	
October	36662.2		7143.8	
November	50491.1		8037.4	
December	73881.4		9989.4	

Source: Ministry of Finance, 1990: 13-14.

declining trend could be observed from July 1989 through April 1990, partly because of reduced purchasing power and partly because of the NBP's decision to raise the nominal interest rates in order to attract deposits. The most significant decline in the real money supply occurred between December 1989 and January 1990, however. Anticipating another wave of hyperinflation owing to the announced liberalization of nearly all prices by January 1, 1990, people found that their real purchasing power fell further. Table 6.2 presents the monthly interest rate for time deposits. The top of the table shows exorbitantly high nominal rates, but even with a 36 percent monthly interest rate in January for a twelve-month savings account, the real rate was a -23.9 percent. January 1990 was typical; with the month's 78.6 percent inflation rate, savers did gain from bank deposits in that they lost less. Panic buying was the norm. In order to reduce the velocity of money the NBP began synchronizing interest rates with inflation rates. The objective was a positive real interest rate. By February, the objective was in sight but depositors' loss in real value was still substantial. By March 1990, the real rate of interest was positive for the first time in months. Nevertheless, the process of achieving a positive real interest rate was not complete. The rate of inflation still fluctuated from month to month, and was not in line with official projections. To the consumer, given the NBP's effort to offer positive real interest, savings deposited in the bank meant a narrow escape from uncertainty and continuing inflation. The number of time deposits increased, reducing cash flow as well as demand for consumer goods. In that sense, the tight monetary policy worked.

Table 6.2
Monthly Rate of Interest for Savings Accounts (in percents), January-April, 1990

	3-month	6-month	12-month	24-month	36-month
NOMINAL					
January	10.0	17.0	36.0	37.0	38.0
February	10.0	13.0	20.0	20.5	21.0
March	5.0	6.5	10.0	10.2	10.5
April	4.0	5.0	8.0	8.3	8.5
REAL					
January	-38.4	-34.5	-33.9	-23.3	-22.7
February	-11.2	-8.8	-3.1	-2.7	-2.3
March	0.3	1.7	5.1	5.3	5.5
April	-3.8	-2.9	-0.0	0.1	0.4

Source: Ministry of Finance, 1990: 8.

For those who received credit from the bank, the monthly adjustable rate of interest was also applied, meaning smaller gains for borrowers. Without the adjustable rate, inflation would have reduced the value of the principal as well as the worth of fixed interest as they became due. Borrowers protested, but to no avail. As a result of the positive and real interest being charged, demand for credit decreased, and the aggregate demand for money was reduced. A tight monetary policy again made its contribution to curbing inflation.

The increase in deposits and the decline in credit also helped stabilize the real rate of interest in time. With positive real interest, a penalty was also effectively imposed on those who withheld goods in anticipation of higher prices. Unwarranted inventory got released into the market as a result; supplies increased and prices became more stabilized. Debtors realized that it would be less expensive to pay off a loan early than to hoard cash, and a further decline in household and enterprise liquidity followed. The excess money supply was soaked up by this credit policy, without help from a capital market awaiting development. Thus, advocates of economic reform have been basking in the success of systemic transformation: the dreaded hyperinflation has been reduced and the process of economic restructuring appears to be moving along on its envisioned path.

Hyperinflationary pressure indeed has been eased. But free-market pricing has been force-fed into an economy where the market does not have the mechanisms essential to function. Raising corporate income taxes, eliminating export tax privileges, partly *indexing* wage increases, suddenly withdrawing state subsidies, and bankrupting nonviable enterprises are all contrived reform measures that attempt to force, more than induce, market responses to desired objectives. Major state enterprises have not become more efficient. Commodity supplies have not improved. Meanwhile, a feeling of instability and uncertainly continues to confront enterprises and consumers alike. Extensive unemployment and impoverishment have befallen many. A small number, on the other hand, have made it through the turmoil and gotten richer while the majority are made poorer. The question is not whether the market system will eventually function properly or not. Neither is the question when it will be on track. The question is, at whose expense and at what cost?

POLICY EVALUATION

The monetary policy employed to stabilize the economy has been effective. The adjustable rate of interest was to the benefit of depositors, and the policy was justifiable with respect to borrowers, too. No injustice or injury was inflicted on society. It had a stabilizing effect on the real value of money, while soaking up the excess cash to reduce inflation.

The success of the monetary policy in Poland, where money and capital markets are still in their infancy, had to depend heavily on the cooperation of member banks. Since the rate set by the NBP had been in line with the demand and supply of money, there was no reason for member banks to deviate. But it should be remembered that the money supply had been reduced to the desired level, not so much because of reserve requirements or discount rate but because of the relatively low level of savings and savers' desire to minimize their money's loss in value. Depositing the money in a bank has been the answer.

Reserve requirements and discount rate cannot be effective tools at the present stage of financial development. There are still too few commercial banks and other financial institutions, and they are too small. The largest bank besides NBP is the Bank Handlowy of Warsaw. Its year-end balance sheet in 1989 was 259 billion zlotys, or U.S. $27.1 million. The next largest bank is the Polska Kasa Opieki SA, also located in Warsaw. Its year-end balance sheet for 1989 was a meager 29,754 billion zlotys, or U.S. $3.1 million. The seventh-ranked bank is the Bydgoski Bank Komunalny SA in Bydgoszcz. Its balance sheet showed a mere U.S. $2.2 million by December 31, 1989 (Stupnicki, 1990: 80). In addition, of the thirty-five commercial banks that obtained permits to provide banking services, only nineteen were in operation by the end of 1989. Therefore, given the fact that commercial banks are few in number and relatively small in size, NBP's raising or lowering the discount rate or changing the reserve requirement would have not been an effective measure to reduce or increase the money supply.

The major reason for successful reduction of the money supply in mid-1990 was because the adjustable interest rate was pegged on the real and positive side. Consumers with savings made the deposits as a hedge against further inflation while earning some interest in the real term. Unless the number and size of commercial banks grows as the economy grows, the central bank cannot be as effective.

The monetary policy has been effective primarily because of the credit policy. But in its effort to reduce the money supply and aggregate demand, the government had no discretionary policy in favor of crucial sectors in the economy. For instance, in order to let market forces allocate the supply of money, the preferential status of the export sector and energy industry, among others, was abolished--they were to compete for credit at the uniform commercial rate. This gives the impression of there being competition in a free-market system, however the present economy of Poland is unique in so many ways. What works well in a developed economy cannot and should not summarily be copied by Poland. In the case of the export sector, the government's ability to service the mounting foreign debt depends on a healthy and growing export industry. Rapid capital accumulation during the early 1970s came to a halt by the mid-1970's, and capital assets acquired then have either become obsolete, are in need of replacement, or are no longer productive. To be competitive, the export sector needs preferential access to credit at rates more competitive than market-determined ones. To phrase it more directly, the export sector needs, and should be, subsidized to a certain extent. A healthy trade surplus helps more than just the servicing of foreign debts. It stabilizes and strengthens the local currency, stimulates the domestic sector through modernized equipment and techniques, helps develop auxiliary industries, provides additional employment opportunities, and energizes the flow of capital. On the other hand, without preferential treatment these potential benefits cannot be easily realized. The long-term interest of the Polish economy is not served.

In the case of the energy industry, easy access to credit and preferential rates of interest should have been continued. It is common knowledge that Poland's energy industry is not efficient. Relative to the West, the amount of energy resource required to produce a given amount of energy is high. More coal is required to extract a given BTU-equivalent level of coal, more coal is required to generate a given level of power, and so on. The industry is in need of capitalization to increase productivity, thus reduce costs to both industrial users and consumers. With the withdrawal of state subsidies and the elimination of preferred status by the banking system, the high cost of producing energy is passed along to industrial users and consumers. As a result, the consumer well-being is decreased.

Conversely, if the energy industry had easier access to the needed credit at state-subsidized rates, then investments could be made to help conserve resources, reduce pollution levels, and lower costs to users. There should be selective credit policies designed to stimulate pivotal enterprises and industries working for the overall well-being of the economy. When such industries are healthy and have become reasonably competitive, preferential treatments can gradually be phased out.

A concluding observation regarding the fiscal and monetary policies of the new administration: There was a definite need to change the economic system. There was a definite need to introduce the market mechanism into the system for efficient resource allocation and equitable income distribution. And there was a definite need to cope with the mounting foreign debt.

But there are no shortcuts to systematic transformation. The approach to marketizing the economy should have been different. Inertia cannot be eradicated overnight. Policies should have maximized what had been inherited. Adjustment schemes and reform measures should have been gradually introduced to constructively phase out old institutions and structures. Instead, the market system was introduced overnight, without benefit of the necessary institutions and accumulated experience. Hyperinflation was the result of haste, and tight fiscal and monetary policies had to be used for damage control. Little administrative energy is left and little attention is paid to constructive reconstruction of the economy.

The tight fiscal and monetary policies demanded that management show little concern over managing supply response. The policies were effective in reducing aggregate demand and inflation, but supply inelasticities persist. To policymakers, inefficient plants should close their doors. The ranks of the unemployed should swell. Real income should be reduced to a desirable level. But the relevant questions of how productivity and production can increase, how income and purchasing power can rise, how prices can remain stable, and how consumer welfare can be restored have not been addressed. Managing demand is easy--the centralized system accomplished that for half a century. But managing supply requires more refined policies with discretionary and differentiated nuances. It requires cultivating an environment conducive to responses to market demand. It calls for incentive taxes and priority spendings, for differentiated credit policies and investment priorities. The system for a market economy cannot be summoned forth at will. It needs time to evolve, incubate and develop. Only then can the end product be healthy and permanent.

Avoidable macro dislocation and disruption have brought undue shock to an already weary and nervous population. The people of Poland deserve kinder treatment. Macroeconomic planning and policy measures should be scrutinized, using workable and constructive micro considerations. The objective of economic restructuring, of adjustment and of reform, is for the good of the people, not for the sake of a system. In that sense, the extreme hardship inflicted on the masses by tight fiscal and monetary policies is not warranted. The reason that "we do not have the time unless radical changes take place immediately" is at best an excuse.

The Polish economy will eventually reach the point where current policymakers wish it to be. And once there, the parts that make the system function will be less well developed than if the transformation were better designed and more thoughtfully executed. For now, the price for blunt policies is paid by the Polish consumer.

NOTES

1. According to the budget law for 1990, passed March 23, 1990, pages 150 and 152, respectively.

2. This section significantly reflects an interview with Professor Wladyslaw Baka, president of the National Bank of Poland, July 1990.

7

PRICING AND INCOME POLICIES

Tight fiscal and monetary policies were designed to curb and then eventually eliminate inflation, so rising unemployment was anticipated. Some administrators even advocated increased unemployment as the avenue to reform. The rationale was to force a more efficient deployment of the factors of production, especially labor. Reduced purchasing power and smaller money supply would thus help reduce aggregate demand. Hyperinflation was public enemy number one, even though it was the result of the government's own free pricing policy as a shortcut to a marketization. As a quick fix for hyperinflation, extremely tight fiscal and monetary policies were applied. And to ensure the effectiveness of the same, a tight income policy was simultaneously implemented.

On the one hand, therefore, free-market pricing was supposed to marketize the economy. On the other hand, there was also tight control over wage increases, so that all markets were free *except* wages. To curb inflation, it was deemed necessary to decrease aggregate demand. Holding down the money supply via low wages would reduce purchasing power as well as shifting the supply function outward--through lowered labor costs--to reduce prices. The faulty assumption was that aggregate supply would increase as a result. Incorrectly assuming supply responsiveness on the micro level, especially where labor was concerned, the desired outward shift in supply did not materialize. Instead, production fell by 40 percent between January and July 1990. Even with significantly reduced real wages, owing to ceilings on nominal wage increases, prices remained high.

Meanwhile, since wage rates are not permitted to reflect marginal value productivity, labor as a factor of production cannot be efficiently allocated. An essential part of marketization is therefore deliberately being omitted from consideration, all in the name of "freeing" the economy. The concern is not so much that paradoxical or countervailing practices have been introduced into the economy. Rather, it is whether consumer well-being has a place in the decision-making process. This chapter discusses the pricing and income policies of the new administration, with an analysis for decision makers and scholars to draw their own conclusions.

PRICING POLICY

Prior to the current reform measures, prices were either subsidized, regulated, administered, or contracted between trading parties (World Bank, 1987a: 27). The size of a subsidy for a given commodity was a function of its relative importance to consumers. Subsidies were granted to essentials such as food, coal, and rent. On the other hand, imported luxury goods such as tobacco and alcohol were hit with high import taxes. Price as a response to market forces did not exist. With widespread strikes and mounting political tension in 1988 and early 1989, acute shortages forced price increases in early 1989.

On June 30, 1989, the Communist government of Mieczyslaw Rakowski adopted an adjustment program. The belt was tightened. The public was asked to make sacrifices in the present in order to have a more promising future. Prices were to be freed gradually, beginning with food. By administrative order, minimum wholesales prices for grain, milk, and meat products were raised by 34 percent. But prices of other commodities were rising at a faster rate, and led to protests by rural Solidarity and industrial workers. To win favor with voters in a forthcoming free election scheduled for June 1989, Rakowski's government yielded to the pressure. Wage increases were permitted to outpace inflation. Therefore, the budget deficit kept mounting and the increased money supply combined with reduced aggregate output to fuel inflation. Contract prices kept rising, as did administered prices. A general price freeze for the month of July was ordered and the Communist party was soundly defeated in the free election. But the party still had General Jaruzelski as president. The lower house, still dominated by the Communist party, appointed General Czeslaw Kiszczak as the new prime minister on August 2, 1989, and he lasted for two weeks. Meanwhile, on August 1, 1989, the "new economic order" came to be. The price freeze was lifted, beginning with food, now to be determined by market forces. Prices of other commodities were to follow.

On August 19, 1989, a new era dawned. Tadeusz Mazowiecki, a journalist and Solidarity leader, was offered the post of prime minister. But Mazowiecki was immediately confronted with general disequilibrium. In anticipation of free-market pricing for food, people's hoarding and speculative activities mushroomed. Price increases ranged between 300 and 400 percent for butter and ham. Undaunted, the government lifted controls on other commodity prices began in subsequent months. "Control" did not mean stable prices. But only a few selected commodities--such as coal, gas, and rent-- were still under control. It meant controlled price increases. There were also progressive price increases for fuels toward the end of November 1989, permitting increases every ten days to two weeks so as to gradually align prices with real costs and value. In accordance, industrial users of these fuels had to keep adjusting their respective product prices as well.

By December 1989, food prices had risen by 877.6 percent over a year ago. Prices of other commodities had risen by 529.6 percent, and services by 440.8 percent (World Economy Research, 1990: 24). By January 1, 1990, prices on 90 percent of all goods and services had been freed. Prices on controlled items such as energy forms and rent were scheduled to be increased in 1990, with the eventual free pricing as well in the immediate future. Therefore, from August 1, 1989--when food prices were first permitted to rise without government control--to mid-August 1990, more than 90 percent of the prices of all goods and services in Poland had been liberalized. In a year's time, the Polish economy had made the transition from relatively tightly controlled prices to nearly none.[1]

The effects of price deregulation may be seen in Table 7.1. Even before the Mazowiecki administration took office, prices had been steadily rising. In row 1, where December prices for the previous year are indexed at 100, the inflation rate for January 1989 was already 11 percent. It was reflective of the economic as well as the political conditions. Strikes were more frequent and more persistent. Row 2 provides monthly inflation rates from January 1989 through April 1990. Even though the monthly inflation rate remained in single digits between February 1989 and July of the same year, the compounded annual inflation rate caused serious hardships, especially for consumers on fixed incomes. Pricing reform was announced in April 1989, and there did not appear to be a buying panic. The monthly inflation rates for the three subsequent months remained in single digits. By August 1, 1989, however, the monthly inflation rate went out of control. Poland's Central Statistical Office reported in October 1989 that for the month of August alone, the prices of bread and flour rose by three times, butter and cheese by four times, and meat products by five and a half times (Warsaw Voice, 1989: 10- 12). For retail prices and services, the month of August 1989, saw a combined inflation rate of 39.5 percent (row 2). It was indicative of the importance of food prices in a consumer's budget. Retail prices kept rising in the subsequent months.

Information in rows 5 and 7 of Table 7.1 indicates that, while the prices for food items surged by 80.3 percent in August 1989, prices for nonfood items increased by a relatively small 17.4 percent. In the two months that followed, however, nonfood prices began their steady climb by 27.6 percent in September and 40.1 percent in October. In November 1989, the rate of

Table 7.1
Retail Prices of Goods and Services, January 1989 - April 1990

	Year	Month Jan	Feb	Mar	Apr	May	Jun	Jul	Aug	Sep	Oct	Nov	Dec
Indices of Retail Prices & Services (%)													
(1) Dec. of Previous Year = 100	89	111.0	119.8	129.5	142.2	152.4	161.7	177.1	247.0	331.8	513.5	628.3	739.6
	90	178.6	221.3	231.7	250.5								
(2) Previous Month = 100	89	111.0	107.9	108.1	109.8	107.2	106.1	109.5	139.5	134.4	154.8	122.4	117.7
	90	178.6	123.9	104.7	108.1								
(3) Same Month a Year ago = 100	89	183.2	170.3	174.2	177.8	185.4	191.3	203.9	282.7	369.2	557.1	657.0	739.6
	90	1189.7	1366.1	1323.1	1302.7								
Prices of Consumer Goods													
(4) Previous Month = 100	89	110.3	108.4	107.6	109.8	107.2	106.7	109.8	104.3	136.0	158.4	121.6	117.5
	90	171.0	125.1	104.7	108.4								
(5) Food	89	105.7	108.0	108.1	114.4	109.8	104.3	107.2	180.3	144.7	165.1	117.4	111.6
	90	179.9	118.1	100.0	112.4								
(6) Alcohol	89	102.2	108.1	1074.5	104.0	102.0	110.6	124.0	132.4	135.0	192.2	116.6	109.5
	90	141.0	126.8	101.5	130.2								
(7) Nonfood	89	115.5	108.9	107.3	108.4	106.7	107.4	108.3	117.4	127.4	140.1	129.6	127.8
	90	172.3	132.4	110.1	106.1								
Prices of Consumers Services													
(8) Previous Month = 100	89	115.9	104.7	110.7	109.8	106.8	102.8	108.2	129.3	136.0	158.4	121.6	117.5
	90	249.0	116.6	105.5	106.1								
(9) Dec. of Previous Year = 100	89	115.9	121.3	134.3	147.4	157.4	161.8	175.1	226.4	275.6	345.4	450.0	540.8
	90	249.0	290.3	306.3	325.0								

Source: Ministry of Finance, NBP, 1990: 3.

increase declined for both food and nonfood items, but inflation by then was being fueled more by nonfood than by food prices, reflecting a shortfall in domestic supply and a corresponding increase in imports.

The monthly inflation rates for services may be seen in row 8. For the year 1989, with the exception of January, March, November, and December, rates of increase were generally lower in the service area than in the economy as a whole. January 1990 was an exception: the entire economy's monthly inflation rate was 78.6 percent, but it was 149.0 percent for services. Prices of services had been freed on January 1, 1990, and public transportation, health care, postal and communication systems were all permitted to increase prices in accordance with market conditions. For the consumer, after having been stripped of more than 40 percent of his or her purchasing power in a twelve-month period, the decrease in demand for services was unavoidable. Aggregate demand took another sharp dive.

Through it all, the Mazowiecki administration did not renege on its promise to implement a market policy. The Polish economy was turned upside down. The long lines that used to be common in major cities disappeared, and it was as if equilibrium had been restored by reaching into the consumer's pocketbook. For a nation that had shown its independent character to the Communist regime, the general public showed remarkable patience and tolerance--not acceptance--toward the government they had freely elected. There were strikes, but they were relatively few in number and mostly short-lived.

The inflationary pressure eased in the early months of 1990, the result of an exceptionally tight monetary and fiscal policy, as approved by the International Monetary Fund and the World Bank. Monthly inflation dropped sharply from January 1990's 78.6 percent to February's 23.9 percent, and further down to March's 4.7 percent. Aggregate demand decreased for months in a row, and policy makers claimed triumph for having succeeded in containing inflation. But economists were concerned about an impending deep recession--the Polish economy was not out of the woods. The economic stabilization policy had yielded positive results in combating inflation, but the economy was not yet stabilized. The question remains: How can the Polish economy get on its feet? The inflation rate is far from stabilized. The first two weeks of December 1990, brought an inflation rate of 4.7 percent. But even a monthly rate of 1 or 2 percent means double-digit inflation on an annual basis. Inflation is far from over unless aggregate supplies become more responsive to the market system.

The Mazowiecki administration's market pricing policy was a 180 degree twin from the centrally planned and controlled system. It was accomplished in record time. With free elections and a free market, the economic system has been changed beyond recognition. But the price has been steep. The changes have been largely cosmetic; the problems remain.

INCOME POLICY

Under the centrally planned system, income was a function of state budgetary considerations. As is characteristic of a communistic system, attempts were made to contain the growth of aggregate demand in order to create social savings for investment. These attempts in Poland, however, were less successful than in other COMECON economies, since Polish workers have a history of going on strike and making demands over economic issues. The Polish Communist party was less repressive, and as a result, political or economic compromises were often achieved between Communist officials and workers. When the government permitted prices to inch up, workers went on strike over wage issues. In the process, both sides won and lost.

Real monthly wages in the socialized economy rose 41 percent between 1970 and 1975 and 10 percent between 1975 and 1980, and fell by 25 percent in 1982. Since then, they have crept up slowly in a cumulative increase of 6.6 percent by 1985, with more than half the increase occurring in 1985. In 1986 there was an increase of 2 percent, 20 percent in nominal terms. This left the monthly real wage in 1986 about 18 percent below its peak in 1981. (World Bank, vol. 1, 1987: 13)

Real wages gained substantially between 1970 and 1975--when Poland fed lavishly on money borrowed from abroad--then they grew slowly between 1975 and 1980. Increases in wages did not reflect increases in productivity; they were a function of budgetary considerations and prevailing political circumstances. Martial law in 1981 led to deep cuts into real wages. Five years later, real wages were still significantly below the 1981 level. Consumer income recovered painfully slowly from 1986 to September 1989 so the workers could not regain the purchasing power they had enjoyed eight years earlier. Then came the new economic order of the Solidarity-backed government. Past mistakes had left a large price tag.

Table 7.2 presents data on nominal and real wages for five economic branches, including industry, construction, transport, communication, and trade. The figures are in 1,000-zloty units. Beginning with January 1989, nominal wages inched upward for two months. It then declined for two consecutive months thereafter. Though inflationary pressure was evident at the beginning of 1989, nominal wage increases had been faster than the inflation rate for the corresponding months. But sustained monthly rates of inflation kept eroding earlier gains in real wages (rows 1 and 15). Real wages declined by 12.5 percent in April 1989. Unstable economic conditions led to the preliminary agreement reached in March between organized labor and government. Wage adjustment was to be commensurate with the rate of inflation, but wage indexing was quickly put on hold by the Mazowiecki administration. By late 1990, the issue was still being hotly debated between the new administration and labor.

The sudden surge in both nominal and real wages for August 1989 was due to announced freeing of food prices on August 1, 1990. The announcement led to arbitrary wage increases, which management was obliged to grant. First, the policy of noninterference with enterprise operations was already in place; second, the workers councils had great influence over management. The wage increase was made in anticipation of a restrictive incomes policy to be implemented by the new government. The resulting hyperinflation was inevitable.

To stem the inflationary tide, income policy was tightened so that future wage increases would be granted only as a given percentage of the previous month's inflation rate. If an enterprise wished to grant a wage increase beyond that rate, it could, but the enterprise would have to pay an additional 300 percent tax. Only foreign or joint-venture firms were exempt from this stringent policy. Given the general economic conditions, and that enterprises were being subjected to market tests for the first time, wage increases above the sanctioned level were not feasible.

Real income dropped by 24.5 percent in September 1989. If we use September as the base, we see that the purchasing power lost another 18.1 percent in October. But if August 1989 is the base, real income was reduced by a combined 38 percent in a two-month period. Wages were permitted to rise to 40 percent of the previous month's inflation, but nominal gains of 1.9 and 25.6 percent in November and December 1989, respectively, still represented a net loss in real income of 20 percent when compared with the month of August.[2] The increase of 25.6 percent in real wages in December 1989, was in anticipation of impending release of prices for most goods and services beginning January 1, 1990. The inflation rate that month was 78.6 percent, causing real wages to decrease by 42.6 percent in January 1990 alone.

February through April saw little improvement. Anticipating high inflation for January through March 1990, the administration froze wages for the duration. The promise was that a partial wage indexing rate would be announced by the beginning of April. The rate was to be such that aggregate demand could be further reduced through continued decreases in real income. It was hoped that prices could then be stabilized from April 1990 onward. The announced increase was to be applied retroactively to these three months, but the permissible increases were not announced as promised because inflationary pressure--even without the retroactive reimbursement of wage increases--was greater than had been expected. When the announcement did finally come in May, instead of the original 40 to 45 percent previous month's inflation rate being factored into the current month's wage increases, the permissible rate was a meager 30 percent. Real income took another significant dive.

Table 7.2
Nominal and Real Wages, January 1989-April 1990

	Year	Month Jan	Feb	Mar	Apr	May	Jun	Jul	Aug	Sep	Oct	Nov	Dec
Nominal Wages Personal Wages in 5 Branches (1000 zlotys)													
(1) Including Profit	89	66.4	85.7	114.9	110.4	105.5	120.9	126.9	257.1	260.6	330.2	411.8	609.0
	90	624.1	716.2	1008.8	932.0								
(2) Excluding Profit	89	66.0	78.8	86.4	92.6	94.8	111.9	119.6	216.4	245.5	328.5	411.2	606.6
	90	618.3	651.9	720.1	754.6								
(3) Industry	89	71.5	92.2	123.3	117.9	113.5	130.4	141.0	282.1	285.4	354.4	463.6	676.2
	90	693.5	800.3	1100.9	1015.2								
(4) Construction	89	70.1	88.0	117.6	112.8	108.1	122.2	127.9	254.3	255.7	312.6	377.6	532.8
	90	570.2	667.7	936.3	906.6								
(5) Transport	89	65.7	86.8	104.4	104.3	95.4	100.5	100.1	253.7	226.9	322.6	360.1	518.6
	90	602.0	639.3	983.6	853.0								
(6) Communication	89	47.3	58.6	92.4	78.2	95.8	76.0	78.5	176.4	181.6	303.9	278.6	546.5
	90	425.7	576.3	915.0	803.2								
(7) Trade	89	51.6	65.1	94.8	91.5	84.3	107.4	101.9	187.3	212.4	267.4	308.5	497.2
	90	6.0	528.1	762.9	724.9								
Previous Month = 100 Real Wages in 5 Branches													
(8) Including Profit	89	62.9	129.0	134.1	96.1	95.6	114.7	104.9	202.6	101.4	126.7	124.7	147.9
	90	102.5	114.8	140.8	92.4								
(9) Excluding Profit	89	62.8	119.5	109.6	107.1	102.4	118.1	106.8	180.9	113.5	133.8	125.2	147.5
	90	101.9	105.4	110.5	104.8								
(10) Industry	89	60.6	128.9	133.7	95.7	96.2	114.9	108.2	200.0	101.2	124.2	130.8	145.8
	90	102.6	115.4	137.6	92.2								
(11) Construction	89	73.5	125.6	133.6	95.9	95.8	113.0	104.7	198.7	100.6	122.3	120.8	141.1
	90	107.0	117.1	140.2	96.8								
(12) Transport	89	71.1	132.0	120.3	99.9	91.4	105.4	99.6	253.5	89.4	142.2	111.6	144.0

	90	116.1	106.2	153.8	86.7								
(13) Communication	89	48.9	123.9	157.8	84.7	122.5	79.3	103.2	224.8	103.0	167.3	91.7	196.1
	90	77.9	135.4	158.8	87.8								
(14) Trade	89	62.8	126.1	145.7	96.5	92.1	127.4	94.8	183.9	113.4	125.9	115.4	161.2
	90	93.3	113.8	144.5	95.0								
Real Wages = 100 Real Wages in 5 Branches													
(15) Including Profit	89	56.7	119.5	124.1	87.5	89.1	108.1	95.8	145.2	75.5	81.9	101.9	125.6
	90	57.4	92.6	134.5	85.5								
(16) Excluding Profit	89	56.6	110.7	101.4	97.6	95.5	111.3	97.6	129.7	84.4	86.5	102.3	125.3
	90	57.1	85.1	105.5	96.9								
(17) Industry	89	54.6	119.5	123.7	87.1	89.8	108.3	98.8	143.4	75.3	80.3	106.9	123.9
	90	57.4	93.1	131.4	85.3								
(18) Construction	89	66.2	116.4	123.6	87.4	89.4	106.5	95.4	142.5	74.9	79.0	98.7	119.9
	90	59.9	94.5	133.9	89.6								
(19) Transport	89	64.0	122.4	111.3	91.0	181.7	66.5	91.9	91.2	122.3			
	90	65.0	85.7	146.9	80.2								
(20) Communication	89	44.0	114.8	146.0	77.1	114.3	74.8	94.2	161.1	76.6	108.1	74.9	166.6
	90	43.6	109.3	151.6	81.2								
(21) Trade	89	56.6	116.9	134.7	87.9	85.9	120.1	86.6	131.8	84.4	81.4	94.3	136.9
	90	52.2	91.9	138.0	87.9								
Dec. a Year Ago = 100 Real Wages in 5 Branches													
(22) Including Profit	90	57.4	53.1	71.5	61.1								
(23) Excluding Profit	90	59.9	56.6	75.9	67.9								
(24) Industry	90	57.4	53.5	70.3	59.9								
(25) Construction	90	59.9	56.6	75.9	67.9								
(26) Transport	90	65.0	55.7	81.9	65.7								
(27) Communication	90	43.6	47.7	72.3	58.7								
(28) Trade	90	52.2	48.0	66.2	58.2								

Source: Ministry of Finance, NBP, 1990: 3.

Nominal money income as a whole, as may be seen in Table 7.2, kept rising for the five economic activities (rows 3 through 7 and 11 through 14). For the average Polish consumer, it meant little comfort. Real income had been declining. Professionals or workers who had relatives in foreign countries thought about finding employment abroad, and a goodly number succeeded in doing so. The Federal Republic of Germany had to place a ceiling on the number of Polish citizens who could be legally employed there. Domestically, real income of those unable to land jobs abroad kept falling (Pacuski interview, 1990). The social mood turned somber.

To better realize the hardship endured by Polish consumers, we convert the nominal income into U.S. dollars. The official exchange rate in January 1989 was $1 to 507.9 zlotys. At the recommendation of the IMF, the Mazowiecki administration implemented internal convertibility of foreign currencies. By January 1990, the exchange was $1 for 9,500 zlotys, a reflection of the real value of the zloty. The exchange rate remained stable for most of 1990, with less than a half a percent fluctuation up or downward.

In Table 7.2, the average nominal monthly wage for the five economic activities given was 624,100, 716,200, 1,008,800, and 932,000 zlotys for January through April 1990, respectively. When converted to U.S. dollars, the monthly wages are $65.70, $76.40, $106.00, and $92.20. That was for the average worker; for persons employed in communication, transport, and commerce, nominal wages were even lower.

Strikes by railroad workers were only one manifestation of frustration by the general public. For the best paid employees in industry, the monthly wage was around U.S. $100. Consumers who had little or no need to purchase imported consumer goods, the monthly income could stretch. Rent, energy,[3] food, and textile products are much cheaper in Poland than in the West. So are public transportation, cultural events, and paper products. But the portion of an average Polish worker's monthly income allocated to food consumption is four or five times higher than in developed economies. Dining out or purchasing imported goods is a luxury for most. The stores are well stocked with basic merchandise, and consumers are making purchases. Most buyers have been dipping deeply into their personal savings, with the anticipation of a better economy in the near future. But pensioners and persons on fixed incomes, are lamenting the more secure days of the Communist administration.

Prices in May and June of 1990 were relatively stable, amounting to between 4 and 6 percent increases monthly. Policymakers toyed with the ideas of raising wage indexation to 60 percent of the previous month's inflation rate, but even so, real wages and income would continue their painful downward slide.

Prices in July and August, however, rose once again faster than the preceding two months. The contemplated increase in wages never came.

Figure 7.1
Monthly Indices of Retail Price and Real Wage, January 1989-April 1990

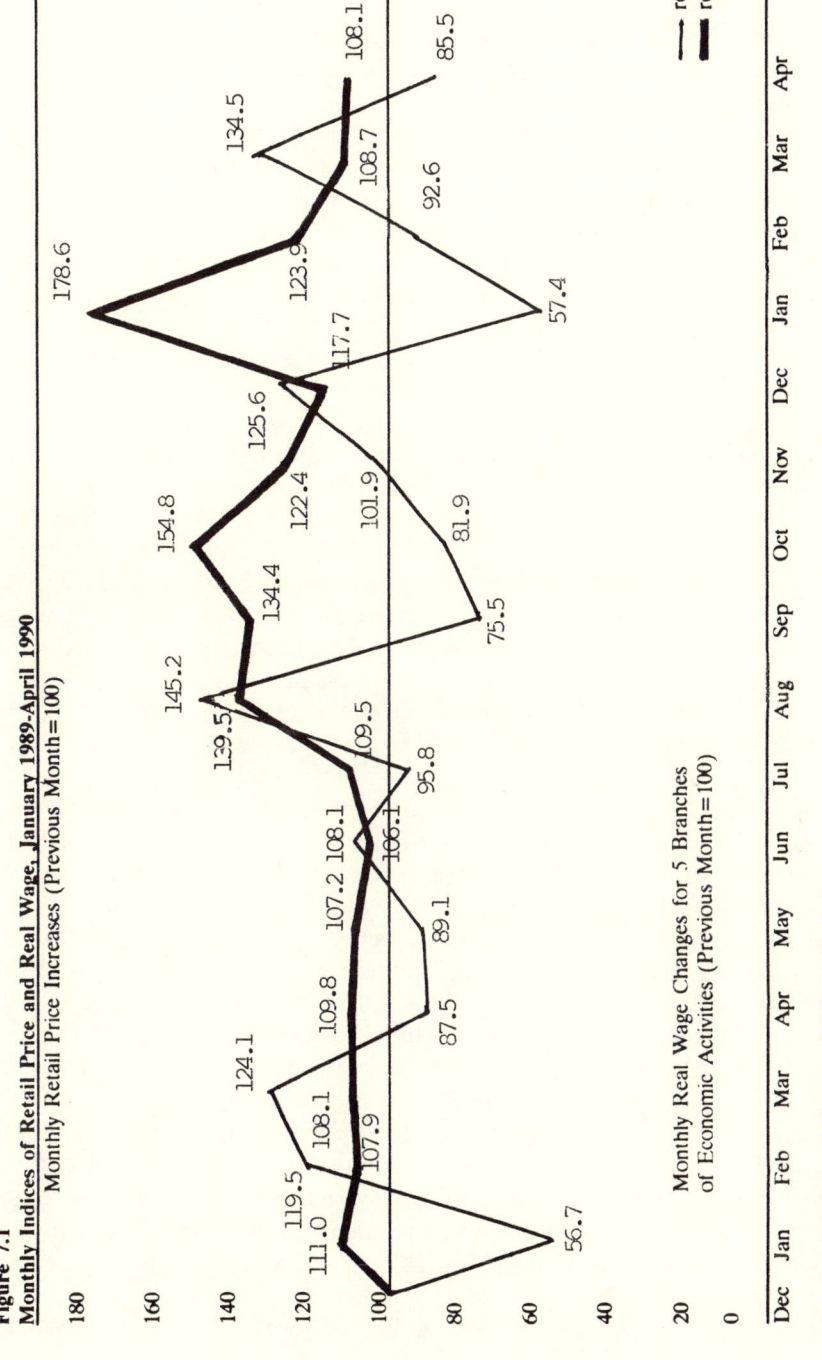

Monthly Retail Price Increases (Previous Month=100)

Monthly Real Wage Changes for 5 Branches
of Economic Activities (Previous Month=100)

real wages
retail prices

Source: Ministry of Finance, NBP, 1990: 3, 8.

Instead, the Polish people were asked to make sacrifices and be patient. On account of Prime Minister Mazowiecki's statue and popularity, and because of their political freedom, people still tolerated the harsh economic climate resulting from the tight incomes policy. However, with declining real wages, workers--particularly those in the socialized sector--have been growing more and more restive and indifferent (Dietl interview, 1990).

Leading economists are calling for a freeing of wages through creation of a labor market. Unless there is motivation to be productive, however, a competitive labor market will not work. Increased productivity cannot be expected from a shrinking pocketbook. Wages must reflect the marginal value produced--that is in line with a market economy. The Mazowiecki administration's preoccupation, however, was on containing inflation. It did not feel secure loosening its grip on wages for fear of rekindling inflation. Tight incomes policy, as it has been, is expected to remain for the foreseeable future.

Figure 7.1 illustrates changes in purchasing power from December 1988 through April 1990. The previous month is used as the base, indexed at 100. Movements along the horizontal line show no change over time. The thick line shows retail price changes during the final months of Communist administration in Poland and the early months of the Mazowiecki administration. The thin line shows changes in real wages for the same period. From February 1989 through July of the same year, the prices line appears here relatively flat. However, with the previous month's price index set at 100, even a relatively flat line would mean significant cumulative inflation for the year. It would also mean decreased and continuously decreasing real wages unless wages were linked to price increases.

In the figure, price increases from August 1989 through February 1990 were significantly higher than earlier months. The changes in real income would then depend on nominal wage increases for the corresponding period.

An upswing in real wages from one month to the next does not necessarily mean that the current month is better for the wage earner than the previous month. It could mean that real wages have actually decreased. For instance, an upswing from April 1989's 87.5 to that of 89.1 in May 1989 indicates that the consumer is worse off in May than in April by 10.9 percent. This is because the real-wage function lies below the horizontal line, and therefore real wages decreased from the previous month. January and September of 1989 and January of 1990 were months when real wages suffered extreme cuts. The particularly unsteady path for real wage changes from August 1989 onward manifests the government's general intent to reduce real wages in order to reduce aggregate demand and hence curb inflation. Tight fiscal, monetary, and income policies made the average wage earner much poorer in a hurry. Since curbing inflation was the primary objective of Mazowiecki's economic stabilization policy, real wages became the sacrificial lamb.

POLICIES EVALUATED

The objective of the Mazowiecki administration was complete and thorough marketization of economic activity, including a free labor market. But the income policy in late 1989 and throughout 1990 has not permitted the emergence of a labor market, private enterprises with foreign capital being the only exception. So long as the threat of sustained inflation remains, the government's lid on nominal wage increases will remain in place. Inflation is being contained through erosion in real income, which is expected to continue to decline because there has been no supply-side response. The time required to regain that lost income will be fairly long.

Indeed inflation needs to be contained, and tight monetary and fiscal policies have been necessary. But the problem that led to these steps could have been prevented. The initiating cause was overnight introduction of the free-market system. The free market is more efficient than the centralized system, so the change is justified. But the mistake is the speed with which it was ushered in. There should have been adequate preparation so that the transition was smoother, less painful, and more fruitful. Instead it was as ineffective and chaotic as shipping tractors and combines to a developing area where plows and mules are still the chief farming instruments. Yield-increasing factors need to be preceded by due preparation. It is likewise for introducing a new economic system to a society where the necessary institutions either have not matured or have not even been established. Free-market pricing needs to be introduced step by step, with attention paid to avoid the potholes along the way.

On a more practical level, since the farm sector in Poland is of primary importance, reform should have been introduced there first. When farm productivity increases as a response to market forces, then farm prices could gradually be freed to match market conditions. A timetable should have been established to announce which major products will have their prices freed, by how much and when. Farm producers could adjust their investment and production accordingly, so that when the time arrives, supplies of their products will be adequate or even abundant. Prices would be stable and inflation reduced. With time, prices for all farm produce could be determined by supply and demand. The equilibrium achieved would be natural instead of contrived.

Government would expend less energy on fighting or fretting over inflation if reform measures were implemented over several years. There would be stability. There would be order. And there would be an accumulation of knowledge and experience, by both the private sector and by the government. The web of social and economic institutions, essential for the development of a market system, would be spun by entrepreneurs and creative investors. Throughout, inflation could be minimized and stabilized. To prevent or regain losses in real income, the labor force would even be expected to work harder and be more productive. The end results would be predictable and sustained.

For now, the threat of hyperinflation has been eliminated, but inflationary pressure remains. Panic buying, hoarding, and supply inelasticities contributed to that hyperinflation and reduced real income. It was a supply bottleneck that prevented prices from drifting downward. Preventive measures could have been adopted beforehand, so that when the prices were freed, producers would respond to market demand, rendering prices stable. Treating the cause of a problem rather than the symptoms will resolve the matter permanently, but takes longer. As it is, some symptoms of economic instability seem to have been removed, but complications lurk in the dark. The reform process does not have to be as cautious or slow-paced as in Czechoslovakia, but neither does it have to be as radical as it has been in Poland. Given that free-market pricing is a reality, the need now is to focus on actual or potential bottlenecks in industrial and agricultural supplies, employing whatever measures necessary to ensure macro stability and micro efficiency. The near-term objective of the new administration should be damage control, not more policy shocks. Only when there is meaningful economic stability can decision makers move forward.

NOTES

1. As of August, 1990, the prices of a few items such as coal, fuel and rental housing were still under some form of price control. But periodic increases were permitted.

2. By extrapolation, using August's real wage as the base.

3. In the form of electricity and coal only, not the price of fuel gasoline, which was close to that in the United States.

8

MANPOWER AND EMPLOYMENT POLICIES

Under Communist rule, there was no unemployment,[1] at least in theory. By July 1990, ten months after the reform policy was inaugurated, more than half a million became unemployed. By standards of developed economies, there still was full employment in Poland. But for the Polish economy, it was a new phenomenon. Mounting unemployment has found no ready solution. In July 1990, the government had expected 1 million unemployed by the year's end; that figure was reached by the end of October instead. The revised estimate for unemployed by the end of December 1990 was 1.2 to 1.3 million. "We are completely unprepared to deal with unemployment, both as a nation and as a Ministry," said Jerzy Pacuski, director of the Department of Employment. "The Ministry has no idea what to do with unemployment or how to take any meaningful action," according to Irena Ostroska of Solidarity's Labor Protection Bureau in Warsaw (Warsaw Voice, December 1990: 12-2).

The unemployment situation *will* get much worse before it gets any better. The number of unemployed is expected to increase by 100,000 per month, with no clear end in sight (Warsaw Voice, December 1990: 12-27). But that estimate was optimistic--it included only open unemployment. There is widespread disguised unemployment in rural areas and in state enterprises, while underemployment is extensive in urban centers. In October 1990, there was only one job offer per fifteen unemployed persons. Bankruptcies and downsizing of state enterprises will help swell the ranks of the unemployed.

The labor market is nascent. Better qualified, more competent and employable persons with mobility have been leaving their positions in cooperatives and state enterprises to join private firms or to freelance in order to earn more. The positions they have vacated cannot be readily filled, for lack of qualified persons. After all, it does not pay to be employed by a state enterprise when wages are higher elsewhere. On the other hand, if a position higher than one's experience and qualifications is offered, then a less qualified person becomes interested. When someone is replaced by a less or unqualified person, the performance of the lower-paying state enterprise is affected. That phenomenon alone renders state-owned firms less competitive in a now market situation: unit costs will not significantly change while productivity will decrease.

CAUSES OF RISING UNEMPLOYMENT

Poland will be faced with progressively more severe unemployment problems in the next few years.   Here are some of the major causes of rising unemployment in the new Poland.

First, there is no organized job-placement service.   There was a distinct manpower policy during Communist administration.   Youth were educated or trained according to the state's needs, as projected by the central plan. College graduates were guaranteed by law to be provided with employment. So were vocational school trainees.   Today, one out of six unemployed is a university or college graduate.   During the Communist era, there was a relatively small segment of the potential work force "who never worked or who worked for a very short period of time."   They were not willing to work at all (Pacuski interview, 1990).   But for those willing to be employed, work positions were assigned.

In contrast, the free-market system has meant hands off manpower planning.   The intent is to create a job market, so that potential labor may be better actualized.   The role of the government is to assist and coordinate the activities of job seekers and firms seeking qualified employees.   The practical results of this laissez-faire stance will be analyzed in a separate subsection hereafter.   Suffice it to say that the government's intended policy on containing unemployment will not and cannot be fruitful for many years.   For now, recently laid-off workers join the ranks of other job seekers.   They cannot be readily absorbed into the free-market system: many are not qualified, even more are not prepared.

Second, there are no good training programs.   Those who did not have to work or who were unwilling to work before are now seeking employment. High inflation and reduced real income have caused those who previously managed to survive on either welfare, social insurance payments, or a spouse's income to now find employment to supplement their lower purchasing power.   Many of these people, however, are not readily employable.   They lack the training, the experience or the appropriate education.   "In December 1989, there were 8,000 people registered as searching for jobs.   There were 450,000 job vacancies.   On June 30, 1990, there were 568,000 registered unemployed with only 42,000 vacancies" (Pacuski interview, 1990).   There are people laid off from steel mills, coal mines, and textile factories who had been working there for ten, twenty, or more years.   They are too young to retire and there is no pension.   They are too old to undergo retraining.   Even so, the new government is not equipped to retrain the increasing number of unemployed, with its extremely scarce financial resources and even more scarce qualified training personnel. Also, on-the-job training and retraining used to be the responsibility of state enterprises--retraining expenses were part of the budget for state enterprises. But that was paper money. Since the introduction of the market system, however, state enterprises have become independent of the government's budget and expenses for training are real costs. Now that these enterprises have to cope with reduced aggregate demand, and therefore decreased revenue, their meeting a payroll is already an achievement. Training or retraining of employees is low on their priority list. Likewise, the training programs that used to exist in many state enterprises have now been discontinued. The burden of training and retraining now rests with the state. But the state has not been coping with the problem, and is not in a position to do so in the near future.

Third, the number of plant closings continues to increase. This phenomenon extends beyond the state enterprises; private enterprises have also been subjected to market pressures. Also, rising production costs has been translated into higher prices. Consumers as a whole, however, have experienced reduced purchasing power, decreasing sales. Unless the demand for a firm's product is inelastic, sales decrease proportionately more than a product increases in price. Reduced revenue combined with increased cost can mean a host of consequences, including layoffs or plant closings.

Fourth, off-farm migration is increasing unemployment in the cities. As of December 31, 1989, 14,573,000 people were classified as rural dwellers --that is more than one-third of the entire population. The younger generation is less inclined to remain on farm, however, and those who are able, flow to urban centers in search of employment. Off-farm migration is not new, but given the depressed economic conditions in rural regions, more join the ranks of employment seekers in the cities. With a severe recession throughout the economy, many cannot be gainfully employed.

Fifth, there is an imbalance in workers available and positions open. Not only private but also state enterprises are in need of qualified personnel with specialized skills and qualifications. While there is an abundant supply of blue-collar workers, there is an acute shortage of persons with specializations. The latter have to come from the younger generation, currently in college or receiving vocational training. It will be years before these manpower needs can be adequately met. Meanwhile, the unemployed for the most part remain unemployable, joined by the newly displaced.

Sixth, there is low mobility among the labor force. It is likely that a minority of unemployed in a region could find employment elsewhere, especially in a major metropolis. However, finding an apartment or a school for one's children is often an insurmountable obstacle. This in effect, holds the unemployed hostage where they are. In developed economies, these obstacles do not exist, but in the Poland they are problems awaiting solutions. But no ready solution is in sight.

Seventh, relative to the West, labor is inexpensive. For Polish enterprises, labor costs account for 40 percent or more of total production costs. Aside from basic wages and salaries, there is a 20 percent wage tax enterprises pay directly to the state treasury. Then, there is the social insurance tax, which has also to be paid by the enterprise. The social insurance payment has varied from time to time, from as high as 53 percent of an employee's basic wage to the present 40 to 45 percent. If an employee's monthly salary is 1 million zlotys, then the cost to the enterprise is 1.6 to 1.65 million zlotys. Given the present economic conditions, most enterprises are preoccupied with limiting how many workers they lay off than hiring more. During central planning, more people could have been employed by state enterprises, since hiring was directly or indirectly at the expense of the state. Now wages are a real expense incurred by the enterprise itself, and cost-cutting is the avenue to survival or growth. As few as possible new recruits are added to the payroll. Therefore, the unemployed have fewer doors open to them.

MANPOWER POLICY

The major cause of rising unemployment is the near absence of a manpower policy. The new economic system is of a laissez-faire mode. The new government wishes to be differentiated from past practices of fitting individuals to state-determined work positions. The choice now should be the responsibility of individuals--they are free to respond to labor market conditions, or not. Dr. Jerzy Pacuski, director of the Department of Employment, summarizes as follows:

There are basically two approaches to the educational system. One is that people should be trained so that they can work in the branches which are needed by the state. The other is that people should learn whatever they wish because of their aspirations, ambitions, and so forth. We were training people according to the needs of the state. Now we will be gradually transistioning to the other system, so that the training of the people in the educational system does not have to respond directly to the needs of the economy. So, people will have more choices. (Pacuski interview, 1990)

Director Pacuski is correct--it is the function of the market to generate information on labor supply and demand in various economic activities. However, at this stage, the government is needed to fill the void until the labor market is fully functioning. A delicately sculptured manpower policy can contribute significantly to avoiding a labor-market bottleneck and to reducing the potential future for unemployment.

Current Legislation and Services

The director of the Department of Employment is responsible for employment issues. Assisting the director is the General Board for Employment at the Ministry of Work and Social Policy, plus regional and local employment offices established by his office. The board advises the director on employment-related legislation, and on disbursements of the Work Fund. Revenue for the Work Fund is allocated by the Council of Ministers and is derived in part from the state budget and in part from social insurance payments made by enterprises on behalf of their employees. The purpose of the Work Fund is to train and retrain persons injured or disabled while on the job, or those who have no particular skills but wish to enter the job market. It is distinct from the training that used to be provided by state enterprises to students in vocational schools, in that the latter prepared students for specific branches of industries or enterprises. Work Fund training is for the general public, with no restrictions or work destination. It is also the responsibility of the board to advise the director of Employment on allocative activities pertaining to the fund.

There are four hundred regional or local employment offices or agencies. For each of these, there is a local employment board. The function of the local board is similar to that of the general board in the Ministry of Work and Social Policy. It is the responsibility of the local employment office to identify employment needs, to register the unemployed, to arrange and finance appropriate training programs, to provide financial assistance to local enterprises that would create useful jobs for job seekers. And when needed, the local employment office also provides welfare or unemployment benefits to those who are eligible.[2]

According to the proposed law, training programs may not last longer than six months. Only in special cases can the training period be lengthened for an additional six-month period. Payments to trainees vary between 40 and 100 percent of the average salary for the occupation. For persons sustaining work-related injuries, compensation could reach 100 percent of average salary. For others, the minimum welfare is 40 and the maximum 80 percent of the respective previous salary (Article 12). Enterprises cooperating with the local employment office to train the jobless may receive loans from the Work Fund. Only 50 percent of the loan needs to be repaid if the trained individual becomes employed and stays employed for twenty-four months or longer (Article 13). Training programs are not to be offered by the local employment offices themselves, however local office helps to create the conditions under which the needed programs would be offered. To date, there is only one such program aimed specifically at university and college graduates; vocational training school has practically ceased, owing to cost considerations.

Coping with the Problem

Enterprises have been attempting to find outside funding, especially from the state. But the budget for the Work Fund is tight. The budget law passed in March 1990 allocated a total of 4.691 billion zlotys to the Work Fund for fiscal year 1990 (Budget Law of 1990, Warsaw)--in dollar value, that amounts to $493.8 million. It is costly to train persons. The monthly training welfare payment amounts to 800,000 zlotys, or approximately U.S. $85. But a three-month training program could run as high as more than U.S. $1,500 per person, depending on the type of training and the field of specialization (Pacuski interview, 1990). The money allocated for the Employment Office is significant, but it cannot be stretched to service the economy's needs. There is sufficient money in the budget for welfare payments, but not enough to train the increasing number of unemployed. Dr. Pacuski comments that:

When you think about paying welfare for these people who could become unemployed, there is money for them. But, indeed, if you have 2 million people who are unemployed, there is not enough money to arrange training for all of them. All of the resources we have for training will cover no more than 1 to 1.3 million people. On the average, it is ten times more expensive to train the unemployed than pay welfare. (Pacuski interview, 1990)

To illustrate how the number of unemployed will rise without government intervention, Dr. Pacuski adds:

The gross output in Poland during the first six months of 1990 decreased by 30 percent. But employment in general decreased by only a few percent. That shows that if every person here follows very strict and rigid market rules, this unemployment should grow very fast. The government is not seeking to prevent the increase in unemployment in order to keep state-owned companies and enterprises open.

With increased competitive market forces, more state-owned enterprises will fold. More people will be unemployed, and unemployment benefits will be available for them. The welfare payment, however, ranges only between U.S. $10 to $20 a month. There will not be sufficient funds in the budget for extensive manpower training programs; meanwhile, the problem of unemployment gets more severe by the day.

The government's inability to find jobs for the displaced is more than just a financial matter. The enterprises cannot help--they are more concerned with cutting costs than making investments in human resources. And the Department of Employment lacks the personnel to deal with this surge in unemployment. In December 1989, there were a total of 2,000 persons working in the regional and local offices of the Department of Employment. By July 1990, the number increased to 4,000. Another 1,000 was expected to join the work force by the fall of 1990. But that is still only one official per 8,000 population. Many of the new recruits have little or no experience in the field. And the seasoned employees are accustomed to old ways of conducting business. As the director explains,

You have to train the people [employees of the Department] and teach them a completely different way of working and thinking about the problems of unemployment in general. Statistics and a new information system for unemployment should be sought. The biggest problem is that the existing offices do not have necessary computer equipment. For 400 employment offices scattered over Poland, all they have are 50 microcomputers. They do not cooperate with each other. (Pacuski interview, 1990)

There is a lack of office personnel as well as functional information systems to coordinate data collection and statistical analysis. The ability of local offices to effectively identify job vacancies and to place the unemployed is severely constrained. And it is too much to expect local offices to coordinate training programs under existing conditions. The state budget is tight; the government is preoccupied with many other concerns.

The government has sought international assistance and cooperation in dealing with its unemployment problem. Agreements have been reached between Poland and the United States, the former Federal Republic of Germany, Belgium, and Great Britain for advice and assistance (Obloj interview, 1990). There are also some other Western economies that have offered cooperation, but no formal agreements have been signed yet. One example of international cooperation is the assistance provided by France, in restructuring the employment situation in the Polish town of Walbrzych, in the province of Silesia. Several mines and coal processing plants are expected to be closed in the near future, and the financial outlook for the town is bleak, so France has attempted to restructure the town's employment profile. Walbrzych, however, is not an isolated instance of mass unemployment. Training and placement is urgently needed. What the Polish government can do in this area is limited. Private employment agencies--five as of July 1990-- have begun to emerge, and hope now rests with private enterprises to train and absorb the unemployed. Limited loans from the Work Fund have been made available for that purpose. It is hoped that private initiatives will be more cost-effective and more productive than government-initiated training programs. But so far the response from the private sector has been minimal.

From 1981 through 1988, a total of 830,000 Poles emigrated to the West in search of a better life. Of those who emigrated, 94,000 were college graduates. Among the 94,000 were 20,000 engineers, 5,500 medical doctors, 7,400 economists, and 8,000 educators. Of the small portion who returned to Poland, most were older or were unemployable (Warsaw Voice, 1990: 7-1). It may be deduced that the brain drain in Poland after martial law in 1981 deprived the economy of potential business leaders, quality engineers, and entrepreneurs.

POLICY EVALUATION

Critics of former prime minister Tadeusz Mazowiecki or finance minister Leszek Balcerowicz come from the left and the right, but both desire the same for the Polish economy. To some, the economic transformation is too slow; to others, it is too fast and inappropriate. To some, rising unemployment is a price to be paid, an economic reality, necessary and unavoidable. To some others, the social cost is too high. Regardless, few have ready solutions.

The administration's decision is an unwavering *hold the course*, with the belief and hope that everything will somehow work out in the long run. An essential consideration, however, seems amiss in the administration's rush to a market economy. Labor is a resource inherently distinct and different from land, capital, technology, or management. Manpower is more than its potential contribution or cost to the economy. It is the aggregate of individuals on whose welfare economic activity should be centered--the end that toward which economic system should undergo change. Unlike in the centralized system, workers are no longer statistics, and they should no longer be considered merely parts of a machinery that is the economy. With this premise, policy measures need be more sensitive to people. A proper understanding of manpower, even in terms of economic reasoning, is of value to decision makers. The ensuing discussion is an attempt at this reasoning process.

It is human resources that actualize the potential value of physical resources. Land and capital are important factors of production. But the objective of production is to benefit consumers, who are also the labor force. Humans are resources. The production factors employed and the institutions formed are all accomplished through that human resource--labor. This factor of production needs to be used to benefit consumers. Institutions need to be formed in the manner that they are at service for humans, not the other way around.

To the unemployed, there is little or no economic opportunity, mobility, freedom, or stability. If there had been adequate preparation for retraining, reeducating, relocating, or at least compensating the unemployed, then the reform measures could have been implemented at the same time. Then would the displaced economic agents bear with the changes but they could actualize their other potential over time. The process is time consuming, but it is more constructive, provides continuity, and is less costly to society in the longer run. Policymakers, therefore, must design and coordinate the preparatory work that can lessen the trauma while society moves forward with reforms.

For now, the effects of economic shock are unavoidable--it is *fait accompli.* Instead, planning for human resource development is needed. A manpower planning and employment policy should benefit consumers rather than economic growth. Conversely, without careful and appropriate planning, the market system will leave a significant segment of Poland's population either relegated to less productive functions or eliminated from the labor market altogether. The centrally planned Communist system had plans that failed because they failed to respect producers and consumers as humans. It is a lesson the new administration should not fail to learn.

Economic policy in Poland needs to take human resource development and human factors into consideration. Without thoughtful planning there can be no successful development. Without development there can be no economic or social benefit to consumers. If the consumers do not benefit the system is not worth introducing. The United States has the purest form of a market economy, yet its economic position in the world community has been on the decline. On the other hand, both Japan and the former Federal Republic of Germany used a planned market system to rise from the ruins of war to become economic superpowers. The major difference between the economic performance of United States and the former FRG or Japan is the human factor--human resource development and deployment. It is the value being placed on individuals as persons and the role of government in anticipating and meeting manpower needs that truly count. It therefore would be a costly oversight if the new Polish government permitted millions of its people to slide into the abyss of frustration and hopelessness. It needs to take immediate action to evaluate its policy priorities so that the most crucial factor of economic activity--human resources--is given due consideration.[3] The success of Poland's economic reform effort depends, to a large extent, on its manpower and employment policies.

NOTES

1.   Valuable information on manpower needs and employment was obtained in an interview in July 1990 with Dr. Jerzy Pacuski, director of Poland's Department of Employment.

2.   Article 10 of Project for the Law.

3.   This information was provided by Professor Janusz Goscinski, University of Warsaw, August 1990. The new government of Poland might learn a lesson from Sweden where after decades in office, the Social Democratic Labor party was rejected by the voters. Yet, in a referendum indicating a preference between full employment and welfare, 95 percent of the voters cast their ballots in favor of full employment--an indication of the maiming effect mass unemployment can have.

9

INDUSTRY: PRIVATIZATION

A developed economy often has a dynamic and efficient industrial sector. But industry's contribution to the GNP is often secondary to the service sector. In 1989, 50.3 percent of Poland's GNP was derived from the industrial sector. Poland is industrialized, it is not developed. After successive centralized administrations, Poland's industry is neither dynamic nor efficient. Economic irrationality, inconsistency and discontinuity in industrial investment, has left its mark on the sector's performance. The new administrations of Tadeusz Mazowiecki and Jan Bielecki have resorted to drastic policy reversals in an attempt to right the wrongs.

Under the Communists, industrial activity was planned, centralized, and controlled. Since September 1989, the new government's basic policy has been decentralization, decontrol, government hands off, and you-are-on-your-own. Disconcerting is the fact that this change came overnight, with no preparation. Just as Poland has been reeling from the consequences of industrial policies of the centralized years, Poland of the future will be affected--contructively or otherwise--by the current wisdom toward industry. To provide a perspective on Poland's new industrial policy, this chapter first briefly outlines the Polish industry under Communism, then presents industrial productivity of the recent past and present. The causes of recent declines in industrial production will be analyzed. Thereafter, the much-heralded policy of privatizing state-owned enterprises will be discussed. And, finally, recommendations will be forwarded.

A REVIEW OF INDUSTRY IN POLAND

Industry Then

In the past, industrial enterprises were mostly state owned. Investments and production quotas were assigned by the Planning Commission. The factors of production were centrally allocated, with no regard to their relative scarcity or abundance. Outputs were sold to the quasi-governmental agency of central purchasing at state-determined prices. Government made all major decisions for management, and all decisions for the workers were made by management via directives from above.

Workers worked, not for the glorification of socialism but for lack of opportunity to be their own masters. In a capsule, work incentives were the same under communism as they had been earlier for those who worked under German and Russian occupation: management represented the master, while workers were subjects. Independent thinking was unnecessary; taking pride in what one did was immaterial. Any increases in labor productivity could be attributed primarily to sustained state investment, particularly in heavy industries. What was produced was distributed according to plan. The need for testing products in the marketplace was abrogated by centralism. Foreign trade took place mostly within the CMEA circle. Consumer welfare and consumer-goods production were sacrificed in favor of rapid industrialization for export. Every year, low income, a low standard of living, and low morale led to prolonged, widespread, and sometimes violent strikes.

Industry Now

With the Soviet Union loosening its grip on its satellites, the Communist-created "Workers' Paradise" was quickly replaced by the Solidarity-backed government. Although this was a 180-degree turn, the structure of industry was not so readily transformed. Deep surgery was inflicted on the industrial sector, with privatization of state-owned enterprises as the scalpel. While foreign governments and investors have been keeping close watch on developments in Poland, industrial workers in state-owned firms have acute anxiety about their future. The government has a general notion as to how privatization should proceed, but there is no clear idea what the end results might be. Foreboding and uncertainty face millions of workers: The past is gone. The present is difficult for most. The future is uncertain.

Recent Industrial Production

Changes in industrial production between 1970 and 1988 are shown for both socialized and private sectors in Table 9.1. Total production sales grew from 1970's 100 percent to 1980's 197.4 percent, but the growth from 1980 through 1988 was only 13.2 percent. That was due primarily to imposition of martial law in 1981 and labor unrest during the ensuing years. Although data for the socialized sector appear to be not far behind the total, growth in the private sector was speedier by far, especially for the post-martial-law

Table 9.1
Sales Production of Industry, 1980 and 1988 (1984 constant prices)

Specification	1980		1988		
	1970 = 100		1980=100	1987=100	percentage
per capita	180.5	193.1	107.0	104.7	---
Socialized Industry	197.8	220.5	111.6	104.9	100.0
fuel-power	161.4	172.2	106.7	100.2	13.7
metallurgical	196.7	179.3	91.2	102.0	8.8
electro-engineering	267.8	350.7	130.9	108.1	27.6
chemical	223.1	267.0	119.7	106.5	8.5
mineral	181.3	187.4	103.4	105.9	3.7
wood and paper	207.3	252.5	121.7	107.8	4.2
light	191.4	210.1	109.7	108.6	10.9
food	175.6	176.2	100.4	101.7	20.2
other branches	196.2	241.7	123.2	107.8	2.4

Source: Poland Statistical Data, 1989: 46.

period. The significant difference may be attributed to a loosening of state grip in private enterprise.

While the entire socialized industry experienced only a 13.2 percent growth between 1980 and 1989, the private sector grew by 224.3 percent. The minuscule difference in production sales between the socialized and the total for the nine-year period is indicative of the dominance by state-owned enterprises in the industrial sector. Data in the second row are evidence of the stagnant position of the socialized sector for the period.

The relative importance of respective industrial activity within the socialized sector can also be observed. More than one-fourth of industrial activities are concentrated in electro-engineering. This reveals the emphasis placed on this subsector, and the subsector's comparative advantage among CMEA members. If successfully privatized, this subsector could be reasonably competitive in Western markets as well. Data in columns 2 and 3 show that, other than the wood and paper industry, no category within the socialized sector comes close to electro-engineering. The food and light industries within the socialized sector had only a combined 32.5 out of the total. Consumer-oriented industries were not assigned their due importance under the socialized system. That explains why ration coupons--ranging from sugar to oil and meats--were necessary for allocating basic consumer goods, and why quality household appliances were difficult to obtain.

A more telling view of the relative strengths and weaknesses within the socialized sector of industry may be seen in Table 9.2. Row 1 shows that, for the decade of eighties, industrial production grew very rapidly in the electro-

Table 9.2
Net Industrial Production for 1980 and 1987 (in 1984 constant prices)

Industry	1970 = 100		1987	
	1980	1987	1980=100	1986=100
Socialized Industrial Enterprises & Establishments	186.6	188.5	99.4	102.9
Fuel-Power	121.1	74.5	61.5	96.4
Metallurgical	179.7	144.8	80.7	91.6
Electro-Engineering	286.0	384.0	134.2	106.8
Chemical Industry	232.9	314.2	134.9	104.7
Mineral Industry	168.3	150.3	89.4	100.8
Wood & Paper	180.9	223.8	123.7	103.6
Light Industry	178.8	196.1	109.7	103.8
Food Industry	115.8	87.1	75.2	102.3

Source: Poland Statistical Data, Warsaw, 1989: 47.

engineering and chemical industries, averaging 18.6 and 13.3 percent a year, respectively. More revealing is the production changes presented in rows 2, 3, and 4. Fuel-power and food declined from 1970's 100 to 1987's 74.5 and 87.1, respectively, while other socialized industries registered impressive to moderate gains.

Hard coal production in 1980 was 193 million tons. Seven years later, production was exactly the same--193 million tons. Hard coal and coke production, on the other hand, declined from 1980's 19.8 to 1988's 17.1 million tons. Natural gas production fell from 1980's 6,329 to 1988's 5,714 million cubic meters. And crude-petroleum processing decreased from 16,126 to 15,006 thousand tons for the same period. Socialized industrial enterprises as a whole saw a loss of .6 percent, from 1980's 100 to 1987's 99.4. While the average gains of the chemical and electro-engineering subsectors average gains were small, significant losses were registered in fuel-power, mineral, and food industries (Central Statistical Office, Warsaw, 1989: 48). The loss in food production during the period must be read with the understanding that beginning with 1980, consumer well-being had progressed from bad to worse.

In May 1989, industrial production decreased by 4.4 percent relative to that month a year ago (Warsaw Voice, 1989: 7-2). Industrial output kept falling. By September 1989, production in the industrial sector fell by 5.9 percent, as compared to the same month a year earlier. By January 1990, excluding the private sector, industrial production fell by 23.2 percent when compared to January 1989 (Warsaw Voice, 1990: 2, 18 and 3.11). Industrial production for the first six months of the year fell by 40 percent. Even advocates of a speedy economic transformation were disturbed by this sharp decline. And the prospect is that cumulative losses will not be regained for years to come.

CAUSES OF PRODUCTION DECLINE

Here, we attempt to identify some of the causes of this freefall in production. First, the decline in industrial production took place nearly exclusively in enterprises formerly under the centralized system. They had no need to compete for inputs or to vie for market share. Their products were not priced via the mechanism of the market place. Therefore, it was a seller's market. Producers could afford to employ scarce resources to produce whatever the plan had directed, since the outlet for their products would always be there. With introduction of the market system, 90 percent of these prices were deregulated almost overnight. Suddenly the state enterprises faced a buyer's market, and there was no guarantee that what was produced would be sold. Inputs for production now had a price tag, and resources became scarce. Sensible action called for an immediate reduction in production of goods not likely to find a ready market, thus production decreased.

Second, with the introduction of a free-market system, prices soared. For state enterprises, with a few exceptions free pricing was equated with arbitrary increases in prices. The price of a light tractor rose by 75 percent in a two-month period in early 1990, even though the new price reflected neither the marginal cost of production nor the marginal valuation placed on it by the consumer. Sales declined by 60 percent during this period, further accentuated by a rise in fuel prices by between 90 to 100 percent in the first two weeks of January 1990. In selected other industrial products, pit-coal prices increased by 700 percent, electrical energy by 300 percent, gas by 250 percent, rail and road transport services increased by an average of 200 percent, and telecommunication services climbed by 100 percent--all within the first two weeks of January 1990. And these price increases occurred in addition to the general rise in prices by 800 percent between December 1988 and December 1989 (Warsaw Voice, 1990: 1-14). With free-market pricing, demand decreased. With reduced demand, inventories accumulated and production in most state enterprises was reduced accordingly.

The private sector, on the other hand, was bursting with energy and vitality. Even with political turmoil in the early part of 1989, output from private industry increased by 30 percent in 1989 (World Economy Research, 1990: 17). Production in the private sector in the first quarter of 1990 did decrease by nearly 8 percent when compared to the same period in 1989, but was largely due to general cost increases beginning January 1, 1990. The reduction in output was an adjustment to changed cost conditions, as well as a reaction to the general decline in aggregate demand.

Third, the sentiment among the working class has been that since it was the people who brought about the change in the political system, the people should not suffer layoffs or plant closings. But with the new economic order introduced so abruptly, traditional job security evaporated. Since the Workers Council in a state enterprise has an active role in the decision-making process, enterprises instead raised prices so wages could be paid. They felt layoffs should be the last resort.

However, the idea of raising prices was based on the generally false assumption that demand for the products was inelastic. Instead, higher prices led to reduced demand. The level of output, therefore, needed to be reduced accordingly. When aggregated for the economy as a whole, production decreases became drastic. Meanwhile, a vicious cycle of price increase and production decrease took over, resulting in a deep recession by mid-1990, which the administration had not foreseen and was unprepared to cope with.

The fourth cause of rapidly declining industrial production was also related to free-market pricing. Product prices rose and demand fell. For state enterprises, particularly those in capital-intensive industries, a decrease in demand meant the accumulation of inventory and a subsequent decrease in production. Faced with asset fixity, enterprises produced less output at higher average fixed costs. Average total cost, or unit cost, correspondingly increased. This led to further price increases and increased prices further reduced demand. That, in turn, further heightened the average fixed cost, to boost average total costs yet higher. Ultimately, production fell and recession followed.

The fifth cause was the government's decision to raise coal prices quickly, bringing them in line with international prices. The objective was laudable, but the basic mechanism incorrect. Polish industry has always been heavily dependent on coal. Formerly, coal production was state planned, subsidized, and distributed. Coal prices were heavily subsidized to keep the machinery of industry going. When coal prices was permitted to rise abruptly, that invariably pushed up the cost of production for coal users. For instance, the coal, power, and steel industries combined normally consume 100 million tons of coal annually, which approximates 56 percent of domestic coal consumption. With a higher price for coal, all three industries had to correspondingly reduce coal consumption, and therefore less energy from coal was used to extract coal. Households and municipalities were forced to reduce power consumption, owing to price increases. Less power was generated, less coal was demanded by the power industry, so less coal was produced. The same sequence of events took place in the steel industry. The steel industry, as in other industries which depend on coal for energy, reduced production.[1]

Sixth, protests from miners, transport workers, and shipyard personnel over deteriorating economic conditions brought appeasement gestures from the government. Layoffs have not been taking place in the largest state enterprises or industrial bases so far. However, employees in smaller state plants have been less fortunate. The number of unemployed is on the rise, exceeding 1.2 million by the beginning of 1991. Accordingly, industrial output has decreased.

The seventh reason for the 40 percent decline in industrial production is the government's intent on balancing the budget. Investment retrenchment has been a deliberate policy to reduce the excessive and unwanted investments of past. The number of government investments in some of the still partly subsidized industries, such as coal and energy have been following a scheduled reduction. The resulting decrease in production therefrom is intended.

The eighth and final major cause may be attributed to low productivity in socialized industries. Low morale and few incentives are the rule. To reduce inflation, the government placed a ceiling on wage increases, effectively reducing incomes. There is no prospect of employees' regaining their lost purchasing power in the foreseeable future. The prevailing sentiment is to minimize effort, thus productivity fell.

All of these factors have, in one way or another, contributed to the unexpected large decrease in industrial production. Many large state enterprises should have gone bankrupt, but the spirit of solidarity exists and workers in these firms lend each other a hand. In time, widespread bankruptcies are inevitable, and when the inevitable does arrive, chaos will result. But for now, the industrial sector is reeling from the unexpected punch of a new free-market system. Remedies need to be sought, and workable approaches be identified. This will be discussed in chapters 13 and 14. For now, the intriguing question is how these ailing state enterprises have managed to survive this long.

The Perplexing Question: Why Not More Bankruptcies?

The bankruptcy of state enterprises is reported in the media fairly frequently. But if state enterprise have been operating according to market practices, many more should have gone bankrupt some time ago. The reason they have survived is that legal ownership of these enterprises is still within the domain of the state, even though day-to-day operation is under the jurisdiction of enterprise directors and their respective workers councils. The state implements macroeconomic policies; the enterprises make micro adjustments. It is akin to a single-parent family with many children--the parent is preoccupied with issuing general directives but has minimal influence over each child's conduct. Each state enterprise is now on its own. Resources that once were allocated by the state now must be secured by the enterprise itself. Output that used to be purchased by the state now must be marketed by the enterprise. If essential resources cannot be secured, either for lack of financial resources or management resourcefulness, production ceases, and bankruptcy is declared. If there are no ready markets for the products, the enterprise folds. However, if a reasonable percentage of required resources can be obtained, and if a reasonable portion of the output is sold, then the enterprise remains open, even if there are financial losses for some time.

Continued survival of many such establishments can also be attributed to workers' solidarity and to the ingenious arrangements among workers. For example, under the centralized system, state enterprise A produces raw or extractive materials. The output from enterprise A was in great demand by a host of industries. When enterprise A was in financial difficulty, the state came to its rescue. Tax deferment and low interest loans were some of the rescue tools. If products from enterprise A were of crucial importance to fulfillment of the plan, debts to the state could be forgiven altogether. Under the new administration, if fewer buyers now demand A's output, its market shrinks and its revenue decreases. If profits decrease or disappear, replacing fixed assets or modernizing becomes a problem. Meanwhile, enterprise A now needs to market the product by itself. Some of the firms that need A's product--coal, for instance--are able to pay for it. Some others, however, are themselves in a financial bind. One of them, state enterprise B, negotiates the purchase of A's product for a price and pays enterprise A partly with cash and partly with a promissory note. Full payment will be made to A when and if B's products sell well. For enterprise A, there is at least sufficient income to pay for most of the production inputs, especially wages, and stays in operation.

Enterprise B employs A's product to produce one or more of its outputs. For instance, A's coal is used to produce B's steel. Enterprise B tries to market its product. Some products steel users make sell well, so they pay B cash. Some others, however, produce products that no longer sell well. One of these, for instance, is state enterprise C, which produces tractors. Company C negotiates and obtains a deferment plan for part of the payment due enterprise B. Part of the payment, however, is made with cash. Company B is at least able to pay its wages and keep operating. Company B is also able to pay part of its debt to A with part of the money from C. Enterprise B meanwhile still owes A part of its payment, because some of B's customers--such as C--cannot pay in full. Enterprises such as C still owe money to B because they cannot sell their products at prevailing market prices. But as long as C is able to sell enough to pay its workers, it remains open. C's inability to timely meet its obligation to B leads to renegotiation (Dietl interview, 1990).

Often enough, enterprises like B do not press their fellow state enterprises like C hard enough to honor their obligations. State enterprises belong neither to the directors nor the workers councils. Workers in other state enterprises are like themselves, suffering from job insecurity and reduced purchasing power. Solidarity. No one is hurt in such informal social-insurance schemes by not calling in debts. State enterprises A, B, and C remain afloat. But for how long can such practices continue? Not long. Plant closings will become more and more commonplace. Unemployment will rise to higher levels. And aggregate loss--to the individuals caught in the quagmire of a chaotic economic reality and to the Polish economy as a whole--is beyond measure. The quick-fix approach to marketization has induced shock. On most fronts, laissez-faire capsulizes the administration's industrial policy. Crudely translated, it means that if the enterprise cannot swim--and most of them have not been taught to--then it will drown.

For state enterprises with a chance to survive or even compete in the future, the thrust of government's policy is privatization. As perceived by most scholars and officials in Warsaw, the government has pinned its hope on successful transfer of ownership from the state to the private sector. The remainder of this chapter is a discussion of privatization. The law of privatization is first briefly discussed. Then, the process of privatization is presented. An analysis of the privatization policy follows thereafter, prognostic recommendations are outlined.

THE LAW TO PRIVATIZE STATE ENTERPRISES

The law to privatize state enterprises was passed on July 13, 1990, after having undergone numerous revisions.[2] The government acknowledges that economic policies could render the economy more efficient. But it also recognizes that such policies are no guarantee for overcoming the economic crisis or for achieving development objectives (Project of the Law, April 6, 1990: 35). The centralized planning system of the past is seen as inefficient, wasteful and passive, but this inefficiency cannot be eradicated unless a structural transformation takes place.

Structurally, the Polish economy is saddled with extensive socialized ownership as a means of production. State enterprises and establishments employ "70 percent of the work force--40 percent in agriculture, 85 percent in industry and 80 percent in trade. Shares of total sales of state-owned enterprises vary from 90 percent in industry, 60 percent in services, and 20 percent in agriculture" (Stupnicki, 1990: 75). Legally, such enterprises are still state owned, but the coordinating mechanism of centralized allocation and purchasing no longer exists. At the same time, a substitute coordinating mechanism in the marketplace does not yet function. The monopolistic structure of many state enterprises allows them to dominate their industry, and their operation detracts from the proper functioning of a free-market system.

Therefore, structural transformation of state enterprises is judged to be the cornerstone of the new economic order.

The law provides the legal foundation for transferring ownership of enterprise assets from the state to the workers, the public, or foreign interests. It delineates the framework wherein the following economic objectives are to be pursued: ownership transformation, increased efficiency through competitive forces in the market, demonopolization, and development of a financial market. The two main agents of ownership transformation are the Ministry of Finance and the National Treasury. In addition, the Bureau of the Plenipotentiary for Ownership Transformation was created to implement the law. The chief executor is the Agency for Ownership Transformation. Also, the Council of National Property was created for the National Treasury, and the chief functions of the council are to preside over the agency's initiatives in privatizing, to approve or disapprove the agency's selection of state enterprises to be privatized, to safeguard the public interest in the process, and to arbitrate differences that may arise between an enterprise and the agency.

THE SCOPE AND METHODS OF PRIVATIZATION

In theory, all state-owned enterprises are to be privatized over an unspecified period of time. The economic activities of these state enterprises range from manufacturing, construction, transport and trade to hotels and small retail shops.   Whether services such as health, education, and communication will also be privatized remains undecided.   Government officials for the most part have not projected much beyond the immediate future.   State farms have not been mentioned as targets for privatization, either, although some lawmakers believe that state farms are within the scope of the law (Sterniczuk interview, 1990).

One gray area is the cooperatives. By definition, they are not state owned, but in practice, cooperatives conduct economic activities much like the state enterprises. Thus, cooperatives in construction, farming, food purchasing and processing, food service, architectural design and law, printing, and flower shops could all be considered legal cooperatives, but they belong neither to the state nor to their respective members. In fact, they are owned by nobody. Some cooperatives like Hortex, a giant food-service chain, enjoyed extensive privileges during the Communist regime. They staked out territories and found market niches that could effectively protect them from serious competition now. Legally, such entities are not subject to privatization. Through legal maneuvering and clever reorganization, they could emerge as oligopolistic giants in their industry. The government, however, is too preoccupied with other issues to forestall such entrepreneurial maneuvering.

State enterprises to be privatized are roughly categorized into four groups.

First, there are small and medium-size economic units: retail outlets, repair shops and other service centers, grocery stores, and small industrial plants come under this category. Disposable assets such as farm machinery, transport vehicles, land parcels, and surplus industrial goods, together with these smaller economic units, are seen as quickly transferable from state to private ownership.

The second group are enterprises considered dispensable: either because of perennial inefficiency or if on the verge of bankruptcy. These enterprises will be permitted to declare or forced into bankruptcy without granting them a chance for reorganization. Many of such firms--textile factories and steel mills--are concentrated in the industrial cities of Lodz, Nowa Huta, and Warsaw.

The third category are enterprises that cannot function smoothly in a market system unless and until they are--at least in part--in the private sector. Such enterprises could survive in a centralized system because they were dependent on the central planning for all major decisions concerning investment, production, and distribution. In the market system, these firms are not capable of competing unless they adapt to market rules. These rules involve not only organizational changes but also operational matters such as responsibility and accountability, incentives, research and development, competitive purchasing of resources for production, organization of production processes, and of products produced. Privatizing these enterprises involves liquidation--either direct sale, in part or in total, or leasing to a third party.

The final group of enterprises includes firms whose ownership will change from state to private hands via common stock competitive bidding on an open capital market. Such enterprises are viable economically in relative terms, and in general should command a market for their stock when offered for ownership transformation.

THE PROCESS OF PRIVATIZATION

At the beginning of each fiscal year, the Parliament establishes the principal lines of privatization (The Law, July 13, 1990: 2-1). The determination takes into account the budget law and the year's budget. Which state enterprises, in which industrial or commercial branches, are to be privatized during the year is the task of the Agency for Ownership Transformation and the Council of National Property. The Council of Ministers and the Agency for Ownership Transformation have been authorized to identify state firms of vital importance to the Polish economy and therefore to be privatized. In general, the more efficient firms are privatized first, with the rationale that such firms can be rendered even more efficient and therefore more able to compete in a free-market situation. Success of these privatization efforts could then serve as demonstration for later ones (Lis interview, 1990). Given successful privatization of the more efficient firms, more players can be attracted to join and compete in the growing Polish marketplace.

The desired approach is that privatization be initiated by the enterprise's management and workers council. If there is the desire and agreement within a firm to go public, then the director and workers council can present a certified agreement to the Agency for Ownership Transformation, petitioning that their enterprise be among those to be privatized. The agency president can approve or deny the petition. The Council of National Property then puts its seal of approval on the agency president's decision.

Two scenarios may arise during this petitioning process. First, the agency may deny the petition. The reasons could be that it is of interest to the national economy that the firm remains state owned, or that the firm is in an economic and financial situation so that it does not serve any constructive purpose to have the property transformed. More plainly, the law implies that a state firm go bankrupt rather than have its equity shares sold to potential buyers.

The other scenario is for the agency president to agree to the petition. Approval of the petition leads to two possible approaches to transformation. First, the legal status of the firm is changed from state owned to a common-stock company. The shares are then offered to the general public. Second, the firm goes through liquidation, via either leasing or sale of the enterprise to the employees. Each of these approaches is briefly outlined below.

From State Owned to a Common Stock Company

The agency president first evaluates the firm's economic and financial status. He then determines the need, if any, of organizational, economic or technical changes. After consulting financial and other specialists, the president determines the value of the enterprise. The firm then becomes a *one-person partnership*, with the National Treasury as the sole shareholder, registered with the National Trade Registry as such. Stock in the company is offered to the employees and the general public two years after registration. Prior to the offering of shares, the agency president, on behalf of the National Treasury, may assume some of the debt of the new partnership. In such case, prior approval by the minister of finance is required. The intent of writing off part of a firm's debt is to render the shares more attractive to prospective buyers. The shares can be sold to three possible interest groups: foreign investors, the general public, and employees of the firm.

Foreign investors may purchase up to 10 percent of the total value of the shares. This applies to shares purchased by any legal entity either directly or indirectly controlled by foreign interests, in effect limiting participation by joint ventures or multinational corporations. Foreign investors, however, may exceed the 10 percent limit if approval is granted by the president of the Foreign Investment Agency. The paradox, as will be shown in Chapter 12, is that the Foreign Investment Law stipulates that--for either joint ventures with foreign interests or direct foreign investment--the minimum foreign investment is 20 percent of equity. In other words, to attract foreign investment, the Foreign Investment Law permits foreign interests to own up to 100 percent of a firm's equity. But in the Law for Ownership Transformation, the ceiling is a paltry 10 percent, even though permits may be secured to purchase shares beyond the 10 percent limit. It would seem that different signals are being given to foreign investors.[3]

As for shares offered to Polish nationals other than the firm's employees, the agency president may request from the minister of finance that the shares be paid in installments. The reason for this concession is that the law itself does not discern a difference between institutional investors and individual citizens. The former are likely to have the financial resources to purchase shares with cash and, at the same time, may write off the expense as an investment. Individual citizens, on the other hand, might not be able to purchase shares with cash. But even with an installment plan, it is questionable whether the majority of low-income citizens could afford to take advantage of this provision. If citizen participation is the intent of the law, which it appears to be, then alternative, more creative avenues may need to be explored. Offering shares to the public is itself simple. They are offered through the capital market, which is still in its nascent stage.

The thrid group to whom shares will be offered are the enterprise employees themselves. A not uncommon sentiment among employees is that they have been the ones who have contributed to the operation of the enterprise, and since they were exploited by the old system for decades, the plant rightfully belongs to them and they should be declared sole owners. The government and the general public, however, do not share this view. Not only were workers exploited under the former system, so were all other citizens. Besides, the low wages paid to the workers were supplemented by health care, free education for children, and subsidized prices for many consumer goods. The enterprise should now be answerable to society as a whole, in the form of shareholding. All who wish should have the opportunity to buy into the company. Privatization means the transformation of ownership to the public, with the concessionary provision that enterprise employees have preferential access to a given percentage of the shares. In light of this, 20 percent of equity shares may be set aside for that purpose.

The conditions for preferential sale of the 20 percent shares of the firm are as follows: (1) 20 percent is the limit; (2) the offer is valid for one year from the date shares are made public; (3) preference takes the form of a specified discount on the face value of the share, of bonus shares to employees who purchase more than a given number of shares, and of ability to pay in installments; and, (4) the total value of concessions made to employees may not exceed the combined payroll of the twelve-month period prior to registration of the enterprise. Under these guidelines, the workers council within the enterprise may specify the range of preference to be given to employees who intend to purchase shares. If employees wish to purchase above the 20 percent limit, then additional shares are bought on the open market, on the same basis as offered to the general public.

A final note regarding this approach to privatizing concerns a difference of opinion between the president of the agency and the enterprise's management and workers' council. According to the law, the Agency President may identify firms to be privatized on the basis of significant interest to the national economy. But the management and the Workers' Council of the enterprise may be opposed to this recommendation. If there is a conflict, the Council of Ministers is empowered to make the final decision.

Liquidation

A different form of privatization, liquidation is initiated by the president of the Agency for Ownership Transformation. The decision of the agency president to liquidate rather than to offer common stock is presented to the Council of Ministers. Before approval is given by the council, there must be consultation between the council and the company director, the workers council, and the various trade unions representing the company.

As in the coomon-stock approach, a partnership is created. A general meeting of employees is held, and the views of the various trade unions are expressed. At least two-thirds of all employees having the right to vote must take part at the meeting, and at least two-thirds of the employees present must declare their intent to buy into the partnership. They pledge payment for their declared share of the enterprise holdings. Then it is determined how many capital shares will be offered for sale to the employees, and how many will be held by the state's representative agency. This determination is made on the basis of voting by the firm's employees. There could be exceptions, but as a rule, at least 20 percent of the shares must be offered to the enterprise employees. The decision then leads to registration of the partnership by the newly formed Board of Supervisors.

The remaining issue is payment for the shares allocated to the employees. For the initial 20 percent, the payment "must equal at least an average month's salary as calculated from the twelve months before the voting takes place" (Project of the Law, April 6, 1990: 20). But for shares beyond the 20 percent, then at least half the employees in the partnership must declare their intent to purchase the additional shares. Payment for these shares should equal at least three months' average salary, as calculated on the basis of the last twelve months before the voting takes place (Project of the Law, April 6, 1990: 21).[4]

To assist employees in purchasing shares, a special Foundation for employee properties is to be established. The foundation's board is made up of three members representing the employees, one representing the National Treasury, another nominated by the District Court, and a representative from the bank working with the foundation. The foundation owns the employees' portion of the partnership. It, in turn, owes the National Treasury the value of the employee shares minus the payments made. And the debt to the National Treasury can be paid off through instruments such as bank credits, employee share of enterprise profits, bond issues, dividends, and foreign investment. When the debts to the National Treasury are paid off, the workers' shares are transferred from the foundation to the participating employees. For the enterprise share purchased by the employees, the process of ownership transformation via liquidation is complete.

A note on the payment by citizens participating in the ownership transformation is in order. Two funds are in the process of being established. One is the National Capital Fund, which is a one-person partnership representing the National Treasury. It receives the shares of a state enterprise on behalf of the National Treasury, then sells the shares, bonds, and other legal papers pertinent to the privatization program. At least one-fifth of the fund's annual income is assigned for the functioning of the second fund, the Fund for Citizens' Shareholding. The basis for the second fund is to promote citizen participation. With income from the state budget, from the National Capital Fund, and from contributions made by private or legal persons, the Fund for Citizens' Shareholding finances transactions in the market through loans. The buyer of shares is given certificates to the shares; the shares, however, are kept by the fund until the loans are paid.

To recapitulate, the ownership transformation program is aimed at privatization of state-owned enterprises. The de facto administrators of the program are the Agency for Ownership Transformation and the Council of National Property. Employees of a firm to be privatized receive preference for no more than 20 percent of the shares. The balance are sold through the capital market. To encourage public participation, the National Capital Fund and the Fund for Citizens' Shareholding are being created. And in the case of privatization through liquidation, employees of the enterprise may purchase 20 percent or more of the shares. The Foundation for Employees Properties is being created to assist in the financing of shares designated by and for the employees. The law also provides that the state's representative agency can simply transfer the shares to a local government; the latter can then select and initiate the privatization approach as deemed appropriate.

The other two forms of privatization are bankruptcy and direct sale of small or medium-size state enterprises. No elaboration on them is needed.

OBSERVATIONS

As of 1989, 85.33 percent of all employees in the industrial sector worked in state-owned enterprises. Manufacturing and mining accounted for 71.0 and 11.7 percent, respectively. Nearly 65 percent of these enterprises employ more than 1,000 workers. More than 100 of these firms have 5,000 or more employees (Central Statistical Office, 1990: 50). The tasks that lay ahead for the agency are not simple. Wisely enough, no timetable was set for completion of ownership transformation. It was also wise to annually establish principal lines of privatization rather than mandate a given percentage of the combined asset value of state enterprises that must be transferred. The principal lines of privatization are likely to be a function of the economy's need for demonopolization, of budgetary considerations, and of how smooth or difficult the process of ownership transformation will be.

There are nearly 7,000 socialized industrial enterprises in Poland. The general guidelines for transformation have been provided by the law, but the relevant question is where to start. Is the program to rely more on initiatives from enterprise directors and workers councils, or is the agency to actively assume the initiative? If the latter, how much weight will economic considerations carry and how much would political? Few people in the administration have knowledge and experience in privatizing state-owned enterprises. Fewer yet have a master plan. Yet marketization of the economy hinges on the success of ownership transformation.

The following hurdles await the administrators. First, with increased unemployment, workers on average are apprehensive about being laid off. Efficiency will be one of the major concerns of privatized enterprises. Efficiency means increased productivity; it also means minimization of the costs of production, which include labor. Layoffs--not a practice in the centralized system--will become a way of life for many. Therefore, the workers councils and trade unions whose opinions and approval of privatization are given consideration, may resist the move by the agency to privatize their firm.

Second, Poland does not have a network of financial and management consulting firms to provide the essential information to the agency on an enterprise's state of health. The agency president's decision to privatize an enterprise ought to be based, at least in part, on such a report. Developing a network of consulting firms takes time. Contracting with foreign firms for these services requires hard currency, which the state is short of. Third, shares for capital privatizing need to course through a stock market. It is far from being well established. The privatization program may be initiated, but it should not be hurriedly pursued because it depends on a healthy, functioning stock market.

Fourth, an efficient communication system is necessary for the smooth functioning of a stock market. Poland is in need of such a system, yet it is in only its initial stage of being developed. Fifth, once equity shares go public, publication of annual balance sheets is necessary, yet the present accounting system in Poland differs measurably from that of mainstream economies. Training qualified accountants takes time. Meanwhile, foreign investors cannot accurately gauge the potential worth of enterprises to be privatized. Buying into such firms thus becomes less attractive, and the potential for foreign money cannot be fully realized.

Sixth, in a free market, share value is a reflection of supply and demand. Presently, there are not sufficient private savings or great enough earning power for citizens as a whole to enter the market, a situation which may soften the demand for shares, making them undervalued. On the other hand, if foreign interests are permitted to purchase controlling shares at rock-bottom prices, the best interests of the Polish economy are not served.

Seventh, the likelihood of mass participation in ownership transformation is remote for psychological reasons. The general public is not accustomed to making business decisions or assuming risks. The idea of reaping a profit or taking a loss on an investment is alien to them. Citizen shareholding is an idea that will take time to become a reality.

Eighth, the real income of average consumers has been reduced severely since late 1989. It will be years before pre-inflation purchasing power is restored. And it will be still longer before consumers can accumulate the savings required to finance share purchases through the Fund for Citizens' Shareholding. The small, wealthier segment of society will benefit immeasurably from purchasing or trading shares, however, and income differences will widen. This could be problematic, especially if the people with money are also former government officials. No longer political overlords, they could conceivably become economic masters.

And, ninth, in economies with developed capital markets, privatization of enterprises has proved more costly and more difficult than anticipated. Privatizing British Airways and Canadian Airways are two examples. In Poland, only the theoretical and desirable aspects of privatization have been articulated; little attention has been paid to the likely obstacles inherent in the process. Not anticipating such stumbling blocks can mean disappointment, failure, and erosion of public confidence later on. The intent of the law is to enhance economic efficiency, to promote a spirit of competition, to capitalize on the profit motive of the masses, to permit the maturing of a free-market system, and to promote economic development for the well-being of consumers. All these objectives are attainable in the long run, and transforming property ownership is an instrument. But active participation of the citizenry is imperative.

RECOMMENDATIONS

Privatization of small enterprises and disposing of surplus public assets are relatively simple. But the horizon needs to be extended so *all* unnecessary properties held by the state are disposed of. This includes the sale of apartments and other rental housing units, public land, and some public buildings. Selling state-owned apartments and other housing units promotes private ownership via thrift and a willingness to defer consumption. The sense of ownership, of possession, of wanting more is a catalyst to stimulate productive incentives on a mass scale. It incubates the spirit of capitalism, even if on a small scale, because there is mass participation.

Privatization through bankruptcy appears straightforward. The process may reduce the state's budget burden, especially if such enterprises were still receiving subsidies. But the government must take into account the subsequent social cost resulting from widespread bankruptcies. Dissatisfaction, frustration, low self-esteem, a sense of hopelessness may corrode the nascent spirit of the new economic order. Therefore, salvageable enterprises should have the privilege of making the decision regarding bankruptcy. It is a way of inculcating responsibility for one's decision. And the decision could instead be drastic reorganization or reorientation of the enterprise. It could be self-imposed wage cuts. It could be a reduction in the labor force. It could also be a host of austerity programs to cut costs and eliminate waste. Layoffs will occur, but the number laid off is minimized, while those remaining can be somewhat more productive than if unemployed. Also, the process of eliminating less competitive firms would be more gradual. Meanwhile, reeducation programs can be developed, and the emphasis would be on the value of workers as persons rather than as items on a balance sheet.

Privatization through liquidation is in essence ownership transformation from state to company employees. Whatever shares not designated for employee purchase will eventually find their way to the capital market. Liquidation involves participation by the employees. It gives them the right to determine the proportion of equity shares set aside and it assists them in financing the purchase. It is more than ownership transformation; it is schooling, since the shares not designated to be bought by the employees are held in trust by the agency for five years. Ownership transformation through liquidation is not going to overburden the service of the nascent capital market. It is ideal. The one recommendation for liquidization, however, is to permit an adjustable mechanism, amended into the law, to apply to shares to be purchased by the employees. For instance, if the proporation of initial shares that two-thirds or more of the employees wish to purchase is 50 percent, then the balance would be sold to the public five years later. But in the meantime, if worker management improves efficiency, employees may want a greater share of the firm. If the workers wish to increase the number of designated shares, then any time prior to going public, the employees should be permitted to increase their proportion to a new level, with the benefits of service from the fund. It is a mechanism to induce hard work, self-determination, and a sense of ownership. This adjustable mechanism may also induce employees who, at the beginning, were either unwilling or financially unable to participate to also take part in the buyout program. It is worker-citizen participation, the basis on which to develop a growing middle class.

Privatization through capital shares applies to all major state enterprises not being liquidated or declared bankrupt. The outcome of this approach, to a large extent, determines the success or failure of ownership transformation as a whole and therefore affects the future performance of the industrial sector.

There are an estimated 7,000 large state-owned enterprises in Poland. In early 1989, 1,020 firms employed a thousand or more workers each. The largest firms, such as the giant tractor producer Ursus, employ over 20,000 employees each. For a multinational corporation, this is not large, but for state enterprise producing domestic goods in a country of the size of Poland this is large, indeed. Many of them are monopolies, awaiting privatization.

One of the objectives of the law is to demonopolize state enterprises and promote competition. But the law does not specify how the demonopolization is to be accomplished. Even if the transformation is successful, the end product is still a giant corporation. If the enterprise has been enjoying monopoly power, it will continue to do so. The operation presumably will be more efficient, more productive and more profitable. Unlike before, accountability to shareholders means stress on profitability. The higher the profit, the more successful the corporation is. Therefore, organizational changes, factor efficiency, cost reduction, price gauging, and setting up entry barriers will be relentlessly pursued. The privatized firm may charge higher prices as a result. Before, at least, there was ceiling on the firm's prices--the centralized command system saw to that. In a free-market economy, even with the equivalent of an antitrust law, the Polish government is not equipped to deal with extensive monopolistic practices. Consumers may be worse off after privatization. Expressed bluntly, when it comes to pricing, it may be better to trust a state-owned monopoly than a privatized one. To ensure that the intent of privatization is fulfilled, large enterprises need to be demonopolized before their stocks go on sale to the public.[5]

To demonopolize these firms, they must be split into smaller units, depending on the nature of the industry and the economic feasibility of such action. There are two methods to demonopolize--vertical and horizontal.

Vertical Decomposition

Theoretically, it is feasible to break each of the major components of a large organization into independent economic activities and therefore into smaller corporations. For instance, within the companies of the Polish Fiat or the tractor manufacturer Ursus, there is a chain of economic activities, from designing, casting, and molding, to parts manufacturing and body stamping, to assembling, shipping, and sales.

However, this approach does not resolve the problem of monopoly. Depending on the nature of the industry, it may accentuate it. In other words, if there is no effective competition for auto designs, the smaller independent auto design firm may still enjoy a monopoly. And because of its previous affiliation with the giant enterprise, it may make deals to discourage competition.   Conceivably, each of new smaller companies could enjoy noncompetitive power, thus cumulatively, the prices for their respective products or services could be even higher than they used to be. This will lead to even higher prices for the end product than if the giant enterprise remained as a legal entity. The heightened cost of a monopolistic chain would be passed along to the consumers, especially when demand for the product is inelastic.

If the foreign competition should become a threat, then the monopolistic chain could put political pressure on the government for protection. It has happened in developed economies, and it can happen in Poland, where workers have considerable political influence.   Vertical decomposition, therefore, may be desirable only to the extent that some horizontal reorganization also occurs. These reorganized companies can then help ease the pressure for cumulative price increases by forward-linked units.

Horizontal Reorganization

The horizontal breakup of a monopoly or potentially monopolistic power needs to be as thorough as realistically feasible. Orbis, the Polish state-owned tourism bureau, for instance, could readily be reorganized into smaller separate travel agencies, the overseas operation remaining as a single unit for economies of scale. To survive, the independents will be forced to be more efficient, more competitive, and more cost conscious. Productivity relative to the industry becomes the basis for judging performance. Motivation, active participation by the work force, improved management skills, and ingenious marketing techniques could be tangible fruits of demonopolization.

Demonopolization ultimately will be more beneficial to the development of a free market than ownership transformation. The ownership of means of production is less crucial to a successful market economy than an increase in competition. Multinational corporations may have oligopolistic or monopolistic power in their own market, yet they are obliged to compete for the consumers' dollar. A free market offers selections and substition, and the dollar can be spent in many ways. It is the market system's strength (Goscinski interview, 1990).

Another recommendation concerning ownership transformation through capital shares is that it begin cautiously and slowly. Well-planned, well-executed privatization of a few large firms is essential to assure the success of future transformations.[6] Selection of the first firms to be privatized should be based on more than just internal efficiency or relative importance to the economy. Those firms that possess the greatest potential to create external economies through ownership transformation should be privatized first. The number selected should be small, so that the task is easily managed by the newly created agency, the council and the Funds. Two legimate questions are: How long will the process take? What happens to the remaining state enterprises between now and then? The answer to the first question is that it will take fewer years than if the administration plunges headlong into transformation activities, stumbles, and falls flat on its face. The answer to the second question is that they should capitalize on the experiences of these who go first.

For example, development of support system for a new capital market will take time. The process is essential and cannot be hastened, and hasty attempts can lead to inefficiency, loss, and chaos. On the other hand, as the capital market becomes operational, the transformation process can begin, with shares traded. With only a small number of firms privatized at the beginning, trading will be manageable. Experience will be accumulated, and weaknesses in the system can be corrected along the way.

The thousands of enterprises waiting to be privatized need not and cannot afford to wait passively; they must condition themselves for privatization. The inducement is economic--20 percent of their shares will be purchased on a preferential basis. Employees need to work for the promise of owning more, through increased profit and profit-sharing. A reasonably long period of a high profit-sharing ratio, if granted, is akin to leasing the enterprise from the state at reduced rent. If needed, tax deferments or reductions can be offered, but no direct subsidy. It is better for government to receive deferred or lowered tax revenues than to have the firms assume a wait-and-see attitude and eventually go bankrupt. With carefully packaged inducement offers, employees will take the initiative and demand reorganization to reduce costs and increase efficiency. The opportunity cost of mismanagement or misallocation of resources is high. Idle resources, waste, lost opportunities--including credit extended to fellow enterprises--will no longer be accepted or tolerated. The fat needs be trimmed; monitoring of work attitude and productivity will be built into the work environment. Thus employees have the choice to either work for profit or to fall behind the competition.

Meantime, the capital market can become more functional and better developed. More shares can then be traded *pari passu* with improved productive activity by enterprises. More state firms will be prepared for privatization, and fewer mistakes need be made, with fewer crisis situations faced by the administration. Cumulative experience and hindsight also help pave the way for smoother future ownership transformations.

By leasing state-owned enterprises to employees, the government exacts only a nominal share of the profits at the beginning, meaning fewer bankruptcies. The future success of Poland's industries will, to a measurable degree, be a function of how successful privatization is implemented.

NOTES

1. Though domestic demand for coal has always been inelastic, there was an inventory of 330 million tons of coal by July 1990, waiting to be sold. Large inventories owing to weak demand has meant further curtailment of coal production.

2. The legal information in this section is based on *The Project for the Law of Ownership Transformation*, April 6, 1990, and *The Privatization Law*, July 13, 1990.

3. During an interview with Krzysztof Lis, Minister for Privatization, this apparent paradox was pointed out.

4. The article does not specify what the payments are for--final or down payments--but it is reasonable to deduce that the law intends the down payment. The value of additional shares of a capital-intensive enterprise could easily exceed the combined salaries of employees for three months.

5. A perusal of the *Project for Demonopolization Law*, December 5, 1989, Warsaw, will convince readers that the final version of the law will be suffused with generalities, out of necessity.

6. In 1990, seven state-owned firms signed the documents in order to be transformed into single-person state treasury companies: Exbud Kielce, Warszawa Metal Rolling Mill, Silesian Cable Factory, Krosno Glassworks, Jeleniogorska Paper Machines Factory, Lodz Prochnik Clothing Factory, and Inowroclaw Meat Factory (Warsaw Voice, 1990: 10-7). During the 1990 presidential campaign, Lech Walesa used this slow pace of privatization as an issue. The hope is that it was simply campaign rhetoric, nothing more.

10

AGRICULTURE

The agricultural sector in Poland is unique.[1] Poland was the only nation among COMECON members whose government was unable to collectivize its farmers. State farms were established, but they constituted only 17 percent of land under cultivation and only 20 percent of the agricultural labor force. State farm workers were accorded the status of state employees, with comprehensive social welfare benefits. Special concessions were granted to state-owned farms through the supply of essential but scarce inputs, subsidized factor costs, and lower taxes. Yet despite these economic incentives, an overwhelming majority of farmers elected to be independent. They preferred owning land to losing independence, and their defiance of collectivization was indicative of the farm sector's political resilience.

The average farm in Poland is only five hectares. Therefore, economies of scale are difficult to achieve. "There is the problem of size of farms. They are very small. It happens quite often that one farmer has his farm divided into separate plots" (Bylinski interview, 1990). This is the result of land inheritance practices in Poland. Plots divided among surviving children, plus land inherited from an aunt or an uncle here and there, add up the average farmer's small holding.

Communist administrators found it problematic to resolve the farm problems then. Attempts to commercialize small-scale farming now pose an even greater challenge.

But given both the size of the agricultural labor force and its potential contribution to the economy, development of the Polish agricultural sector is a *conditio sine qua non* for successful reform. Development entails the growth of all important segments of the economy--all major sectors are interrelated and interdependent. To ensure successful privatization, industrial restructuring, price stability, and attainment of long-term development objectives, an effective and sound agricultural policy is indispensable.

A healthy industrial base, established in accordance with sound economic principles and time-proven economic relationships--certainly in the

Polish setting--requires a dynamic and efficient agricultural sector. Economic reform and restructuring needs to consider the efficient coordination of rural and urban, farm and nonfarm. Focusing on one sector to the neglect of others runs the risk of repeating the mistakes of past administrations.

The reform measures concerning agriculture included subsidy withdrawal, free-market pricing for both production factors and market products, and establishment of a reserve stock.

On 22 December 1989, the Parliament approved--with some amendments--government guidelines on agricultural policy. These envisage *inter alia* the establishment of an Agricultural Market Agency. Purchases and sales of agricultural products at market prices and a buffer stock policy are to constitute the principal instruments of central intervention in this sector. Minimum or guaranteed prices would no longer be established. (United Nations, 1990: 2241-42)

RECENT CONDITIONS

Distribution and Production

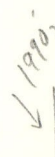

As a preliminary note, there is a distribution network for farm products. The farm purchasing and processing industries are in the hands of the so-called cooperatives. Both industries are de facto agencies of the Communist era. Under the new administration, all enterprises are autonomous and these cooperatives have become cooperative *monopolies*, or cartels. Legally, they cannot be privatized; they are cooperatives, not state-owned enterprises. Now that they are free of government control, they procure farm products at stable prices while selling their produce to outlets via free-market pricing. Meanwhile, prices for tractors, chemical fertilizers, equipment rental and other yield-increasing factors of production--mostly produced or provided for by monopolistic state enterprises or cooperatives--have risen severalfold. With stable output prices but hyperinflated factor costs, farmers are caught between a rock and a hard place. For most of the farm producers, there are no other channels of distribution. There is greater exploitation of the farmers, but now the exploitation is by nongovernment-controlled cooperatives. Negative reaction to the guidelines were immediate, not only from farm producers but also from the academic circle. The concern was that farmers were not prepared for those drastic policy changes, and food prices would soon be out of reach for many consumers. This concern was quickly justified by the subsequent unfolding of events.

Annual grain production in Poland is approximately 25 million tons. Grain storage capacity, owned by the purchasing cooperatives, is 5.5 million tons. The problem for farmers became apparent in late 1989 and early 1990. Owing to hyperinflation, farmers collectively held back the sale of grain for fear that payment received would be of little value in the months ahead. The government, in an attempt to stem inflation, suggested the grain loan program. The program would take the hoarded grain off the hands of farmers, and the government would pay for the grain six months hence. Unfortunately, things did not work as planned.

But information about the grain load was very poor. So the farmers did not quite understand what it was all about. Also, if the government had told the farmers that the grain price was to be determined, they would sell. But the government did not. (Bylinski interview, 1990)

Farmers were not interested in the proposal, and the grain was lost to mold, insects, and pests.

To curb inflation, particularly skyrocketing food prices, the government turned to the West for assistance. The assistance arrived, including a grain shipment of 22.5 million tons. The farmers were once again caught in a no-win situation. By the summer of 1990, they needed cash to pay taxes and rent equipment for harvesting. But the rental costs set by the cooperatives had by then doubled in a six-month period.

The problem now was that the farmers desperately needed to sell last year's (1989's) grain. But there is only one monopolistic company that buys the grain from them. Since the government had received a grain shipment from abroad, the purchasing company depressed the prices so low that the farmers would not be able to purchase anything with the proceeds. (Bylinski interview, 1990)

The farmer's reinvestment ability was curtailed, and the prospect of fuller and speedier participation in marketization was nipped in the bud. Both farm producers and consumers were caught in the grip of a Communist relic-- the cooperative monopolies.

Grain production fell by 41.69 percent between January 1989 and January 1990. With the new economic order, demand for farm machinery and yield-increasing inputs fell correspondingly in 1990. Food prices remained high. Consumers, like the producers, were subjected to extreme hardship as a result.

The farmers asked for preferential credits and tax relief. They sought guaranteed minimum prices for their products in place of free-market pricing. But their cry found little sympathy from the government. In July 1990, they took to the streets, blocked thoroughfares with tractors, and occupied the Finance Ministry building. In response, the government passed a new law creating the Agricultural Market Agency.[2] The farmers have also been accorded the privilege of purchasing up to 20 percent of equity shares in farm-related, state-owned industrial enterprises on a preferential basis--that is, when such enterprises eventually get privatized. In addition, a small subsidy was restored to dairy farms. The government response to the farmers has been compared to spreading a patty of butter on an entire loaf of bread. The farmers have suffered greatly.

Needs

Umbrella legislation and broad administrative measures are needed to create an atmosphere conducive to increased agricultural productivity. Laws need to aim at activating and enhancing the farmers' innate entrepreneurial spirit. However, both private and public financial resources are limited, and no extensive investment in the farm sector is likely in the foreseeable future. Instead, there has to be better utilization of existing factors, pricing incentives, preferential tax measures, efficient government services, demonopolizing of the cooperatives, genuine and spontaneous cooperative efforts by independent farmers in producing, harvesting, purchasing, and marketing their produce. The government needs to be the catalyst. But so far, Polish farmers have no effective means to respond to the new economic order.

A NEW FARM POLICY

To meaningfully marketize agriculture in Poland, farmers need equitable influence over the supplies and prices for the means of their production as well as genuinely competitive marketing practices. So far, farmers' fears and concerns have been well founded. "The real problem lies in the fact that everything concerning agriculture--beginning with fertilizer, equipment, and so forth--is monopolized." (Bylinski interview, 1990) But politicians have been preoccupied with politics, and the farmers' plight reflects the lack of a constructive and effective farm policy. Just as it was under the centralized system, the farm sector is being neglected. The following is a discussion of needed actions.

Economic Rationale

Increased agricultural productivity and production means more than stable prices for food and industrial raw materials. It also means increased income and purchasing power for the farm sector. Farmers would then be able to increase their savings for reinvestment. Further increases in farm productivity, income, and purchasing power can also provide increased demand for nonfarm products, and increased demand for nonfarm products creates nonfarm jobs. More of the unemployed and underemployed in industrial centers can find gainful employment, and the disguised unemployed farm labor can more successfully migrate to cities for more productive activities. Throughout this orderly process of structural transformation, productivity as a whole would witness steadier and more sustained increases. The revenue base would widen as well as deepen, so that fiscal and monetary policies could be more effective in manipulating the economy. Increased government revenue would also grant an enhanced ability to initiate new programs.

This much-simplified growth scenario for Poland is not mere theory. It has proved correct in developed economies. It is workable in Poland, particularly because a relatively high percentage of the labor force is still engaged in agriculture. But since the demise of the centralized system, the focus of the legislature and the administration has been on stabilizing prices, on attracting foreign investment and joint ventures, on balancing the budget, on privatizing of state enterprises, and on rescheduling the foreign debt. Unless more attention is focused on the farm sector, a high economic price will have to be paid by the Polish people for years to come.

Avenues of Potential

This section does not imply that little is being done, using the ideas mentioned here. Rather, it is to emphasize that, for sound economic reasons, much more can and needs to be done to energize the agricultural sector.

First, with liberalization of the economy and democratization of the political system, Poland can seek extensive external assistance to develop its agriculture. Agricultural engineers, extension specialists, agricultural economists, farm financial experts, and forestry management and maintenance teams are some personnel resources that the Ministry of Agriculture can draw on from both the Food and Agriculture Organizations of the United Nations and academic institutions in the West. Each fresh idea, each studied recommendation, can be translated into a wealth of returns, economic as well as social.

Second, state farms have been less efficient when compared to private independents (Central Statistical Office, 1990: 53). The land holdings of the socialized farming sector still accounted for 23.8 percent of the total in 1989. Privatizing state enterprises, primarily industrial complexes, has been high on the government's agenda. But discussion of privatization of state farms needs to be addressed as well. So far, no such discussion has taken place.

Following the land-to-tiller principle, agricultural land holdings of the socialized sector can be transferred to the employees for more efficient use. The land can be sold. Or the state may exact rent from purchasers, decreasing annually as a fixed percentage of its equity. And this percentage can be levied in such a way that prospective purchasers still have enough money left for investment. Procedures need to be mapped out, and the flexible parameters within which local administrators can implement the program need to be determined, but one of the results will be greater competitiveness within the agricultural sector. It is an inexpensive approach to promoting a more effective, market-oriented farm industry.

Third, instead of only producing staples for domestic consumption, farmers need to explore foreign markets for higher-valued, higher-priced products,--especially those for which Poland has competitive advantage. As an example, garlic was exported:

Even though it [garlic] was sold for very little money [abroad] because the prices had dropped, what the farmers could receive there was still more than what they could get in Poland. In [former] West Germany, for one kilogram of garlic the farmers there could get 1 mark 92 pfennigs.[3] But there are still people in Poland who are willing to export garlic for the price of 32 pfennigs per kilo. Even with the current foreign exchange ratios, the 32-pfennig price is better than they could get in Poland. (Bylinski interview, 1990)

Timely market information, therefore, can help Polish farmers keep abreast of domestic and foreign demands, with an appropriate product mix to their benefit. Information regarding production supplies and their prices also needs to be efficiently gathered and disseminated. Speedy investment and adjustments in production in light of market conditions may help minimize costs and maximize returns.

Fourth, traditional family farming is not the most efficient use of land, labor, or capital. Prior to World War II, to compensate for such limitations, there were fairly extensive cooperative efforts on the part of independent farmers. Retreating from the threat of collectivization, these voluntary cooperatives dissolved. The government needs to encourage the reappearance of these cooperative efforts. Depending on local needs and conditions, cooperative efforts could be made in the areas of procurement, equipment rental, production, processing, transport, and marketing. Economies of scale can lead to reduced costs, increased efficiency, lower prices, and enhanced income. The government needs to design an incentive program that will promote such cooperative endeavors.

Fifth, the number of educators and specialists in farm-related disciplines need to be increased, qualitatively and quantitatively. Academic exchange programs between Poland's agricultural institutions of higher education and their counterparts abroad can be initiated or expanded. Since these operate on the basis of exchange, they are cost-effective. Research programs in crop science, agricultural finance, economics, and marketing can be a natural by-product of such programs. On another front, extension specialists need to upgrade their skills to provide a vital link between theory and practice.

Sixth, animal husbandry is another area with potential. The absence of meat shortages is not due to abundant supply but to increased prices. Lacking financial resources for feedlot poultry production or imported fishmeal for cattle, farmers can still increase meat production practically and feasibly. For example, the Polish farmer can readily raise more chickens and hogs in his backyard. Both require modest initial investment and minimal operating cost. Tax incentives and easy-term credit are inexpensive programs the government can initiate. In whatever form, actualizing the productive potential in this subsector can lead to better utilization of farm labor on farms and increased employment opportunities in the meat-processing, freezing, packaging, transport, and distribution subsectors.

The seventh and final frontier that policymakers should explore is the fishery industry. Polish consumers have a preference for fish, yet average restaurants do not even have fish on their menus and shellfish is nonexistent in the market. Poland is not as well endowed with lakes and waterways as the United States or Canada, but it does have its fair share. Expanding the culture and seeding of fish stocks is inexpensive, yielding increased production as well as more job opportunities. Commercial fishing in international waters, the building of fishing fleets for which Poland is well known, and the commercial processing, freezing, packaging, and marketing of seafood can all be vastly expanded. Japan and Taiwan are such success stories in this respect that they now find themselves experiencing a labor shortage and increased demand for seafood imports. Poland should realize the potential of this expanding demand and enter world competition.

International financial institutions such as the World Bank, the Paris Club, and regional development banks could be approached with specific proposals to expand Poland's fishery industry. Canning corporations in developed economies may also be potential financers for the expansion. The pivotal step is government's planning, implementation, and coordination of a fishery policy.

These are promising concepts the administration may explore. They represent opportunities. Needed are knowledgeable and dedicated individuals to plan, organize, and seek external assistance--both technical and financial. These individuals need to motivate, to espouse flexible fiscal and monetary policies beneficial to agricultural development, and to provide leadership. Government's role is to identify a few such individuals to serve as catalysts.

Selected Desiderata

First, there needs to be an improved system of secondary or tertiary feeder roads, linking small villages or mountainous regions to large towns.

Purchasing cooperatives have access to relatively remote regions, using trucks or mechanized vehicles. But local farmers mostly have only horse-drawn carts. If rural feeder roads are improved, farmers will have a better chance of delivering their products themselves, without having to use purchasing agencies or monopolistic suppliers. Production costs, as well as prices, can be reduced as a result. An improved transport system also facilitates the flow of labor, innovative ideas, and useful information. Visits to remote villages by extension personnel, credit agents, small commercial traders, and other government agents can increase with construction or improvement of feeder roads.

Rural progress is propelled by ideas, and ideas are prompted with the prospect of financial gain. Financial gains are achieved when small farmers are given opportunities. In mountainous regions to the south and in isolated regions to the east, ideas and incentives may come through radio or printed literature, they are not attainable, for lack of adequate roads and transport facilities. Indirect as an improved rural transport system might appear to marketization, it is a crucial link in developing a more efficient distribution system in rural Poland.

Second, institutional farm credit should be more available and accessible to family farms. The need is more urgent now that there's a free market for farm supplies and equipment. Many of Poland's small farms are financially unable to purchase yield-increasing elements. With the liberalization of the banking system, however, banks are interested in high profits. Food processing and food distribution are of interest to banks, but food production is low on their priority list. "At the beginning of this year [1990], the rate of interest charged farm borrowers was 40 percent. That adversely affected the most efficient small farmers" (Bylinski interview, 1990). If there is not adequate investment at the grassroots level, there can be no gains in productivity and production. Both producers and consumers lose. Conversely, if institutional farm credit is made more readily available, seeds of high-yielding varieties, pesticides, chemical fertilizers, and basic farm implements can be secured via short-term investments. Thereafter, medium-term loans for more ambitious endeavors--livestock or land improvement projects, among others--will be sought. When the merits of investments with institutional farm credit are demonstrated, and when confidence in their usefulness builds more enterprising farmers will try using long-term loans for land consolidation and for cooperative efforts in using capital-intensive inputs.

The process not only is economically beneficial, it is also educational. The role of the government is to train the needed personnel and to secure foreign credit, especially from the International Bank for Reconstruction and Development (IBRD) and the International Finance Corporation (IFC). The cost to the state treasury would be negligible; to the farmers, however it would mean survival.

Third, to achieve increased distribution efficiency of farm products, there needs to be farmer-owned or farmer-operated food-processing facilities.

The need is the demonopolization of everything concerning agriculture--the separation of companies buying grain from the ones processing them--and the separation of the latter from retailers. The food-processing industry is very weak. Up until now, farmers did not really have anything to say about it. (Bylinski interview, 1990)

The government has invited prospective foreign investors to enter Poland's food-processing market, but it has not enabled or encouraged independent farmers along the same line. Introducing competition in the food-processing industry will benefit small farmers, but if farmers are to form their own cooperative processing facilities, then the competition will be more keenly and meaningfully felt by themselves as producers. The ideal is that, through cooperative efforts by independent farmers, farmers will own and operate their food-processing enterprises. An alternative would be that farmers buy into the existing monopolistic processing cooperatives, but these cooperatives cannot be privatized.

The need to demonopolize is there, but small farmers are financially unable to initiate food-processing plants on their own. Government should provide assistance.

It is not really the farmers who should be directly subsidized. In Italy, when the government wished to develop companies and enterprises servicing the farm producers (after World War II), the subsidies were for these companies. The farmers could sell their output to the companies at fair prices. And the companies could afford to sell processed farm products to consumers as stabilized prices. (Bylinski interview, 1990)

As the agricultural sector in Italy became increasingly viable and competitive, the indirect subsidies were gradually withdrawn. In Poland, owing to the monopolistic food-processing industry, indirect subsidies could be channeled to the establishment of farmer-owned and operated processing facilities.

Long-term loans are an effective and quite indirect form of subsidy to promote competition. Seed money is needed. Financial resources "need come from the state budget" (Bylinski interview, 1990). But so far, the farmers' pleas have not yielded the desired results. The government needs to search for international assistance and cooperation. Long-term, low-interest loans from international financial institutions such as the World Bank are obtainable. The money can then be channeled to rural credit institutions. It is cost effective.

Fourth, adequate food storage facilities are needed. They are a crucial link in the internal distribution system. But, as had been alluded to, Polish farmers have been callously exploited by the cooperative cartels in recent years.

One of the most important factors in providing farm producers with investment incentives is steady income via stable commodity prices. Farmer-owned and farmer-operated storage facilities are an effective means of stabilizing commodity prices. If storage facilities are adequate to hold surpluses during peak seasons, they can distribute those supplies during lull periods and hold reserves for emergencies, thus avoiding price fluctuations. The farmer, a risk averter, can then have the assurance that his investment will net an acceptable return, instead of seeing profits pouring into the coffers of the cooperatives. However,

Given the monopolistic companies, marketization of the agricultural sector is really impossible. At the same time, the budget allotted for the newly created Agricultural Market Agency is way too small. The agency, among others, wishes to expand the storage capacity. That means assistance to the farmers who wish to build their own storage facilities to store the grain by themselves. The agency will help to create a more favorable condition for the farmers with the banks. But the government gives the agency only 870 billion zlotys for all the programs the agency has to undertake. But the need should be at least five times more. (Bylinski interview, 1990)

Again, the role of the government needs to be expanded to initiate, assist, and coordinate the cooperative efforts of independent farmers in owning and operating suitably sized, no-frills storage facilities. Farmer-owned and operated storage facilities not only increase storage capacity, but also provide direct competition with the monopolistic cooperatives. It is farm marketization in action. Long-term farm credit, therefore, has this useful and productive function as well.

CONCLUSION

The agricultural sector in Poland's economic transformation is of crucial relevance and importance. To date, the legislative and administrative energy directed to developing the farm sector has been less than concrete and less than adequate.

The government has not faced up to the real problems. It thinks that a free-market concept is a remedy for everything. "Up to now [July, 1990], the government thought that it was only the agriculture lobby trying to turn everyone's attention onto them" (Bylinski interview, 1990). The government needs to listen, and to increase its role. An increased government role here does not mean unreasonable or non-productive subsidies. Rather, it means government initiatives--with adequate budget money for long-term investments--in exploring inexpensive and cost-effective opportunities and in stimulating investment and production through an improved infrastructure support system. Additional financial resources for the latter may be secured with relative ease from IBRD and IFC.

The Polish farm sector needs no extensive privatization. Eighty percent of these farms have been private all the while. But the sector is not marketized. Because of structural rigidity inherited from past administrations and hasty policy measures of recent years, agriculture is handicapped, ineffectively functioning within an artificial market framework. Structural changes need to precede functional ones. The market cannot function smoothly unless prerequisite conditions are met.

The ideas outlined here could induce orderly and smooth structural changes within the agricultural sector. The government has a stake in, as well as the responsibility for, the well-being of more than one-fifth of the nation's labor force. It is an investment in success, in Poland's future. Unless the interests of the farm sector are nurtured, full marketization of the Polish economy is not a reality in the foreseeable future.

NOTES

1. The author wishes to acknowledge the valuable information shared with him by Janusz Bylinski, member of Parliament, Minister of Agriculture, and chair of the Parliamentary Committee for Agriculture.

2. The law establishing the Agricultural Market Agency was passed on June 7, 1990, not on December 22, 1989, as alluded to in the quotation near the beginning of the chapter.

3. U.S. $1 equals approximately DM 1.6-1.8.

11

FOREIGN INVESTMENT POLICY

With a U.S. $42 billion foreign debt, unemployment expected to reach 2 million by the end of 1991 and an acute shortage of patience, the new administrations of Tadeusz Mazowiecki and Jan Bielecki have been attempting to stabilize the economy while restructuring it for normal functioning.[1] One of the first acts of the Mazowiecki administration was to seek immediate assistance from abroad. The world was riveted on Poland then, the first COMECON member to successfully back away from the suffocating embrace of the Soviet Union. To the West, Poland's success in democratization and economic restructuring could serve as a model for other communist economies. Poland could count on financial assistance from the West, with confidence. It was August 1989.

However, the domino effect was instant. Within a year, the winds of democracy swept across Eastern Europe, and the world's attention was divided. The financial assistance from the West would now have to be parceled out among Poland's neighboring new democracies as well. Investors in the West were presented with more waters to fish from. No longer in a privileged position, Poland was still in desperate need of foreign money. On December 27 and 28, 1989, the Polish Foreign Investment Law was adopted by the two houses of the Sejm. With it, the Foreign Investment Agency was created, with a president nominated by the minister of finance. But to accentuate the importance of foreign investment, the agency president was appointed by, and is responsible to, the prime minister. The duties of agency president include:

Formulating the objectives and implementing the policies of the State on investment cooperation with foreign countries; stimulating and undertaking measures to increase the interest of foreign parties in pursuing economic activity in the Polish People's Republic in the areas, within limits, corresponding with the interests of the national economy. (Foreign Investment Law, 1990: 4-4)

The interests of the national economy at the time included stabilization of economic activity within the framework of a free-market system, a balanced budget, stabilized prices, rescheduling and repayment of foreign debts, privatization of state enterprises, and attracting direct foreign investment or joint ventures.

The contribution foreign investment can make is important to any growing economy. To Poland, it could be pivotal, creating jobs, modernizing the means of production, upgrading the quality of labor, improving the organizational skills of management, reducing the need for imports, increasing exports, widening the tax base, strengthening weak links, and even helping develop an infrastructure. A well-planned and implemented foreign investment policy could provide the Polish economy with that much-needed injection of foreign funds as well as a boost to self-confidence.

That the foreign investment law was passed within three months of the new administration's installment was a statement in itself: foreign investment is crucial. The discussion that follows presents the essence of the law, its performance, factors contributing to or detracting from an investment inflow, and considerations to provide a more conducive investment environment.

PERSPECTIVES ON THE LAW

The law affirms that investment in Poland by foreign sources is for mutual benefit. It acknowledges that investors' profit motivation is a legitimate reason for conducting business in Poland. Foreign nationals, foreign corporations, and foreign nationals of Polish descent are all eligible investors. Provided the foreign investment activities are not harmful to the interests of the nation, "at this state, we invite any kind of investment" (Piotrowski interview, 1990). The need for foreign capital is pressing, but it is not without direction. According to the law,

A permit to establish a company is issued whenever the business activity ensures in particular: (1) introduction of modern technologies and management methods into the national economy; (2) provision of goods and services for export; (3) improvement in the supply of modern and high quality products and services to domestic market; and, (4) protection of the environment. (Foreign Investment Law, 1990: 5-2)

The direction is clear: modernization of production to benefit consumers and expand exports. Economic activities are to be for the well-being of consumers. Therefore, consumer goods and services resulting from direct foreign investment or joint ventures are given priority consideration when reviewing for permits. High on the preferred list are agriculturally related production and processing, housing-related industries, health-care products, and office and paper products industries. Other than high-technology industries such as energy and telecommunication systems, which are also on the list of high-priority items, the majority of preferred foreign investments are not as capital intensive. For investors from developed economies, initial capitalization could be as low as U.S. $50,000, equal to or exceeding 20 percent of a venture's total equity. The foreign investor could also elect to be sole owner of an enterprise, if so desired, or to own al least 51 percent and be a majority owner with the decisive voice in management and decision making.

A foreign investor's contribution could be either in cash or in kind. To provide further incentives to foreign capital, a firm with foreign participation is entitled to a three-year exemption form corporate income tax. At the discretion of the minister of finance, that privilege may be extended for up to three more years--that is, if the goods or services produced by the firm are much needed and are a preferred investment. When the tax exemption expires, firms with direct foreign investment pays a 30 percent corporate income tax. In the case of a joint venture, the Polish partner's share pays 40 percent while the foreign partner still pays only 30 percent. The latitude provided the foreign investor is inviting. Even joint ventures with negligible initial capitalization or direct investment are received with open arms. To protect and to promote the interest of the foreign investors, the law also established the Chamber of Industry and Commerce of Foreign Investors. According to the law, the

Objective is to represent the economic interests of its members, to take up actions aimed at protection of those interests by offering its members assistance in solving economic, organizational and legal problems involved with the undertaking and conducting of economic activity. (Foreign Investment Law, 1990: 37)

Foreign investors may even obtain loans from a Polish bank, having its financial obligations guaranteed by the same (Law, 1990: 22). In principle, the Foreign Investment Law has provided as many guarantees and privileges to prospective foreign investors as conditions permit. It should have been an investor's paradise, yet the flow of foreign investment has been below expectation.

Performance and Observations

The original foreign investment law was enacted in 1976. Over a six-year period, only nine firms with foreign capital were registered, and they were peripheral industries (Sadowska-Cieslak, 1990:14). Poland was no paradise for foreign investors then. The terms and conditions were stringent, not to mention the less-than-pleasant social and political conditions at the time.

The 1976 law was replaced by the law on the Principles of Operating Small Scale Industry Enterprises by Foreign Persons of July 1982. That same law underwent revisions and modifications in 1983, 1985, 1986, and 1988. Over time, a more conducive environment for foreign investment was created. As a result of the 1986 revision, fifty-four joint ventures came to be. With the more favorable conditions set forth in the 1988 version of the law on Economic Activity with the Participation of Foreign Parties, 866 new permits were issued in 1989 alone (World Economy Research, 1990: 47). As of May 1990, a total of 1,145 firms--either as direct foreign investments or as joint venture--were in existence. By September 1990, the number grew to 1,903 (Warsaw Voice, 1990: 100, 21). There seems to be an upsurge in foreign interest.

In terms of national origin, until the end of May 1990 investment from the Federal Republic of Germany accounted for nearly 41 percent of the 1,145 enterprises. Scandinavian economies, the United States, Great Britain, France, and Italy accounted for most of the balance. Notably low in profile was Japan. By the end of 1989, there was only one Japanese investment in Poland (Drewnowska, 1990: 37; World Economy Research, 1990:47). Also notably absent was investment from other COMECON members, with the exception of the Soviet Union, which had fourteen by the end of 1989.

If the initial capitalizations of foreign investors are examined, three observations can be made. First, only a small number of medium-size foreign investments have been made in Poland. The average initial capital outlay is approximately U.S. $163,000. The larger foreign investors have been Kvaerner, Intercell, Polovat and Furnel International, but most of the 1,145 firms with foreign capital are small. By the end of 1989, the ten largest foreign investments added up to a negligible U.S. $68 million. And the thirty-nine largest accounted for more than half of the combined total of U.S. $186.6 million invested (Drewnowska, 1990: 37, 43). Second, despite the presence of millions of Polish descendents in the United States, only seventy-three sources from the United States have made investments in Poland, totaling less than U.S. $11 million. And third, investors from Great Britain, France, Belgium, and Canada--three of those countries close enough to be termed neighbors with Poland--made a total of 149 investments by the end of May 1990, a mere 13.1 percent. The combined value of these 149 investments amounted to a meager U.S. $17 million.

The responsiveness of foreign investors in general, and of Polish-American entrepreneurs in particular, has been less than overwhelming. And the large foreign investors still seem to be holding back, at least for now.

There are possible reasons for this lukewarm attitude on the part of the United States and Japan. To begin, the investors in the United States, relative to their European counterparts, have become more conservative over time. Corporate administrators are concerned more with their domestic market share than with foreign investment opportunities. The entrepreneurial drive in the United States has also been stymied by oligopolistic corporations. New products or new processes are released into the market step by step, while companies hold onto technologies that quickly become less competitive on the international market. This lack of entrepreneurial drive is in sharp contrast with Japanese engineering and production, which will readily discard existing techniques in search of new frontiers. The spirit of venturesomeness in the United States is on the decline. Indirectly, Poland suffers as well.

Poland has also experienced a shortage of Japanese investments, at least for now. Japanese investments abroad are closely coordinated by its Ministry of International Trade and Industries (MITI). MITI's interest and intent differ from the market economies of Western Europe, who may be more interested in investing in Poland as a springboard for commercial and industrial operations in the European part of the Soviet Union. Japan, on the other hand, is more focused on the far eastern region of Siberia, where energy and raw materials await exploration and exploitation (Goscinski interview, 1990).

The economic activities of foreign investors have ranged from shipyard work to mining, from furniture making to plastics, and all the way to color photo processing. Material activities surpass those of nonmaterial by nearly ten to one. Industry accounts for slightly more than 51 percent of total activities, but only a small portion of it is in metal, electronic, or engineering works. Leading industrial activities include food processing and textile products. No foreign investment to date has benefitted in a measurable way the development or improvement of Poland's infrastructure.

The pace of foreign investment has accelerated since August 1989, but most new investments have been made in markets that are relatively competitive. Industries dominated by socialized enterprises have so far remained untouched. For instance, the still traditionally important industries of energy, farm equipment, automobiles, and residential construction are like virgin snow, untouched by foreign investment. To move the Polish economy forward and to ensure a smooth economic transformation, it is desirable that significant foreign capital flow toward such industries to increase competition. The Foreign Investment Agency needs to integrate its policy with that of the privatization program so that foreign capital can help demonopolize the large state enterprises.

One of the successes of Poland's foreign investment policy is that nearly 90 percent of the joint ventures are in the areas of food processing, textiles, wood products, commerce, and commercial building industry, all on the list of preferred investments (Drewnowska, 1990: 54-55). However, with the exception of several luxury hotels in Warsaw and Gdansk, the majority of permits issued to joint ventures during the first quarter of 1990 were small in size (Bossak, 1990:72). A corollary observation is that many small foreign investors seem attracted to noncapital-intensive, short-term, rapid payback investments. A harsher assessment of these investments is that "foreign-capital direct investments in the form of foreign small manufacturing enterprises and companies with foreign-unit shares have been of little importance to the Polish economy" (Burzynski, 1990: 64). This does not negate the meaningful contributions made by more substantial investments but many small foreign investors do project an image of being there just to take advantage of the situation: three-year tax holidays and low-cost factors of production. But as the president of Poland's Foreign Investment Agency says: "We have a growing unemployment, a strong recession. So, for us now to say 'no, we do not need you' is difficult at this time. We hope that the interaction with the foreign capital will cause the economy to grow" (Piotrowski interview, 1990). The question is how to translate this hope into more concrete results to the benefit of the Polish economy. In short, there are tangible successes in the government's effort to induce foreign investment, but there are also shadowy corners which deficiencies and concerns lurk.

CONDITIONS FAVORABLE TO INVESTMENT INFLOW

First, Poland is strategically located in Europe. The Germans and Russians used to cross east and west for their military expeditions. And the Swedes and Austro-Hungarians crisscrossed south and north for similar reasons. Modern-day Poland has a well-developed rail system and deep-sea ports to the north. With the trend for liberalization in the Soviet Union and neighboring Eastern European economies, Poland is an ideal distribution center for Europe: east and northeast to the Soviet Union and Finland; northwest to Scandinavian markets; west to Germany, south to Czechoslovakia, Austria, Hungary; and southwest to France, Italy, Yugoslavia, and Greece.

Second, land may now be leased with ease for business purposes. Foreign investors have been guaranteed ready access to both public and private:

State land may be made available to the companies [foreign investments or joint venture] under a perpetual lease in accordance with the regulations applicable to the administration of state-land or they may lease such land. (Foreign Investment Law, 1990: 26-1)

Investors may--in accordance with existing laws governing real estate--lease land as Polish nationals do--there are no restrictions. Indeed, since favorable consequences often result from such foreign capital, investors from abroad have an edge over locals in leasing choice properties. More important, foreign investors may still find land--as a factor of production--cost-effective.

Third, there is a three-year corporate income tax exemption, and an additional three years may be granted if the goods and services produced are much needed. Since preferred industries include a wide range of economic activities, many foreign investments can be exempt from corporate income taxes for up to six years. It is a substantial reduction in production costs, rendering the investor's products highly competitive, domestically as well as internationally.

Fourth, the process of obtaining a permit has been expedited by the law. The Foreign Investment Agency is obliged to provide an applicant from a foreign country with a decision "within two months from the date of the filing of the application" (Foreign Investment Law, 1990: 10). It is comparable to the supermarket express check out line. And insofar as the proposed venture does not pose a threat to Poland's national security, subvert its economic interests, or violate its environmental protection law, it may find ready acceptance.

Fifth, there is an exemption from import duties on machinery equipment "as well as other items required for the conduct of business activity," as stated on the permit (Foreign Investment Law, 1990: 3). There is no expiration date for this privilege, and all factors of production considered essential may be eligible for import duty exemption. The potential savings to a foreign investor could be significant.

Sixth, no item in the law stipulates import restrictions by foreign investors. Therefore, it is feasible for an investor to import cheap raw materials from nearby Eastern Europe for lower production costs. Building materials, minerals, and some forms of energy are such items.

Seventh, labor costs in Poland are highly competitive. In 1988, an average worker's monthly income was 52,291 zlotys. A nonworker, meaning a management or office employee, had an average salary of 54,475 zlotys (Poland Statistical Data, 1989: 36). When translated into dollars, the monthly wages are United States $120 and $125, respectively--that is, if conversion takes place according to the official exchange rate. Using the black market exchange rate, the monthly wages only amount to $26 and $27, respectively. Despite the significant wage increases in recent years, labor costs are still one of the lowest in the region. As of July 1990, the monthly wage of a university teacher averaged $100. Wages in industries such as mining, transport, and construction are higher, but not significantly so. To foreign investors, this represents savings in operating costs (Szemplinska interview, 1990). And for the next few years, wages and salaries are likely to remain competitive.

Eighth, quality of workmanship is prized in Poland. *Prima facie*, the Polish worker maximizes utility by performing the minimal work possible. This was true for decades. This is even true today in many state-owned enterprises. This phenomenon is due to high inflation and declining real wages--the work incentive is low.   But it is far from true in private enterprises, especially in foreign-owned or joint-venture firms where there is no ceiling on wage increases. This positive work attitude is rarely noted in the West.   And performance is more than comparable with the West.   The cleanliness at the Marriott Hotel in downtown Warsaw, for instance, cannot be readily found in the West. Precision industrial products from joint ventures or foreign-owned enterprises are of readily exportable quality. Awareness of wages and profits as a function of one's productivity is manifest, from factory floors to service centers.   Given adequate economic incentives, there is even pride in workmanship.

PROBABLE DISINCENTIVES FOR INVESTMENT INFLOW

Considering all these favorable conditions, Poland could well be a foreign investor's paradise. Why large foreign investors have not been flocking to this promised land? There are unfavorable conditions as well.   First, the Foreign Investment Law permits the perpetual leasing of land, but unlike in developed economies, land ownership by direct foreign investment is not one of the privileges. Only joint-venture firms may purchase real estate on the condition that the "Polish partner(s) has or have a majority share in the equity" (Sadowska-Cieslak, 1990: 24). For transnational corporations, this *provision* could be a disincentive. Unlike smaller investors, multinationals are capital intensive by nature. Their fixed assets are invested for long-term production. There is an advantage for them to purchase land, since it can be listed as an expenditure, therefore a major tax write-off. Land ownership also signifies permanency. It provides a sense of long-term commitment by the Polish government to the foreign investor. But, so far, it is not permitted.

Second, housing conditions in general and business facilities in particular are not conducive to attracting foreign investment. This is particularly clear to small or medium-size investors who lease rather than construct their buildings. Many commercial or industrial buildings were poorly constructed and have been more poorly maintained.   They need extensive repairs or remodeling to suit the needs of foreign enterprises.   But the commercial building industry is still in its development state. Years will elapse before the supply can adequately meet the potential demand.

Third, small or medium-size foreign investors have no ready access to market information on the Polish economy. This is particularly true in recent times with their rapid changes. Extensive, in-depth market research would be cost prohibitive for small investors. Therefore, even though competitive costs, tax privileges, and quality workmanship are inviting, investors would have a difficult time determining which branch of industry to enter and what the ideal initial capitalization should be. Accessible information of a specific nature would help those in doubt.

Fourth, if a joint venture fails, the proceeds due the foreign investor may be transferred out of the country no earlier than ten years after the company's initial registration date (Foreign Investment Law, 1990: 21,2-3). That is, investors in a failed joint venture that began in 1990 need to wait until the year 2000 to transfer the value of their shares out of Poland. No investor can afford to have financial resources tied up for that long. Exceptions to the ten-year waiting period may be made by the minister of finance, but they have to be specially justified cases.

Fifth, state-owned enterprises or cooperatives still have a monopolistic grip on many marketing channels. Breaking into these markets takes a giant corporation from abroad with significant financial commitments. But such ventures need the services of a support system, and some of these support services are still within the domain of monopolistic socialized firms. Existing monopolies also have an advantage over newcomers in local connections and legal arrangements. Therefore, the Polish government needs to demonopolize state enterprises, and foreign investment need to assist in this effort. Without the injection of substantial foreign capital to increase competition, the monopolies will not disappear easily.

Sixth, Poland's telecommunication system is inadequate. There are not enough automatic switches to accommodate the volume needed for international telecommunication. International telephone calls, for the majority of firms, still must be sent through operators. In a world of instant communication, where time is money, this is a weak spot in Poland's infrastructure.

Seventh, there is a ceiling on the amount of profit foreign investors can repatriate. The law states that:

The foreign partner has the right to purchase foreign currency at a foreign exchange bank for the amount of profit paid to him by the Company . . . equal to the surplus of export proceeds over import outlays obtained by the Company in convertible currencies during the previous fiscal year . . . .

The foreign partner has also the right to purchase foreign currency at a foreign exchange bank in the amount of up to 15 percent of the remaining part of profit for the previous fiscal year that exceeds the surplus mentioned in paragraph 1, in exchange for the profit paid to him by the Company. (Law, 1990: 19-1, 2)

According to paragraph 1, if the foreign investment is made in the production of goods or the provision of services to domestic markets, then there can be no "surplus of export proceeds over import outlays." The profits due the foreign investor cannot be exchanged for a foreign currency. Paragraph 2 permits the exchange of up to 15 percent of the previous year's "remaining part of profit" due the foreign investor over and above the "surplus of export proceeds over import outlays." This means that, even if there are no export proceeds, only 15 percent of the previous year's profits may be exchanged. What is the foreign investor to do with the balance of profits reaped? The 85 percent profit could be trapped in zlotys, representing a high opportunity cost. This scenario can also apply to foreign investors who market their Polish products both domestically and abroad. As long as there is no surplus of export proceeds over import outlays, 15 percent is the limit. It is a significant disincentive to transnational corporations.

Eighth, there is a near absence of money and capital markets. This gap keeps major foreign investors from trading shares, which is an essential function of major enterprises in the West. It means they are unable to mobilize domestic financial resources. It also means no investment opportunities for foreign investors with nonrepatriatable profits. Primary and secondary stock markets, options and futures markets, auctions and spot markets are all essential for circulation of financial resources. They are still being developed.

Ninth, the banking system lacks sophistication. Exaggerated accounts describe one to three months as the time required for local transfers of funds. Realistically, a few weeks is not uncommon. No interbank instant crediting-debiting facilities, no computerized equipment or interbank linkages, shortages of adequately trained personnel, and no efficient auditing and accounting system all render the banking system unattractive to foreign investors. They are accustomed to electronic transfers and instant verification of completed transactions. Tied-up financial resources mean high opportunity costs.

And, tenth, the prevailing social and economic conditions in Poland are unstable. This might be a factor in the wait-and-see attitude of many prospective foreign investors. Attempts at social and economic transformation have been radical, rapid, and extensive. Meanwhile, relics of past regimes remain in place, including leftover middle-level bureaucrats. Rising unemployment, high inflation, declining purchasing power, and sporadic strikes all assemble a collage of negative images.

The sluggishness in flow of foreign capital may be traced to one or more of these real or perceived obstacles. Research into the causes of low foreign investment and the concerns of prospective foreign investors needs to be conducted on a continuous basis. Investing to strengthen the positive, while removing or improving the negative, will help change the wait-and-see stance.

CONCLUDING REMARKS

That the Polish economy needs a massive injection of foreign money is a foregone conclusion. The country has witnessed a meteoric rise in foreign investments. But aggregate value has been significantly below expectations.

Rethinking on the part of government is in order. To better understand the foreign investors' mentality, government must think *with* them to learn what will induce them to make investments.

In an attempt to attract foreign capital, Poland has to recognize the reality that capital is a resource. By definition, resources are scarce. On the one hand, there is limited availability of investment funds worldwide; on the other hand, alternative investment opportunities abound. If neighboring COMECON nations were still in the fold of Communism, then Poland would be in a much better position to court foreign capital. But the focus of the West has been diluted to multidimensional. Weaknesses in the Polish economy will not be overlooked by foreign investors. Poland has to compete with others for foreign capital, and foreign investors need to be patiently and earnestly courted. Like flowing water seeking low ground, investment firms constantly search for where conditions are most favorable for profit. Further concessions may be needed to make that place be Poland.

What is perceived as obstacles by investors can discourage foreign capital. When investment conditions are interpreted as high opportunity costs, then the wait-and-see posture replaces an eagerness or willingness to invest. This is particularly true for multinational corporations. Therefore, the risks of investment need to be recognized by the government for possible trade-off inducements.

Social and economic stability is an important consideration for major foreign investors. And social stability means more than the absence of prolonged strikes. It means a general sense of security and well-being. It means a healthy attitude toward work and life. It means that the investors can count on Polish society, on the Polish work force, and on the Polish government that economic activities undertaken will yield predictable and rewarding dividends. And economic stability means more than stabilized prices. It means reliable delivery and communication systems, an efficient banking system and functional money and capital markets, consistent legislative action pertaining to economic activity, and no unexpected fluctuations in macro variables. All these may appear to be asking too much of the Polish economy today. To compensate for weaknesses in these areas, advantages could be expanded or fortified.

It also should be remembered that foreign corporate investors are held accountable to their shareholders. Once a major commitment is made, foreign capitalization could amount to hundreds of millions of dollars. Management could not, and would not, commit sizable financial resources to an economically risky or even less profitable venture. Consequently, the Polish government needs to weight the considerations that routinely enter into the decision-making process of prospective foreign investors. Taking into account all the investment opportunities that exist for foreign investors--in Poland or elsewhere--the Polish government needs to offer a package that is competitive yet beneficial to its own economy. Requirements and restrictions, concessions and privileges can then be packaged accordingly so that investment in Poland is appealing.

The office of the president of the Foreign Investment Agency is aware of the obstacles to the inflow of foreign capital. Toward the end of 1990, a new draft bill was presented to Parliament for debate (Warsaw Voice, 1990: 10, 21). The main features of the draft are:

-- waiving foreign investment permits for all direct investments or joint ventures with Polish nationals and cooperatives, so that only joint ventures with state enterprises need permits from the Agency;

-- reducing the tax holiday from three to two years in exchange for a speedier amortization rate; and

-- most important, full repatriation of profits by foreign investors instead of the existing 15 percent ceiling (Law, 1990: 189-91) and immediate withdrawal of foreign capital, if so desired, instead of the present ten-year waiting period (Law, 1990: 21-23).

Not being in a strong bargaining position under the present circumstances, the Polish government is bending over backwards to encourage foreign investment. All conceivable concessions are being offered. The proposed amendments to the law will help remove some of the major obstacles to investment inflow. But short-term objectives also need to be viewed in perspective to assure that the long-term economic interests of Poland are not pawned for insignificant short-lived gains. In essence, the long-term economic colonization of Poland by foreign capital needs to be avoided. It is a delicate balancing act between immediate gratification and sustained benefit. Continuous monitoring and constructive adjustments are in order, without diminishing the confidence of foreign investors that there is consistency in Poland's foreign investment policy for mutual benefit.

NOTE

1. The author wishes to acknowledge the insightful and frank comments made by Dr. Zbigniew Piotrowski during an interview in July 1990. Dr. Piotrowski is president of Poland's Foreign Investment Agency, Ministry of Finance.

12

FOREIGN EXCHANGE
AND FOREIGN TRADE

Foreign trade has become a major component of every nation's economic development. For Poland, at least in the near future, foreign trade is less a concern for generating wealth. Rather, a growing export sector is needed to service the foreign debt. As of early 1991, each Polish citizen owed foreign creditors U.S. $1,150. For a two-income family of four, that is equivalent to two wage earners working for two years without pay. Unless the current account is sufficiently positive to repay the principal and interest as they become due, the value of the zloty will depreciate and Poland's creditworthiness will be called into question. Since foreign debts have to be paid in the foreign currency, foreign trade is of key importance in Poland's effort to rebuild its economy.[1]

As discussed in Chapter 4, Poland's inability to service its foreign debt in the late 1970s resulted in a moratorium on further credit. Belt-tightening was effectuated to reduce imports. Economic incentives were provided to export-oriented industries. The combined policy of import restriction and export promotion led to Poland's regaining its earlier position as a trade surplus nation. But that was not achieved until the early 1980s. And the trade surplus was not sufficient for servicing Poland's debt. By late 1989, the new administration of Tadeusz Mazowiecki moved swiftly to introduce legislation and issue administrative decrees liberalizing trade-related activities. One of his first policy actions espoused the internal convertibility of the zloty.

FOREIGN EXCHANGE

During the Communist administrations, the exchange rates between various foreign currencies and the zloty were fixed by the state. When a domestic enterprise imported goods or services, payment was made in zlotys at the official exchange rate--the importer gained at the expense of the state treasury. In September 1988, for instance, the official exchange rate between the U.S. and Polish currencies was pegged at $1 for 460 zlotys. The black market, however, was offering 2,000 zlotys for $1. The enterprise with an import license was able to make the payment in zlotys to a Polish bank. The bank was obliged to pay the foreign supplier in hard currency. The importer, therefore, needed to pay less than one-fourth of the real value for the imported goods, and then he could sell the goods on the domestic market at a much higher price. Significant profits were reaped. With profits in hand, the demand for further imports would always be strong.

On the other hand, domestic exporters had to convert their proceeds from exports to zlotys, also at the official exchange rate. They lost to the state treasury. Demand for imports would always exceed exports, and a trade imbalance materialized. Nonconvertibility of the local currency was a major contributing factor.

To achieve some semblance of a trade balance, the centralized government restricted the issuance of import permits and determined import quotas. State enterprises were the chief beneficiaries of such permits, but within the socialized sector, they had to vie among themselves for a greater share of the import quotas. For enterprises producing exportable goods and needing imported materials for production, the balance of whatever they could not obtain through import permits had to be secured from the black market. It was a disincentive to exporters.

The Mazowiecki government, therefore, implemented a policy of internal convertibility of currencies in order to equalize trade opportunities and harness the potential of the export industries. The exchange rate between the U.S. dollar and the Polish zloty was 1 to 507.9 in January 1989. It rose to 844.6 in June of the same year, and to 6,500 by the end of December 1989. On January 1, 1990, the rate was finally set based on the demand for and supply of convertible currencies. The NBP fixed the official exchange rate at $1 for 9,500 zlotys.

To ensure the stability of foreign exchange rates, a stabilization fund of $1 billion was extended to Poland by the industrialized economies of the West. The IMF also provided a standby line of credit for approximately $750 million. The NBP could draw on theses funds to buy or sell convertible currencies so as to maintain the relative value of the zloty. Thus the rate of exchange has been stabilized. As of December 27, 1990, the NBP "paid a free market price of 9,650 zlotys for 1 USD, selling it for 9,750 zlotys" (Warsaw Voice, 1991: 1, 6). With internal convertibility of the zloty, the government also removed import and export restrictions on Polish nationals. All agents, whether enterprises or individuals, can now import or export goods and services without a foreign trade permit. There remain only a few restricted trade items that require an import or export license.

As before, the banks authorized to engage in foreign exchange serve as the intermediary between the Polish and foreign trading partners. Through an authorized foreign exchange bank, the Polish national who imports pays in zlotys. Similarly, a Polish exporter must deposit the proceeds from exports with a foreign exchange bank in Poland and all foreign accounts are settled in the local currency.

For their part, foreign exchange banks are obliged by law to buy or sell foreign currencies from or to Polish nationals in order to settle trade accounts. The NBP in turn is obliged to buy from, or to sell to, commercial exchange banks any convertible currencies at the official rates set by itself. As a result of zloty devaluation, and of the policy of internal convertiblity, Polish exports have become more competitive abroad while imports have become more expensive.

With internal convertiblity of the local currency, and the government's determination to adjust exchange rates to match supply and demand, the confidence in the zloty has been established. To further demonstrate the government's resolve, Polish nationals may now open foreign currency accounts with domestic exchange banks, with interest paid in that currency as well. There has been no rush to dump zlotys for hard currencies. Instead, within the first six months of 1990, more than a billion dollars in hard currency have been deposited in Polish banks. That was the same convertible currency that used to be kept in a shoe box or under the mattress. The estimate is that another billion or more dollars will soon find its way to bank vaults for interest-bearing earnings. The policy of internal convertiblity of the zloty has been a success, achieved without the government's having to draw upon the standby stabilization funds mentioned earlier.

FOREIGN TRADE

Poland's foreign trade performance during the Communist administrations was presented in Chapter 3. The following is a brief discussion on policy measures and administration since September 1989.

Subsidies

As late as 1989, there still were subsidies to selected exporters. Agricultural products, leather goods, textiles, chemicals, and some metal products destined for socialist economies received state subsidies. Subsidies were also granted to enterprises that restructured their operations for export-goods and came in the form of favorable exchange rates and reduced export taxes (World Economy Research, 1990: 44).

With the new administration, all export subsidies were removed in 1990. The only present concession granted to exporters is that they can be refunded the tariffs on imported essential factors of production of export goods.

Administration

The promotion of exports is under the guidance of the Ministry of Foreign Economic Cooperation. The ministry is charged with:

--preparing the guidelines for a general foreign economic policy;
--elaborating the directions of an export-oriented strategy for the
        national economy;
--developing foreign economic relations;
--stipulating new forms of economic cooperation;
--collaborating with the ministry of finance in the implementation
    of a foreign exchange policy;
--concluding multilateral and bilateral agreements;
--formulating and implementing a tariff policy; and
--controlling foreign trade (Piotrowski, 1990: 28, 29).

There are also a number of offices and organizations affiliated with or subordinated to the ministry. The more important ones include the Central Customs Office, the Foreign Investment Agency, the Center for Advanced Training in Foreign Trade, and the Foreign Trade Research Institute (Piotrowski, 1990: 29). The ministry's sphere of influence is not as extensive as Japan's MITI, but its responsibility is more pivotal because Poland's ability to service its foreign debt depends to a large extent on the success of its foreign trade policy; and Poland is in need of closer ties with world economies in order to modernize its own economy.

To achieve a positive balance of payments, the importation of alcohol, tobacco, automobiles, and luxury items is penalized with a surcharge tax, once the goods are sold on the domestic market. On another front, to open the Polish market to foreign interests and gain readier access to foreign markets, the Polish government reached agreements with numerous Western economies, mutually granting most-favored-nation status. Tariffs on imports are standardized in accordance with General Agreement on Tariffs and Trade (GATT) regulations. Trade with some forty less developed economies has also been made easier by granting the latter preferential treatment, either in the form of reduced tariffs or zero customs duty on selected items unique to the exporting less developed countries (Piotrowski, 1990: 15).

As a result of this liberalized trade policy, there has been a shift in trade patterns. Poland's chief trading partners used to be CMEA members, but with adoption of the free-market system, trade activities with the West has been on the rise while trade with COMECON members has correspondingly declined. Poland can now turn to the West for a wider range of quality goods at competitive prices. The economic integration of Poland into the world economy will increasingly veer toward the West. Available data suggest that Poland's foreign trade policy has already yielded handsome dividends. For the first four months of 1990, trade with socialist economies showed a monthly surplus of 47, 351.3, 572.4, and 449.1 million rubles, respectively. Trade with the West for the same period recorded a monthly surplus of U.S. $13.4, 243.8, 520.7, and 431.0 million, respectively (Ministry of Finance, NBP, 1990: 21). For the year 1990, a record surplus was expected. Whether accounts for the years to come will be sufficient to meet debt obligations is too early to predict. The following briefly presents what is involved in servicing Poland's external debt, and what measures need be taken.

Foreign Debt Financing

For now, Poland is burdened with foreign debt of U.S. $42 billion. Direct foreign assistance has been significantly below expectation, and foreign investments have trickled instead of poured in. There was a debt-servicing moratorium for 1990, which is now over. The current account is significantly in the red.

But first, the domestic scene needs to be understood. The Polish government is faced with a dilemma. On the one hand, it needs to honor its loan obligations on time. The ideal is to significantly increase exports while holding down imports. But on the other hand, there is an urgent need for increased imports of productivity-increasing factors, some of which are needed to increase production of exports. How are the two reconciled?

Debt repayment is made by the Polish government. Total long-term debt service as a percentage of GNP in 1988 was 2.5 (World Bank, 1990: 223). It is significantly higher now. Ultimately, the money has to come from the government, so a substantial portion of the budget is earmarked for repaying the foreign debt. Thus, a tight fiscal policy will have to be in effect for decades. That, in turn, is translated into decades of belt tightening by consumers, and socially, that is unacceptable. On another front, a tight investment policy leads to reduced productivity and employment. Economically it is unwise. For the export sector, reduced investment will lead to obsolete equipment and outmoded production processes. The export sector can be rendered less efficient, more expensive, and less competitive, but foreign earnings will be adversely affected and it makes future debt servicing more difficult. One way or the other, the constraints on the economy enforced by the overwhelming foreign debt are nearly insurmountable. This is where foreign trade is capable of making a difference. *If* the trade surplus is sufficient to cover the need to import essential raw materials, as well as to sell the balance of the proceeds to the government for debt servicing, then the export sector may remain competitive.

On the part of government, buying foreign currencies from export proceeds means fewer resources will be available for domestic consumption. To achieve a balanced budget revenues have to be raised somehow or cuts made somewhere. A higher tax burden will not be acceptable, nor will a prolonged reduction in government spending. The government, however, may resort to borrowing from the public. Bonds can be issued at rates attractive enough to compensate for deferred consumption, and may also be exchanged for equity shares in state enterprises, with very favorable terms of exchange. The sale of such bonds, however, needs be restricted to Polish nationals. It is more desirable to have Polish citizens buy into state enterprises-- inexpensively--than to be delinquent on debt payment. Foreign interests thus will not be able to dictate the terms of future economic relations with Poland. Assuming a significant and sustained trade surplus, foreign obligations will be met and the state-owned assets will to a large extent remain Polish owned. Greater participation by the public in purchasing shares via government bonds will provide an incentive to be more productive on the one hand and to be thriftier on the other. Also, reductions in government spending need not be as severe if there is increased borrowing via long-term bonds. The remaining question is how to achieve a significant trade surplus on a sustained basis.

Import Substitution

A simplified solution to maintaining a trade surplus is a policy of combined import substitution and export promotion. If imports are essential to establishing or strengthening an industry that can reduce the future need for imports, then such imports need be granted economic inducements, and no reduction is justifiable. If imported services are required to initiate or develop such ventures, then such imports should not be spared. Over time, as the domestic supply of such goods and services grows, sales taxes--not import duties--can be proportionately increased to discourage importation of the same in the future. On the other hand, imports that can be produced domestically need to be contained. Tax surcharges are not sufficient to discourage undesirable imports, which can undermine the fledgling viability of some domestic industries. Some subtle form of temporary protectionism needs to be in place, with the purpose of discouraging undesirable imports and providing selective domestic producers with a chance of being more competitive within a certain time. Many developed economies protected infant domestic industries; temporary protective measures are not harmful in the long run. The government of Poland needs to regard its economy as being seriously wounded and in need of a respite.

Export Promotion

It must be acknowledged that the effectiveness of curtailing imports as a means of reducing the outflow of hard currency is limited. To increase the trade surplus, there needs to be greater promotion of exports. A number of approaches may be considered. First, Poland's low labor costs are a vast potential. The country can pursue the same route that Japan, the Republic of Korea, and Taiwan once took. Production activities that are too expensive in the developed economies can be imported for domestic employment. A portion of the finished products can supply domestic needs, reducing the need to import the same with convertible currencies. The balance is exported for foreign earnings. Meanwhile, the skills and sophistication of domestic labor is enhanced.

Second, economic incentives and preferential treatment need to be provided to export-oriented enterprises. Outward-looking entrepreneurship needs to be actively cultivated. The Ministry of Foreign Economic Cooperation, therefore, must rely on the profit motivation of domestic investors to provide the needed growth in the export sector. The recently abolished Export Development Fund needs to be restored. While in theory it is plausible to require export-oriented industries to compete for credits from commercial banks, the practice eliminates the advantage that the export sector used to enjoy. Given the urgent need for repayment of foreign debts, there is the justification for differentiating treatment for investors. Readier access to a more ample supply of less expensive credit steers investors to desired industries. Entrepreneurs producing exports need this privileged position to expand and accelerate their activities.

Third, the tax exemption for exporters needs in some measure to be restored. It is not a blanket elimination of export taxes for all exports. Rather, similar to product differentiation, different export tax rates are applied to different exports. It is a form of subsidy that numerous developed economies have employed for decades.

Fourth, there should be a reduction or elimination of import taxes on the factors of production needed in export industries. This is more effective than the tariff refund mentioned earlier. Such import tax reductions or exemptions, depending on the degree of need, free the money for immediate and more productive uses.

Fifth, forty developing nations have been granted preferential access to Poland's market. It serves the interests of Poland to intensify the search for raw materials and intermediate goods from among these less developed countries (LDCs). Many of these LDCs are short on convertible currencies, but they would increase imports from Poland if no real payments are required. Bartering Polish exports for needed imports can help expand trade while reducing the need for some imports currently financed through the outflow of hard currencies.

And, sixth, more efficient state enterprises can be encouraged to look outward for investment opportunities, in the form of subsidiaries or branches in economies less developed than Poland. Of particular interest are ventures in raw material extraction and processing. This expansion can reduce the need for imports while providing a direct link between domestic resource needs and a steady and less expensive source of supply from the LDCs. Profit repatriation therefrom is also a valuable source of foreign earnings.

A CONCLUDING REMARK

The trade surplus achieved in the early months of 1990 was indicative of the entrepreneurial responsiveness to economic incentives. The positive current accounts, however, pale in comparison to what is needed. Greater incentives need to be provided for the export sector. A trade policy that vigorously and effectively promotes exports while, in a calculating manner, curtails unnecessary imports can help restore Poland to a healthier internal as well as external state. Poland's decision makers need to be less fervent in adhering to free-market principles, at least with respect to foreign trade. Given the present economic conditions--including foreign debt obligation--Poland cannot afford to practice laissez faire on all fronts. The foreign trade sector needs nurturing today, for a healthier and freer Polish economy tomorrow.

This and the six previous chapters have dwelt on macroeconomic policies since the economic reform program began in 1989. Their respective consequences, implications, and needs have also been duly noted. The following chapter addresses some of the issues that need to be decided on the enterprise level.

NOTE

1. At this writing, major foreign creditors, including the United States, are willing to forgive a substantial part of the debts owed to them. However, the balance due will continue to pose major problems to Poland's foreign sector.

13

NEEDED: ENTERPRISE-LEVEL ADJUSTMENTS

For Poland's economic sectors to be efficient and productive, the market system needs to function in a meaningful manner. For the sectors to perform well separately, jointly, and interdependently, enterprise-level economic activities have to be operationally unified and functionally forward looking. And for the enterprises to be both productive and competitive, management needs to make sound economic decisions. Decision makers need the skills to structure economic activities in such a way that all productive parts of the enterprise are like an organic unity. They must effectively direct and control all operations to reach desired objectives. Labor as a factor of production, however, must be recognized and accepted as made up of humans, not machines. Management must skillfully guide, economically motivate, and artfully shape the workforce as a smooth, contributing unit. This chapter discusses micro considerations on the enterprise level, with the view that human resources are as important as nonhuman factors in decision making. General problems are first presented, then the functions that management must now learn to perform well are outlined. Thereafter, areas that require special attention are discussed, and selected recommendations are forwarded.

GENERAL PROBLEMS

First, presently many enterprises are still overstaffed with white-collar personnel. In the past, top-heavy adminstration was commonplace. Blue-collar workers were assigned specific functions; they could at least look busy, using their hands and making physical motions. White-collar workers, in particular party bureaucrats, just sat behind their desks and stared into space. Their functions were vague or redundant, and their productivty was difficult to measure. There was no fear of being laid off. Valuing personal relationships, new management in Poland is less accustomed to the sometimes impersonal approach of western firms in hiring and firing people. Many lower-level white-collar functionaries and blue-collar workers remain. They need to look busier now than they used to, but their pay still does not reflect their marginal productivity. Layoffs have become more common, but disguised unemployment remains.

Second, petty theft of enterprise stock is commonplace. One of the practices during the communist regime was the siphoning off of enterprise assets by employees. "Everybody did it." Since enterprise property "belonged to all the people,"--or to no one in particular--and since employees were the people, taking home what belonged to no one was done without hesitation. The practice was also deemed justifiable because workers felt exploited by the state. Items taken included nails, small tools, cement, wood, metal scraps, lubricant, moveable parts of equipment, laboratory chemicals, and leather. Even textiles and small finished products were taken. And the practice was not limited to blue-collar workers. Office supplies and equipment were removed by white-collar workers. The practice extended all the way to top management, whose actions were more discrete but represented a more substantial diversion of enterprise resources. Little was done to prevent this pilfering, and such practices continue somewhat. They translate into increased costs and, hence, higher prices for products produced.

Third, doing business is difficult. It is a new game with a new set of rules, quite alien to management. State subsidies--especially in key industries --used to be part of an enterprise's income. If losses occurred, tax deferment or tax forgiveness would come to the firm's rescue. Ready access to cheap credit was also a privilege. Now, all privileges have been revoked and credit is secured on the basis of a firm's financial strength and competitive prevailing rates. Tax rates have been equalized between state and private enterprises, and corporate income tax rates have been raised for all. Tax collection procedures have been tightened, and the government is quite prepared to allow state enterprises to go bankrupt. Efficiency and competitiveness have become the rule. Coping with these new business conditions has been difficult for many people in management.

Fourth, management is frequently unable to adapt to new conditions and is resistant to change. The freeing of prices and controlled indexing of wage increases have led to decreased purchasing power for the consumer. Decreases in demand for nonessential goods and services have led to decreased sales. To aggravate the already difficult situation, a state enterprise no longer has a guaranteed distribution channel for its products, and must compete with emerging private firms and the growing volume of imports. Instead of actively seeking ways to adjust to the new business environment, management often assumes a wait-and-see attitude.

Fifth, there is generally low morale in the work force. The real income of workers continues its downward slide while inflation steadily climbs. Not only are workers uncertain of the future value of their income, but many are uncertain about their employment and employability. Low morale adversely affects productivity, causing a firm to become increasingly less competitve over time.

Sixth, there is a general lack of quality management, indispensable in summoning forth the productive potential of the work force. Directors of state enterprises used to be routinely appointed by the government; they could be technocrats or party functionaries. Political connections and affiliations were helpful, or even essential, but special knowledge or experience in budgeting, marketing, economics, finance, or other business fields was not required. Costs and prices were centrally determined, and centralized distribution took care of marketing, so to speak. The manager's primary role was to organize production to meet quotas. If there was reasonable productivity, bonuses and profit sharing were the rewards, with top management getting a lion's share. And in the event of poor performance, either the state would come to the rescue or there would be musical-chair reassignments to maintain basically the same group of managers.

Each large state enterprise had a workers council elected by the workers. But until the early 1970s the councils were integrated into trade unions or the Conference of Workers' Self-Management, which was controlled by government bureaucrats. Enterprise directors, therefore, were de facto workers' management as well. In the late 1970s and throughout the 1980s, economic reform permitted the election of directors by the workers councils, confined to enterprises not of key importance to the national economy. But martial law in 1981 once again reduced the workers councils to a passive role in management.

Today, the workers council is a functioning part of enterprise management. There is worker self-management and autonomy from the state. There is freedom in decision making. But there is not much more. The councils have had little or no experience in making business decisions. As a rule, they are more politically astute than financially experienced. The enterprise management team must now deal with free pricing, loss of state subsidies, low worker morale, layoffs or plant closings, limited credit, and other market forces for all major decisions. The tasks are overwhelming, and management, on average, is ill prepared.

FUNCTIONAL ADJUSTMENTS AND ADAPTATIONS

The adjustments that state enterprises need to make vary from industry to industry, and from one enterprise to another in the same industry. But the common denominator is adaptability. Firms with more adaptability and flexibility are more likely to survive. The following are some adjustments management must now consider making:

1. Decisions must be based on economic objectivity, particularly regarding human relations. The operational rule is efficiency, and the objective is profit and growth. The premise is maximum return with minimum outlay. A system of rewards and accountability needs to be defined and understood by all employees in the company. Hiring, promotions, and dismissals are to be implemented impartially. Management must encourage a sense of responsibility among workers, and instill discipline as a work attitude. The aim is to motivate employees to realize their potential.

2. Distribution practices need to be significantly improved. New channels of distribution have to be explored, while existing ones reexamined and less profitable clients replaced. In a free marketplace, there is no room for blind loyalty between buyer and seller. It is similar to sending oil through pipelines with multiple outlets; whichever outlet promises the highest economic return has its valve turned wide open, while less rewarding ones are perhaps only a trickle or closed, as economic conditions dictate. Enterprises must improve their markets for enhanced profits.

3. Consumer confidence in a product must be established, maintained, and strengthened. This is now a buyer's market. If the product is of exportable quality, foreign channels of distribution should be sought, with the purpose of simultaneously expanding the domestic market. Consumer demand, especially now, favors imports over domestic goods. If a product is accepted in foreign markets, Polish consumers will accept and trust that same product as well because presumably it is of higher quality. Therefore, enterprises need to establish a quality control mechansim to retain consumer confidence.

4. There must be attention to marketing. Products need to appear attractive to consumers, who may now choose among competing brands. How consumers perceive a product is crucial, and management needs to explore innovative ways of presenting a product to the consumer. Adaptation to and modification for varying consumer tastes and preferences can enhance a product's image in a competitive market. Market survey, advertising, improved packaging and quality control are some of the ready examples. State enterprises that experienced no such need before, must now be reoriented to make their products desirable.

5. Management in larger enterprises must seek up-to-date information on prices, sales, and market share. In a centralized system, this market information was of little importance, but now it is the basis for important decisions regarding earnings. Producers need to anticipate increases in demand for their products and services. Accurate and timely market information helps a company eliminate waste, reduce risk, and enhance market opportunities. Prices can be set in accordance with market conditions;

inventory can be built up or allowed to run low; production can be accelerated or slowed. Prompt adjustments to fluctuations in demand, rather than adherence to predetermined production quotas can help minimize losses and maximize market opportunities.

6. Management may need to redefine its product mix to match changing market conditions. If so, new investments and production should be synchronized accordingly. Product differentiation and enterprise diversification are ready avenues for increased market share and expanded economic opportunities.

7. Attention must be paid to keeping costs down. Cost cutting used to be a less important consideration for management than was meeting production quotas. In a market situation, however, efficiency dictates minimization of costs and overhead. Management must actively seek new reliable and competitive suppliers. It not only helps contain costs, but also forces all suppliers to improve their services and products. To further reduce production costs, where warranted, quasi subsidiary enterprises can be established in small cities and towns, where labor costs are lower and materials are apt to be cheaper.

8. Compatible smaller firms may consider joining together in cooperative efforts or even merging to realize economies of scale. Such efforts can include both forward and backward stages of production and horizontal collaboration or coordination.

9. Management should run a tight ship. Surplus resources in the form of machinery, equipment, land, buildings, inventory and personnel need to be eliminated. Laying off surplus or less productive personnel may prove traumatic, but when an enterprise's survival is in question, the lesser evil is to continue operations on a leaner basis so that at least some of work force may continue to be productive. Where costs can be reduced without adversely affecting quality or service, then effciency and competitiveness are accomplished.

10. Management needs risk takers. The decades-old tradition of avoiding new ventures and playing it safe does not work in a free-market system. Undue conservatism in an increasingly competitive environment leads to a loss in market share, or eventual demise. A willingness and ability to assume reasonable risks are essential for success and growth. New products, new pricing practices, and new markets need to be tested and explored, and that means taking calculated risks.

11. Enterprises must service the after-purchase needs of their customers. Trained repair personnel, technicians, part suppliers, and the like need to be part of the enterprise work force, to ensure customers that their purchases will remain functional for their life span. It is not sufficient to maintain the existing corps of product service personnel at their current level of qualitfication. New products need new knowledge. Management must

update the knowledge and skills of its service personnel, thereby cultivating consumer confidence in its products.

12. Management needs to consider spinning off smaller operations or reorganizing into separate functions. Some state enterprises are inefficient by themselves but could become competitive as smaller units. Chemical or electronic engineering enterprises, for instance, were built to manufacture endproducts of a capital-intensive nature. Many such firms are of considerable size, involving numerous stages of production and producing varied intermediate products as well. If market conditions no longer justify production of the endproduct, then the firm may consider breaking into smaller, independent units that can serve as suppliers of intermediate goods for others. Micro units can be highly competitive and profitable, especially suppliers of parts for transnational corporations. The latter have the financial resources, advanced marketing information, and established distribution channels. Also, the demand for intermediate goods often exceeds the productive capacities of these micro units. Therefore, breaking up the large enterprise into these smaller units offers an option for developing the more efficient and profitable departments of a state enterprise.

These possible adjustmetns or adaptations are far from exhaustive. Each enterprise will face unique constraints and opportunities. Each will need to adapt to its given economic circumstances. The point is that, to be competitive and grow in a free market, enterprises must modify their business practices. Flexibility and progressiveness are essential ingredients in this transitional phase of economic reform.

HARNESSING HUMAN RESOURCEFULNESS

Macroeconomic policy provides a framework for reform, but for the program to succeed management needs to call on mincroeconomic policy. This section briefly discusses three aspects of human resource management, a crucial element of success.

Incentive Systems

Profitability in this new economic situation requires joint efforts by labor and management. Management needs to provide incentives on all levels of operation so that everyone is duly engaged and constructively motivated. What motivates some people might not motivate others as much, so there is a need to identify motivational common denominators.

Economic incentives rank high among motivating forces. So does the prestige of promotion. But owing to partial wage indexing, financial reward in the form of higher wages is not presently feasible. And for many enterprises, financial constraints do not permit promotions, even if justified. Management, therefore, needs to initiate programs and practices which are cost-free or cost-efficient and, at the same time, effective in bringing forth the best from all workers. A ready example is keeping records of current efforts, which will then be translated into pay increases or promotions in the future. Management should provide clear job descriptions and spell out responsibilities that are measurable by objective criteria. Each employee is accountable for his or her actions and is periodically evaluated for completion of assigned duties, with records of performance kept for future reference.

Supervision and coordination need to be accomplished within the framework of a partnership, with mutual respect, trust, and value of common good. Cogent information, whether it be of a technical or a business nature, should flow freely between the work force and decision makers, so that all employees feel important, involved, and valued. To the extent feasible, management should foster an atmosphere of job satisfaction and pride, with high degree of individualized involvement. Merit points can accrue to individuals, as well as to operational units, so that peer pressure, group acceptance and cooperation are translated into new ideas and shared attitudes. Personal interests and individual motivations are then integrated into a group effort. A sense of belonging and team purpose can inject vitality in a project, for a shared vision of a set objective.

* Entrepreneurship

Entrepreneurship under the centralized system found its expression in moonlighting to make ends meet, in black market and other underground activities, and in capitalizing on whatever loopholes existed. The people of Poland are resourceful, creative, and innovative. And management must channel this spirit of resourcefulness for constructive results.

Entrepreneurs in present-day Poland need not be big-time financiers or import-export giants. The entrepreneurial spirit can express itself in small ways, on all levels of economic activity. Street vendors who peddle inexpensive merchandise are entrepreneurs; they pay no taxes and reinvest their profits in expanded operations. The government is aware of them as small-time tax evaders and wisely tolerates the situation. For this spirit can help all individuals to be more resourceful in their respective activities. In the enterprise, an entrepreneurial spirit can lead to new products, new markets or channels of distribution, new sources and approaches to financing, and greater efficiency. A rapidly increasing number of joint ventures and an increased volume of foreign trade are convincing evidence that entrepreneurship in Poland is alive, well, and growing.

Through entrepreneurial activities on the enterprise level, weaker linkages in the market can be strengthened, resources more efficiently allocated, shortage problems mitigated, oversupply reduced, and commodity circulation channels increased and multiplied. They activate, enliven, and invigorate profitable propositions. They bring potential ideas to fruition. Management must develop creative ways to cultivate and encourage entrepreneurial energy.

Pareto Better Exchange Programs

A third way to mobilize human potentials is exchange programs. Polish managers of state enterprises know the rules of a free-market economy, but most of them have not played the game. With the passage of time, many firms will lose ground unless managers become more adept. A feasible solution, at least for a good number of state enterprises, is to obtain assistance from business leaders and academics abroad. Quality graduate students in foreign business schools and seasoned managers from foreign enterprises can be invited to assist in advising, organizing, and training. In return, foreign business students, under the guidance of knowledgeable teachers, can gain valuable field experience through on-the-job training. And host enterprises need only provide accommodations, since the exchange is mutually beneficial. It is a Pareto Better scenario, with minimal demand on the scarce financial resources of state enterprises.

Visits by managers from abroad can likewise benefit both sides. With help from these experts, Polish management can gain valuable knowledge and insight into the operation of the free market. For the visiting foreign managers, on-site visits may lead to future suppliers at low cost. Distribution outlets for their own products may also materialize. Increased interaction is a Pareto Better frontier awaiting exploration.

In brief, the future success of Poland's economic transformation rests, to a large extent, on the individual success of its enterprises. And the success of an individual enterprise is in turn a function of that firm's ability to adapt to a new market condition, and to tap the productive potential of its employees on all levels and fronts. This is the aggregate success of microeconomic theory that ultimately passes judgment on the wisdom and effectiveness of macroeconomic reform policies.

14

REFORM PROSPECTS, RECOMMENDATIONS, AND CONCLUSIONS

Economic restructuring in Poland is in its gestation. The form of a free market has been introduced, but the likelihood that the embryo will develop uneventfully, and on schedule, is remote. The aspiration to be rich is within the Polish people, but the means to achieve that objective are beyond most. The design has a grandiose exterior, but the infrastructure is absent.

Reform has been radical. Government's rationale was that "we simply did not have the time" to be less than radical. But in being radical, it has not been smooth. For example, there was a dilemma: whether to establish the institutional framework for a market system first and then introduce the market mechanism, or introduce the market first and then build the supportive system. The institutional changes needed for a smoothly functioning free market take time, especially when changes involve attitudes, values, and belief systems. The new government has attempted to transform overnight a basically centralized system into a totally decentralized one. The result has been frustration, confusion, and chaos. This chapter first presents a review of the prospects for political, social, and economic reform of Poland, then offers brief recommendations and a few concluding observations.

PROSPECTS FOR LASTING REFORM

Political Prospects

Despite the parting of ways between former prime minister Tadeusz Mazowiecki and new president Lech Walesa--polarizing the two camps of

Solidarity supporters--there will be relative political stability in Poland. There will be strikes, there will be protests, and there will be significant social discontent. But with memories of the unsatisfactory centralized system still fresh, there will be no clamor for a return to the past. Differences and discontents will be brought into the open through the democratic process. Administrations will come and go, but the basic democratic system will remain. Freedom and democracy are hard-earned dividends of decades of resistance and struggle. They have been the beacon of hope in a storm of economic uncertainty. The people of Poland look in one direction: westward. Politically, Poland is as free and as democratic as any other democratic country in the world. The aspiration now is to catch up with the West.

Social

In today's Poland, communist philosophy and the communist system properly belong to history. But the effects of nearly half a century's social and quasicultural conditioning under that system cannot be eradicated quickly. Patterns of behavior have been deeply branded into people's subconscious. For forty-five years, workers perfected their skill playing one game: how to deal with authority. They maximized personal utility with minimal effort. The new game plan for many is wait and see. Shifting people from one mode of behavior to another takes years, if not decades. It is a barrier to change and to progress.

The difficulty does not lie in people's unwillingness to change. Rather, they do not know how to adapt quickly to new economic circumstances. Risk taking, entrepreneurial ventures, corporate well-being through personal effort are just concepts to the majority. Quoting Stefan Nowak, professor Krzysztof Obloj accurately portrays it as a social vacuum:

The two main frames of references for the Poles are the nation and the family. There is nothing in between. There is the global scale *we* as a nation. Poland. Poles. Our history. Tragic history. Won battles and lost wars. Grand things. And then there is a second level: *family*. I am here. My son, my daughter, my wife, my very small circle of friends. And there is nothing in between. There are no anchors at the level of enterprises, firms, institutions, and so forth. (Obloj interview, 1990)

The people do know what they want, but getting what they want is now through economic endeavor not political action. They learned that political actions led to results. Now they know that the means for change are economic, but they are not skilled in economic maneuvering. In the absence of knowledge and experience to attain economic objectives, they do nothing different. Many state enterprises have thus far succeeded in remaining open with such a posture. They might ultimately lose the game, but for now they are still in it. Their immediate concern is *their* survival, not the nation's.

Harsh macroeconomic policies have been effective in curbing inflation, but no effective tools have been devised to induce attitudinal changes. Meanwhile, it will take decades for younger generations in school to acquire the correct economic mores. The appearance of economic stability--vis-a-vis stabilized prices--should not be taken to mean there is a stabilized economy. Meaningful economic stabilization in Poland is still on the horizon, since economic reform cannot abscise itself from social and cultural development.

Economic

Here's a *what if* scenario: The Solidarity-backed government inherited many major economic problems from past administration, but those areas requiring immediate attention were hyperinflation, a growing budget deficit, and a nearly insurmountable foreign debt. The primary cause of inflation was the freeing of food prices, and the main cause of the bulging deficit was irresponsible spending. The government reimposed price ceilings on food, and inflation was significantly reduced. Earlier subsidy increases owing to inflation were then gradually withdrawn, reducing government spending. Inflation lingered, but was not as strong. And budget deficit remained, but was no longer a permanent problem because moderate and appropriate measures were implemented over time. There were difficulties, but not severe. When the economy was stabilized, the brakes were released in a measured way for orderly transformation of the system. Once there, the government would proceed with deliberation and clear vision to continue growth and development.

How receptive would foreign creditors and the IMF have been to this scenario? It's likely that the foreign creditors would have been more receptive than the IMF. If the likely consequences of an alternative policy had been reviewed beforehand, creditors would have seen it would be to their advantage to take a steadier and slower-paced approach to reform. The IMF, on the other hand, is known for making severe demands on debtor nations. Nevertheless, Poland was prepared to institute internal convertibility of currencies and free trade, two of the IMF's standard demands. Another major IMF demand is a balanced budget--and a balanced budget was to be achieved, though not instantly. There was room for negotiation. If this scenario had been adopted, then Poland would have sent a signal to its creditors, via increases in free-market forces introduced over time, that it was allocating more efficiently. Productive workers, managers, service personnel, and government officials could then have learned, adjusted, adapted, and progressed without confusion, losses, and resistance to change.

Given what happened instead the prospects for Poland's economy are less obstacle free.   Since the justifications for these conclusions have been discussed in earlier chapters, only summary statements are made here.

The architect of current reform is Leszek Balcerowicz.   He was appointed deputy prime minister and minister of finance in September 1989. Despite a year of severe macroeconomic dislocations thereafter, Lech Walesa promised a continuation of the Balcerowicz program if elected president. Walesa was elected, and Balcerowicz was reappointed by the new prime minister, Jan Bielecki.   The program is on course, but the desired consequences for the most part have been, and will continue to be, elusive.

The budget has been nearly balanced and hyperinflation has ended. But for lack of adequate supplier response, price decreases will not occur to any measurable degree.   Any decline in prices will be a result of reduced consumer purchasing power rather than increases in supply.   The corollary to this is that the significant loss in real income during late 1989 and the first half of 1990 will not be recouped in the near future.   Demand for nonessential goods, therefore, will remain weak for the corresponding duration.

Employment opportunities will become more bleak unless effective job-retraining programs are made extensively available.   But such programs are nowhere in sight.

Plant closings will become more commonplace.   Unemployment will continue to rise.   And given the consequences of a nearly balanced budget, a growing number of the unemployed will waste away, festering in political discontent.

For privatization to proceed smoothly, markets for trading stocks and notes must be developed.   But developing such markets takes more time than impatient politicians would like.   The outcome of privatization --constructive or otherwise--will be a matter of economic strategies versus political considerations.   Success is far from a foregone conclusion.

The private sector will grow, but gains in production will not be sufficient to offset the continued loss of state enterprises.   Most rapid industrial growth will be in the export sector.   Trade surpluses will increase, rendering debt service less problematic.

Heavy labor taxes imposed on enterprises will continue to seriously distort labor-productivity ratios and make labor-intensive products less competitive on the international market.   But as a source of government revenue, these taxes are unlikely to change, at least in the foreseeable future.

The farm cooperative cartels ensure that agricultural producers, as well as consumers, will continue to be exploited--there is no effective means of breaking up this monopoly power. Agricultural production will inch upward over time, but more of the production will be for export rather than for domestic consumption. Food prices will not meaningfully decline; the well-entrenched cartels will see to that. Meanwhile, the government is preoccupied with other facets of public policy. The resilient Polish farmers will survive, but they will not thrive. To the detriment of consumers, the potential for significantly increased farm productivity will remain dormant.

Finally, recent amendments to the Foreign Investment Law have created a favorable climate for the inflow of foreign capital. Assuming political and social stability, foreign investment will continue its upward climb,

The birth of a free-market economy in Poland has been belabored and premature. The infant, with the essential features of a free market, needs a life support system for an extended period of time. The infant will survive, but how long will it take before normal development takes over? And will this entity be able to run races with neighborhood kids?

RECOMMENDATIONS

Many of the recommendations given here will not be heeded by Poland's policymakers. But the role of economist is not to forward only those recommendations favored by officeholders. Instead, they are made because they are needed. Lessons can be learned from history, and the Polish economy is history in the making. Specifically,

1. The labor market must be permitted to seek equilibrium.

2. The policy of partial wage indexing needs to be repealed, in favor of wages as a function of the marginal value of productivity.

3. Employment policies must include the effective retraining programs.

4. Mild inflation should be considered a lesser evil to prolonged recession, stagnation, and massive unemployment.

5. Displaced labor should not be permitted to waste away. Labor- intensive, useful public works can be initiated, minimizing social costs while enhancing external economies.

6. The government should resort to aggressive foreign borrowing for capital formation, not for consumption, as in the early 1970s.

7. Effective antimonopoly measures should be implemented and endorsed, rather than merely introduced on paper.

8.   Crop insurance, subsidized farm credit, price supports, and price ceilings for factors of production are needed on a short-term basis to stabilize and stimulate the farm sector.

9.   Equity shares in state enterprises can be offered to retiring farmers in exchange for their land. A land consolidation program would then be more realizable in the longer run.

10.   Price ceilings should be temporarily reimposed on strategic factors of production as well as on consumer goods. The ceilings can be raised over time as supplies increase.

11.   Subsidies to the export sector should be reinstated, at least on a temporary basis.

12.   Differentiated credit policies need to be introduced in order to foster stabilization, recovery, and growth of key industries, with the National Bank of Poland as the prime lender.

13.   To compensate for the loss in real income, vouchers for equity shares in state enterprises should be distributed to all Polish nationals. The distributed vouchers should be nontransferable for a specified time, to prevent undesirable activities by a small class of superrich.

14.   The terms of worker buyouts of state enterprises should be repackaged, making ownership transformation more attractive to employees. This will enhance the work incentive and help foster the emergence of a working middle class.

15.   The first firms to be privatized should be core enterprises in key industries, providing an example for further institutional and structural reform.

16.   For further financial concessions from foreign creditors, the government should assemble convincing examples of privatization.

17.   Financial aid to Poland, insofar as possible, should be untied to increase fungibility for more efficient and productive allocation of same.

18. Aid needs to be less in kind than in assistance for human resource development.

19. More training programs provided by donor nations should take place in Poland rather than in donor nations.

20. The old propaganda machine should be resurrected for a constructive media campaign, directed at developing new social norms and values.

21. Increasing attention should be directed to micro levels of economic activity to promote macroeconomic policies.

CONCLUDING OBSERVATIONS

The Polish economy is on a long journey through unchartered waters. The destination is known, but visibility is reduced by unknowns and uncertainties. Poland will reach its destination. The questions are, how many detours are along the way? How long will the journey take? And how turbulent will the waters be?

The Polish experiment has been radical. Its speed and scale are unprecedented. The frame work for economic restructuring is in place, but many support units are missing. The potential for success depends heavily on individual responsiveness. The jury is still out. And the world community waits for the verdict.

CHRONOLOGY OF SIGNIFICANT EVENTS, JANUARY 1989– DECEMBER 1990

KEYS TO SOURCES

BW--*Business Week*　　　　　　　　TRIB--*Daily Tribune*
E--*The Economist*　　　　　　　　　V--*Warsaw Voice*
FP--*Detroit Free Press*

January 18, 1989	Decision by the Communist party's Central Committee to begin the process of legalizing Solidarity. (BW 2/6/89, p. 51)
February 2, 1989	Inauguration of the roundtable talks. (V 4/16/89, p. 3)
February 24, 1989	Legislation granting the government extraordinary powers in economic management. (V 4/16/89, p. 3)
March 1989	Negotiations begin between Poland and the EEC involving trade and economic cooperation. (V 7/16/89, p. 11)
March 2, 1989	First meeting between interior minister Czeslaw Kiszczak and Lech Walesa. (4/16/89, p. 3)
April 5, 1989	Agreement is signed by the government and the Solidarity-led opposition. (4/22-28/89, p. 48)

Agreement includes free elections and economic reform. (BW 4/24/89, p. 47)

A constitutional amendment is adopted, making the President the chief executive. (V 7/8/89, p. 3)

April 17, 1989   Solidarity becomes legal again and is registered in Warsaw. (E 22-28, April 1989, p. 48) (V 4/30/89, p. 4)

April 27-28, 1989   Jaruzelski visits Moscow and discusses economic issues with Gorbachev. (V 5/7/89, p. 4)

June 4, 1989   Free elections are held. In first round of voting, Solidarity wins 99 out of 100 seats in the Senate; the communists retain a guaranteed majority in Sejm, the lower house. (E 7/15-21/89, p. 39)

June 6, 1989   Jaruzelski formally invites Solidarity to take part in a coalition government. Solidarity refuses. (E 6/10-16/89, p. 43)

June 23, 1989   The Civic Parliamentary Club, formed by Solidarity Senators and MPs, announces that it is not endorsing a candidate for the presidency. (V 7/2/89, p. 4)

June 28, 1989   Rural Solidarity calls on farmers to continue their month-long protest against the unprofitability of agricultural production. The protest involves refusing to pay the year's financial obligations to the state. (V 7/9/89, p. 4)

June 30, 1989   The government adopts provisions for an economic program for 1989/92 suggested by the IMF and World Bank (V 7/9/89, p. 4)

July 11, 1989   President George Bush visits Gdansk. (E 7/15-21/89, p. 39)

July 19, 1989   The National Assembly elects Wojciech
                            Jaruzelski president of Poland.

July 25, 1989   During a meeting with Jaruzelski, Walesa
                            proposes that Solidarity be asked to form a
                            government. (V 8/27/89, p. 3)

August 1, 1989   The president of the Polish National Bank
                            issues a regulation that gives commercial banks
                            freedom to establish interest rates for loans and
                            deposits. (V 7/23/89, p. 11)

August 2, 1989   General Czeslaw Kiszczak is appointed prime
                            minister.

August 14, 1989   Kiszczak announces his intention of resigning.
                            He proposes Roman Malinowski as his
                            replacement. (E 8/19-25/89, p. 33)

August 15, 1989   Solidarity negotiators propose Lech Walesa as
                            prime minister. (E 8/19-25/1989, p. 33)

August 19, 1989   Jaruzelski accepts Kiszczak's resignation and
                            offers the position to Mazowiecki. (V 8/27/89,
                            p. 3)

September 12, 1989   Mazowiecki delivers a policy speech in the
                            Sejm assuring that the government will raise
                            the standard of living, streamline the economy,
                            and curb inflation. (V 12/31/89, p. 10)

September 19, 1989   The economic cooperation and trade agreement
                            is signed between the EEC and Poland. (V
                            10/1/89, p. 3)

September 26, 1989   The European Commission convenes a second
                            meeting with twenty-four Western nations
                            trying to help reform the Poland and Hungary.
                            (E 9/30-10/6/89, p. 4).   Finance Minister
                            Leszek Balcerowicz meets with IMF in
                            Washington to seek $2.5 billion in aid over the
                            next six months (BW 11/2/89, p. 44)

October 6, 1989

Poland's new government announces plans for a market economy. (FP 10/7/89, p. 21A)

December 8, 1989

Solidarity-led government announces belt-tightening policies. (FP 12/9/89, p. 2A)

December 12, 1989

Walesa proposes that the government be granted special powers permitting it to restructure the economy without the approval of Parliament because legislative debate is slowing adoption of laws needed to end the economic crisis. (FP 12/13/89, p. 7A and V 12/24/89, p. 4)

December 15-17, 1989

Solidarity Independent and Autonomous Private Farmers' conference is held at Mistrzejowice, near Cracow. Delegates demand preferential treatment for credits and taxes.

December 18, 1989

Farmers' representatives become the first major interest group to object to the government's economic reform program. They ask for guaranteed minimum prices for farm products instead of free marketing pricing.

December 28, 1989

After heated debate, Poland's lower house approves the economic reform measures. (FP 12/29/89)

December 29, 1989

The Senate approves the reform package. The lower house votes to change the nation's name from the People's Republic of Poland to the Republic of Poland, and votes to end the leading role of the Communist party. (FP 12/30/89)

January 6, 1990

At a three-day congress, Communist leaders vote to disband their party. In its place, a leftist party with a new name and platform is to be formed.

January 25, 1990

The Polish United Workers' Party is officially dissolved. A new party, the Democracy of the

	Republic of Poland, is formed. (FP 1/27/90, p. 1A and FP 1/28/90 p. 3A)
April 1990	Lech Walesa confirms that he will run for president. (V 4/22/90, p. 4). Poland is unable to pay the interest on its $40 billion national debt to the Paris Club and other Western creditors. The interest has amounted to $4 billion, equaling 7 percent of Poland's annual national income and 50% of its hard-currency export earnings. (V 4/15/90, p. 12)
June 7, 1990	Agricultural Market Agency Law is approved.
July 13, 1990	Law of Privatization of State Enterprises is approved. Office of Minister of Ownership Transformation is created.
July 1990	The Centrum Alliance (the group that is putting Walesa forward as candidate for president) holds meeting with 400 participants, discussing the basis of a political and economic program. (V 7/1/90, p. 4)
November 14, 1990	Law on the election of president is passed by the Senate.
November 25, 1990	Presidential election. Walesa and Tyminski are to face each other in a runoff election. Mazowiecki announces his resignation as prime minister.
December 22, 1990	Walesa takes the oath of president.
December 29, 1990	Walesa appoints Jan Bielecki as prime minister. Bielecki promises to continue economic reforms of Mazowiecki administration.

SELECTED BIBLIOGRAPHY

Barnett, Clifford R., et al. *Poland: Its People, Its Society, Its Culture.* New Haven: Hraf Press, 1958.

Bossak, Jan W. "The Program for Stabilization and System Reforms." In *Poland: International Economic Report, 1989-1990.* Warsaw: World Economy Research Institute, 1990, pp. 56-74.

Brumberg, Abraham (ed.). *Poland: Genesis of a Revolution.* New York: Random House, 1983.

Budget Law of 1990. Warsaw: Government Documents Daily of the Republic of Poland, 1990.

Burzynski, Wojciech, and Ewa Sadowska-Cieslak. "Results of Foreign Direct Investments." In *Foreign Investments in Poland: Regulations, Experience and Prospects.* Warsaw: Foreign Trade Research Institute, 1990.

Directorate of Intelligence. *Handbook of Economic Statistics, 1988; 1985; 1980; 1975.* Washington D.C.: U.S. Government Printing Office, 1989, 1986, 1981, 1976.

Drewnowska, Ewa, Jerzy Hylewski, and Ewa Sadowska-Cieslak. "Analysis of Licenses Granted by Foreign Investment Agency." In *Foreign Investments in Poland: Regulations, Experience and Prospects.* Warsaw: Foreign Trade Research Institute, 1990, pp. 10-34.

Flakierski, Henryk. *Economic Reform and Income Distribution. A Case Study of Hungary and Poland.* New York: M. E. Sharpe, 1986.

Foreign Investment Law, 1990. Warsaw: Government Documents Daily of the Republic of Poland, 1990.

Gabrisch, Hubert (ed.). *Economic Reforms in E. Europe and the Soviet Union.* Westview Special Studies in International Economics, 1989.

Hunter, Richard J., and Leo V. Ryan. *Poland's Balcerowicz Plan: Risks and Uncertainties.* Paper presented at 1991 Annual International Conference, International Academy of Management and Marketing, April 11-14, 1991, Detroit, Mich.

Kolankiewicz, George, and Paul G. Lewis. *Poland: Politics, Economics and Society*. London: Pinter Publications, 1988.

Landau, Zbigniew, and Jerzy Tomaszewski. *The Polish Economy in the Twentieth Century*. trans. by Wojciech Roszkowski. London: Croom Helm, 1985.

Law Concerning the Privatization of State Enterprises, Warsaw: Government Documents Daily of the Republic of Poland, July 13, 1990.

Marer, Paul (ed.). *Polish-U.S. Industrial Cooperation in the 1980's*. Findings of a joint Research Project. Bloomington, Ind.: Indiana University Press, 1981.

Marer, Paul, and Wlodzimierz Siwinski (eds.). *Creditworthiness and Reform in Poland*. Bloomington, Ind.: Indiana University Press, 1988.

Ministry of Finance and the Institute of Finance. "Basic Statistical Data Concerning the Implementation of the Stabilization Program". *Financial Policy: Destabilization-Stabilization*. Warsaw: Ministry of Finance, 1990.

Nelson, Harold D. (ed.). *Poland: A Country Study*. Washington, D.C.: U.S. Department of the Army, 1984.

Piotrowski, Janusz. *Poland's Foreign Trade Regime in 1990*. Warsaw: Foreign Trade Research Institute, 1990.

Poland: A Market for Products from Developing Countries. Geneva: International Trade Center UNCTAD/GATT, 1989.

Poland: International Economic Report. 1989-1990. Warsaw: World Economy Research Institute, 1990.

Poland Statistical Data, 1988; 1989; 1990. Warsaw: Central Statistical Office, 1989.

Sadowska-Cieslak, Ewa. "Proposals for Changes of Principles of Functioning Companies with Foreign Capital Participation." In *Foreign Investments in Poland: Regulations, Experience and Prospects*. Warsaw: Foreign Trade Research Institute, 1990, pp. 96-98.

Sadowska-Cieslak, Ewa, Roland Pac, and Wojciech Kozyra. "The Goals of Direct Investments and Analysis of Relevant Legislation". In *Foreign Investments in Poland: Regulations, Experience and Prospects*. Warsaw: Foreign Trade Research Institute, 1990, pp. 10-34.

Stupnicki, Krzysztof. "Privatization of the Public Sector's Enterprises." In *Poland: International Economic Report, 1989-1990*. Warsaw: World Economy Research Institute, 1990, pp. 75-81.

United Nations. Secretariat of the Economic Commission for Europe. *Economic Survey of Europe in 1970-1989*. New York: United Nations, 1971-1990.

Warsaw Voice. Warsaw: The Warsaw Voice, Inc.

World Bank. *Poland: Reform, Adjustment and Growth*. Vol. I, Main Report: The Economic System. Washington, D.C.: The World Bank, 1987.

Poland: Reform, Adjustment and Growth. Vol. II, Agriculture, Manufacturing and Minerals, Energy, Transport, Telecommunications and Construction, Housing, Health and Education and Training. Washington D.C.: The World Bank, 1987.

World Development Report, 1988, 1989, 1990. Washington, D.C.: The World Bank, 1990.

World Economy Research Institute. *Polish Economy in the External Environment in 1980s.* Warsaw: Central School of Planning and Statistics, 1990.

Zielinski, Janusz G. *Economic Reform in Polish Industry.* London: Oxford University Press, 1973.

INDEX

ABOUT THE AUTHOR

RAPHAEL SHEN is a member of the Society of Jesus and a professor of economics at the University of Detroit. He received his Ph.D. from Michigan State University. He has authored and presented many professional papers in the fields of economic development, comparative economic systems, and the economics of natural resources. This is his first book.